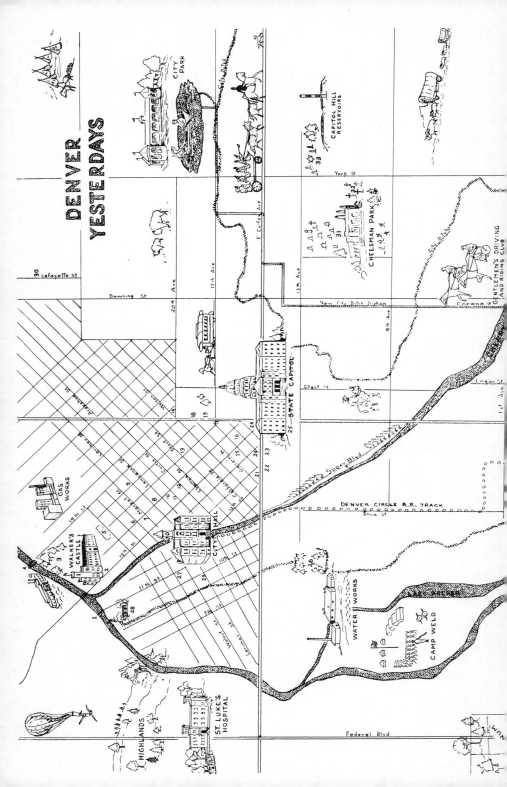

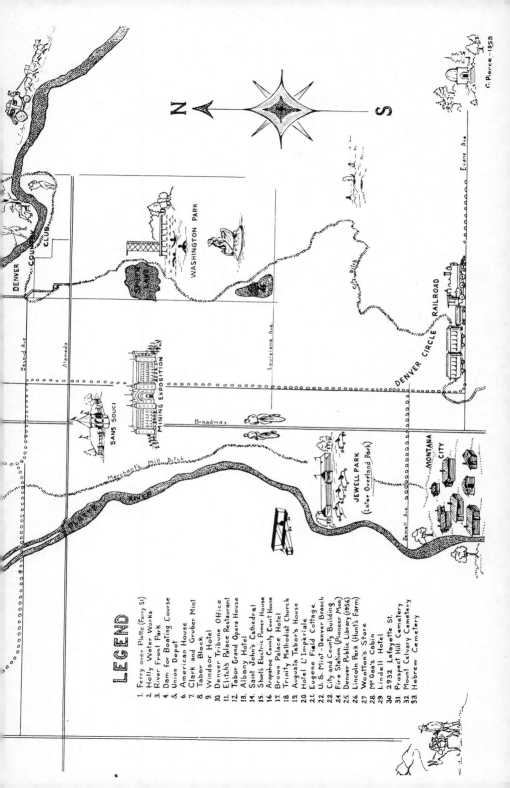

G. Pierce - 1959

N ◄ ► S

DENVER COUNTRY CLUB

WASHINGTON PARK

SANS SOUCI

MINING EXPOSITION

Broadway

Merchant's Mill Ditch

Platte River

JEWELL PARK
(Later Overland Park)

City Ditch

DENVER CIRCLE RAILROAD

MONTANA CITY

Evans Ave.

Exposition Ave.

Alameda

Louisiana Ave.

LEGEND

1. Ferry over Platte (Ferry St.)
2. Holly Water Works
3. River Front Park
4. Dam for Boating Course
5. Union Depot
6. American House
7. Clark and Gruber Mint
8. Tabor Block
9. Windsor Hotel
10. Denver Tribune Office
11. Elitch's Palace Restaurant
12. Tabor Grand Opera House
13. Albany Hotel
14. Saint John's Cathedral
15. Sho's Electric Power House
16. Arapahoe County Court House
17. Brown Palace Hotel
18. Trinity Methodist Church
19. Augusta Tabor's House
20. Hotel L'Imperiale
21. Eugene Field Cottage
22. U.S. Mint-Denver Branch
23. City and County Building
24. Fire Station (Pioneer Mon.)
25. Denver Public Library (1956)
26. Lincoln Park (Hunt's Farm)
27. Wootton's Store
28. McGaa's Cabin
29. Lindell Hotel
30. 2932 Lafayette St.
31. Prospect Hill Cemetery
32. Mount Calvary Cemetery
33. Hebrew Cemetery

DENVER IN SLICES

Indians in Denver

On Blake Street, Denver City, Kansas Territory, the Indians and the gold-rushers were neighbors. In the foreground are a few of the three hundred Arapahoe lodges that were in or near Denver in the summer of 1859. (Sketch by A. C. Warren, in Richardson's *Beyond the Mississippi,* 1867, p. 186. *Denver Public Library.*)

On September 28, 1864, after nine days en route from eastern Colorado, two wagons crowded with Cheyenne and Arapahoe leaders paused on 14th Street, Denver. (The large building is the newly built Lawrence Street Methodist Church.) The curious of Denver lined up in buggies to follow the Indians to Camp Weld, where the Indians asked for peace and the governor promised them nothing. Two months and a day after this council, some of these Indians were among those killed at Sand Creek by Colonel Chivington and Colorado volunteers. (Photo from Smiley's *History of Denver*, 1901. p. 405. *Denver Public Library*.)

The 1882 Mining and Industrial Exposition at South Broadway and Exposition Avenue exhibited Ute Indians as though they were a circus sideshow. Only the Ute women and a few dignified men appeared without frock coats and high silk hats. (Photo by W. H. Jackson, *Denver Public Library.*)

An Indian on the balcony of the Colorado Capitol looks down 16th Street toward the South Platte River where his ancestors used to camp. Arapahoe County Court House (1883–1933) shows on the left of the street, and the Kittridge Building (1890) on the right. (Photo from *Mrs. Philip Fitch. Denver Public Library.*)

DENVER
IN SLICES

LOUISA WARD ARPS

Swallow Press
Athens, Ohio   London

A Sage Book of Swallow Press

Copyright © 1959 by Louisa Ward Arps
All rights reserved
Published 1959 by Alan Swallow
Second Printing, 1983, by Swallow Press
Printed in the United States of America

Library of Congress Cataloging in Publication Data

Arps, Louisa Ward, 1901–
  Denver in slices.

  Includes bibliographical references and index.
  1. Denver (Colo.)—History. 2. Denver (Colo.)—
Description. 3. Denver (Colo.)—Buildings. I. Title.
F784.D457A77   1983   978.8'83   83-11058
ISBN 0-8040-0840-X
ISBN 0-8040-0841-8 (pbk.)

Swallow Press Books are published by
Ohio University Press, Athens, Ohio 45701

Table of Contents

Table of Illustrations

Preface to the Second Edition

This is a new edition of a book published two dozen years ago. The worst historic errors have been corrected, and two new pictures added—the picture of Buffalo Bill's burial and of the merry-go-round at Elitch's Gardens—but these changes do not amount to a revision.

Further changes would have destroyed the book's value as an historic monument to Denver before the Energy Boom. So many of the buildings taken for granted in 1959 have disappeared. For instance, the buildings connected with Horace Tabor's ghost in Chapter VI included the Tabor Block, the Windsor Hotel, the Tabor Grand Opera House, Hotel L'Imperiale and the old Post Office Building. Today—all gone. And certainly Denver no longer uses TA-5 as a telephone exchange.

For this edition the original pictures (all 98 of them) had to be located. This involved searching the files of the Colorado Historical Society's library and of the Western History Department of the Denver Public Library. The author is grateful to both institutions and especially to "Augie" (A. D. Mastroguiseppe, Jr.) and Kathey Swan of the Western History Department. With patient detection, they located 87 of the pictures and one map. The rest of the staff, including the director, Eleanor Gehres, continued the happy relationship with the Denver Public Library that the author has enjoyed for decades.

Preface

"Goldrick has got home and in Sunday's
TIMES promises his readers 'Denver in Slices'
for a week or two."
Rocky Mountain News, January 23, 1867

Since the author of this book has borrowed practically everything
else in it from earlier writers—only the inevitable mistakes are
hers!—it seems fitting to borrow the title. *Denver in Slices* is
appropriate to the present book, which is not a history of Denver
—just a slice here and a slice there with enough of the "Whole
Loaf" to indicate the position of the slices.

The fastidious Irishman, Owen J. Goldrick, who thought up
the title in 1867, was Denver's first school teacher. After two years
of nearly starving on the proceeds of his private school, he super-
intended the organization of a public school system in 1861, then
turned to journalism for a living. At his death in 1882 he was
editing the *Rocky Mountain Herald.* The only reason the present
author has presumed to borrow a title from this professional
writer, this traveler, this man with a classical education from
Dublin University who talked Latin to his oxen, and whose
flowery style was saved by an Irish wit, is that, like her, he enjoyed
living in Denver. Perhaps, from whatever corner of the Hereafter
he enlivens, Goldrick joins the author in hoping that the reader,
too, will have fun with *Denver in Slices.*

*   *   *   *   *

The compilation of material for this book started in January,
1956, when the Denver Public Library decided to sponsor a series
of television programs designed to demonstrate the resources of
the Western History Department of the Denver Public Library.
Librarian John Eastlick asked the astonished author of this book

12

to prepare and present the programs, called "Denver Yesterdays." This she managed to do with his encouragement; with the friendly energies of Alice Norton, the Library's Publicity Director; and the skill of the staff of Denver's educational television station, KRMA. "Denver Yesterdays" filled the eight o'clock spot the evening KRMA made its debut, January 30, 1956.

Some of the subjects used in the thirteen television programs have been re-used in this book, others have been substituted. Most of the material came, of course, from the Western History Department of the Denver Public Library. Its expert staff used indexes and intuition to find books, pamphlets, clippings, newspaper articles, maps, and manuscripts. As for pictures—practically all the pictures used in the book are from the Department's tremendous collection and are used with its generous permission. For their patience, interest, and friendliness the author thanks the four H's of the staff, the Mesdames Hanley, Harber, Hawkins and Howie, as well as Ina Aulls, Alys Freeze, Margaret Campbell, James Davis, and John Joyce.

The Library and Museum of the State Historical Society of Colorado graciously shared their treasures for this book, as they had for the television program. The author will never forget being allowed to exhibit the Society's collection of Clark-Gruber gold coins on the air, nor the man who came to guard them. Officials of the City and County of Denver were uniformly helpful, especially those in the Parks Department, the Auditor's Office, the Water Department, and the County Court. Thanks also go to the staff of the Denver Branch of the United States Mint.

Many, many other people have given help and memories to the author. Their companionship has brightened her travels through the little town that Denver used to be. She is grateful to them all, and especially to Elwyn Arps, Caroline Bancroft, Frederica Le-Fevre Bellamy, Jack Gurtler, Henry Hanington, Paul Harrison, Esther Holt, Edwin S. Kassler, Cedric Kaub, Anne Byrd Kennon, Rosamond Denison McLean, Katharine Morrell Perenyi, Gertrude Pierce, Geraldine Lane Sauvage, Helen Tillotson, Edith Hanington Ward, Orlando Ward and Mary Freeman Wegg.

The Whole Loaf

"Our camp is beautifully situated on the bank of the river, which is here about 100 yards wide—our tents are pitched in a grove of cottonwood trees that shade us from the scorching rays of the sun," wrote Capt. John Bell, the official journalist of Major Long's expedition, on July 5, 1820.[1] The river was the South Platte and the place was near the mouth of Cherry Creek. The sun was the western sun on a hot summer day and the trees were the only kind of deciduous trees that grew large enough to give shade in what Major Long on this trip christened the Great American Desert.

In 1858, at the same place in the spring of the year—the second week in May—young Lieutenant John Du Bois complained about a blizzard. "Since this storm we have been struggling on," he wrote his mother as his troops slogged down the Cherry Creek road. "Our animals exhausted & the roads almost impassable from snow and mud. We reached the South Fork of the Platte & found it twelve feet deep. Here we remained three days building a boat & ferrying all our wagons acrosst. We swam all our animals over & lost quite a number."[2]

Such reports show that long before Denver began, the mouth of Cherry Creek was an oasis for the men who roamed the Great American Desert. As we drive "acrosst" the Speer Boulevard viaduct of today above the railroad tracks and warehouse yards, it is hard to visualize the meager South Platte River running a hundred yards wide and twelve feet deep, lined with cottonwoods that sheltered Indians, beaver trappers, traders, buffalo butchers, explorers, dragoons, and just plain tourists.

Then came the gold seekers. By late fall of 1858, the ones who had not gone home for a civilized winter were established at the mouth of Cherry Creek. Early the next spring, when rumors of

15

gold in the Pikes Peak Country had fired the Midwest, the camping spot at the mouth of Cherry Creek was the logical destination for the endless lines of emigrants. (Never, during the early years, were they called immigrants.) Here they found two towns. On the southwest side of Cherry Creek, between it and the Platte River, Auraria had been laid out by gold-seeking Georgians who wanted a place to hole up for the dreaded winter. Denver, on the northeast side of the creek, was started by real-estate promoters who strong-armed the claim of a previous company. The fact that the land belonged to the Indians bothered nobody, not even the Indians. "Early in the summer of 1859 there were nearly 300 lodges of Arapahoes in or immediately around Denver and Auraria."[3]

The rush of early 1859 petered out in a matter of weeks because the few flakes of gold found in the piedmont streams were insufficient to support even a rumor. Leaving the two towns on Cherry Creek to the optimistic few, many emigrants retraced their tracks across the plains. In disgust they must have torn up the guidebooks to the gold mines of western Kansas and Nebraska they had so eagerly bought in the Missouri River towns.[4]

The Struggling Sixties

As soon as placer gold in paying quantities was discovered in the Front Range, traffic lines from the Missouri River turned west again. This was "no gentle tide of emigration . . . it came as a tidal wave."[5] Very soon, however, the gold that could be easily washed out of stream beds or scooped up at the grass root level, as in the hills of Gilpin County, had been stowed away in the pokes of prospectors. (The story of how this free gold was compressed into coins by the first Denver mint is told in Slice V.)

Few of the original prospectors knew anything about metallurgy. Some knew about mercury having an affinity for gold and dumped it in their gold pans. Then they collected the gold-mercury, retorted the mercury to use again, and pocketed the gold. This worked with free gold. It also worked with partially decomposed quartz shot through with gold, after they had crushed the quartz in primitive mills. They found this "blossom rock" on

16

the surface, but when it was gone and they dug deeper along the gold vein, they met hard rock. Even when they pulverized this, they could not recover enough gold to pay the processing bills.

As for silver, there was a rush to Georgetown in 1864 after pure silver veins were found nearby, but the same story of metallurgy was repeated in embedded silver. No one knew how to extract the riches from the dross. On the upper Arkansas River prospectors cursed the heavy-as-lead ore that held no gold, unaware that it would later make Leadville's silver kings. After the easy metal had been picked up, and the hard rock refused to give up its riches, prospectors wandered away from the Rockies, leaving their shacks to ghosts.

Denver, too, dwindled, since the history of Denver reflects the history of the surrounding regions. The mid-sixties gave the town a grim time. The bodies of criminals swinging from cottonwood trees did not deter other criminals from their dark intent. Yankee Denver had its Civil War problems. Though the town was never raided by the Indians, it was almost scared to death by threats of raids, and almost starved when the Indians cut off supplies along the various stage roads.

Though the winters proved less severe than the shivering Georgians in Auraria had anticipated, nature was not always kind. Fanned by wind, a frightening fire swept through the town in 1863. Ever since then, brick making has been big business around Denver. A city ordinance against frame buildings was passed in 1876. Today, by observing wooden houses, one can tell which parts of town were built outside the city limits and annexed later.

Harmless little Cherry Creek produced a devastating flood in 1864. (The tale of this and subsequent rampages of that eccentric stream may be found in Slice III.) It seemed unfair when the Christmas jollity of that same year of 1864 was ruined by a terrific two-day windstorm, and the next summer grasshoppers poured in from the prairie along with the dust. Summer or winter, the streets of the prairie town were either dusty or muddy.

The severest blow was delivered to Denver in November, 1866, when the Union Pacific Railroad announced its logical decision to build across the continent by way of the plains of Wyoming instead of up and over and down the mountains west of Denver. That blow staggered the town, but aggressive citizens, led by ex-Governor John Evans, quickly raised enough money to finance the Denver Pacific Railroad which tapped the main line at Cheyenne in 1870. Soon other railroads stretched in and out of Denver, but not across the barrier Rockies to the west coast. It was not until 1932, five years after the Moffat Tunnel was bored through the Great Divide at public expense, that Denver achieved a transcontinental rail route.

The Constructive 1870's

The reason that railroads expanded after 1870 was that deep-rock mining had begun to pay. This was chiefly due to one man's curiosity. Nathaniel P. Hill's inquisitiveness led him to cart ore from Gilpin County across the plains to the Missouri River and ship it to Swansea in Wales. Here he watched smelter-men, experienced in hard rock, crush and wash and treat the ore. Hill asked so many questions that, in January, 1868, back in Black Hawk, Gilpin County, Colorado, he fired his first smelter.[6] The county was turned into "Golden Gilpin," because the mines paid. And Denver was the supply point for the activity in the foothills and beyond.

Denver business men of the 1870's, perhaps subconsciously aware that Denver had little reason for growing, were determined to make a city of it. A British tourist of 1872 observed: "Denver is a city of 10,000 to 12,000—I was told 40,000—for all the effort here is for one 'city' to outgrow another. They build recklessly & boast in proportion."[7]

In the autumn of 1873 another Britisher, this time a lone woman riding south of Longmont across the dry plains, recorded: "At the top of every prairie roll I expected to see Denver. But it was not till past 4 that I looked from a considerable height on the great 'City of the Plains,' the metropolis of the territories . . . There the great braggart city of 16,000 souls lay spread out brown and treeless upon a brown and treeless plain."[8]

Had the lady come in summer, she would have seen a faint glimmer of green. Denver was trying hard to remedy its "brown

18

and treeless" state. Householders planted lawns and pumped well water by hand to keep them green. Denverites became slaves to their lawns—they still are!—and were delighted when the mayor bought an irrigation ditch that carried water from the South Platte River to the bluff east of Denver. From it they dug little canals that led the water to the city streets. (An account of this, Denver's first irrigation ditch, is told in Slice II, The City Ditch.)

Behind the braggadocio of the "metropolis of the territories" to which the tourists of the 1870's objected, lay some truth. The population of Denver in 1874 was 14,197. This figure represents an actual count of noses.[9] The isolated town had the same conveniences that eastern cities enjoyed. Ever since 1863, when telegraph wires were strung 600 miles across the plains, Denver had communication with the "States," except when Indians cut the "talking wires" or buffaloes pushed down the poles in their efforts to scratch their itching backs. Since June 22, 1870, when the Denver Pacific Railroad connected Denver with Cheyenne, Denver had rail connections east and west.

Denver had streetcars—horse drawn to be sure, but they ran on rails. Denver homes were lighted with gas, as were some of the streets. Lamplighters carrying short ladders came around each evening to light the street lamps. "When the moon came out they all scurried back and put out the lights so as to conserve gas."[10] (To Colonel James Archer, Irishman, went the credit for the first gas. How he also furnished Denver with its first piped water will be told in Slice I.)

It was not until 1879 that telephones came to Denver. When, that same year, six letter carriers started the first free delivery of mail, historian Vickers asked, "Railways, telegraph, water and gasworks, streetcars, fire-alarm, telephone and free delivery—is there anything more to come?"[11]

The Energetic 1880's

In Colorado, the answer to that question was silver. Someone found that the heavy rock around Leadville which had been cursed because it bore no gold was loaded with silver. Colorado, nicknamed the Centennial State when it joined the Union in

1876, changed its nickname to the Silver State, ignoring Nevada's claim to the name. In 1881 Denver became the official capital of Colorado, but not without bitter and statewide competition.

Because Denver was the supply point for the Leadville and Aspen mines, Denver boomed. Ore came down to the smelters erected north of Denver, where the name of Swansea School still bears witness to Nathaniel Hill's trip to Wales to learn metallurgy.

Not only ore rode down the narrow-gauge trains into Denver, but men who owned the ore. Practically none of the mining men who made big money stayed in the mountain towns to spend it. Some went back East with their loot. Some, politically ambitious, moved to the state capital. Nathaniel P. Hill moved his Boston and Colorado Smelting Company from Black Hawk to a point north of Denver in 1878, giving his new industrial town the classical and apt name of Argo. The next year he went to the U. S. Senate to represent Colorado. Some mining kings came to Denver to invest in banks and real estate. Their silver built business blocks in downtown Denver in the 1880's just as Texas oil does today. (For the story of Leadville's "Ten-Millionaire Tabor" in Denver, where he built buildings and played politics and poker, see Slice VI.)

To erect these office buildings in central locations, older structures were bought and demolished. The Denver Mansions Company tore down Kehler's brick home to build the Windsor Hotel; Tabor bought the pioneer hotel of genial Jake Broadwell at 16th and Larimer to build the Tabor Block, and paid $14,000 for A. B. Daniels' attractive home and grounds at 16th and Curtis as part of the site for the Tabor Grand Opera House.

What did people live in? Tents and huts and log cabins in earliest Denver and brick houses, especially after the fire of 1864. Frame houses with bargeboard cutouts gave way to brick houses with the same kind of trim, usually heavier. Fourteenth Street was the fine residential avenue of the 1870's with two-story brick houses trimmed with iron grillwork. An extant sample of such a house is the gracious Evans home at 1310 Bannock Street, crowned with a captain's walk.

When Denver started to grow with the advent of silver in the 1880's, it was anyone's guess which way it would grow. Real estate subdivisions sprang up on the outskirts of town in all directions, all necessarily linked by public transportation. Horsecars had already made substantial houses possible around 20th and Champa, which was far from town. Horses pulled cars over the 15th Street bridge that spanned the Platte and labored up the bluff to the Boulevard (which was called simply that until years later when it changed to Boulevard F and then Federal Boulevard). Because that section was nearer the mountains, and above the smelter smoke that filled the Platte River Valley, it was obvious that Denver would grow north and west, obvious to a few men who built large homes and planted trees on the Boulevard in the Highlands (North Denver).

A steam-powered railroad ran south, its revenue augmented by patrons of the big Exposition Building on South Broadway. This was called the Denver Circle Railroad because, in theory, it was destined to circle the town. (How Jewell Park, later Overland Park, was developed because of this railroad is told in Slice IX.)

Before electricity replaced horse or steam power, cable cars reached out from town. The cables stopped their endless underground circles in 1900 when the trolley cars took over completely. South Denver developed as four lines of double tracks stretched out Broadway. As soon as streetcars jangled out east on Colfax Avenue, East Denver burgeoned. Baron von Richthofen's promotion of the town of Montclair (northwest of present Lowry Air Force Base), with its trolley lines and a steam railroad to Fairmount Cemetery, was not the most successful but certainly one of the most colorful real estate promotions. (This story is told in Slice VIII.)

Amusement parks around the outskirts of town entertained the bourgeoisie. Such a park was River Front, situated west of downtown on the Platte River. (For the story of this park and navigation of the River, see Slice IV.) In South Denver a beer garden named Sans Souci stood near the great Exposition Building for which Exposition Avenue is named, of course. Later the wooden bowl of the Tuileries on South Broadway held many a bicycle and motorcycle race. The Denver Tramway Company built a baseball park at Broadway southwest of Cherry Creek. Two amusement parks, started when North Denver was farm land, still flourish—Lakeside and Elitch's. (For the story of Elitch's see Slice XI.)

Today, at 3rd and Emerson, there is a public garden in the dry bed of an old lake. This was the lake at Chutes Park, so named because of the high chute that led into the water. Boats plunged down the chute at such a speed that Mrs. Edwin S. Kassler, one of the two ladies selected to make the opening ride, "lost the trinkets from her hair."[12]

With all these suburban schemes, served by public transportation and advertised with a flair comparable to modern publicity methods, where did the fine residential district of Denver settle in the 1880's? Not the Highlands to the northwest, nor South Denver, nor the eastern plateau of Montclair. The silver kings chose the bluff just east of Broadway, one reason being that a man named Brown gave some of his homestead to the state of Colorado for a capitol site. He also built a house at 17th and Broadway—"the only conspicuous building east of Broadway was the dwelling built in 1875-76 by Henry C. Brown."[13] (For the ghosts that haunt the site of this house, see Slice VI, The Tabor Ghosts in Denver.)

Suddenly in the 1880's Brown's bluff was covered with mansions, built by the silver kings from the mountains or by Denver men who were riding the crest of the boom. Grant Street and environs became the fashionable district. The homes that sprang up on Capitol Hill were as vigorous in design and generous in proportion as the whiskers of the men who paid for them.[14]

With the building of the great mansions, somewhat to the astonishment of the democratic frontier town, a tight little social set developed, tighter among the ladies on the hill than among men downtown. Newspapers devoted more and more space to social affairs, featuring Nathaniel P. Hill's daughter-in-law as the social queen who reigned for several decades. Society editors were especially interested in a whist-playing set called "The Sacred Thirty-Six."

Influenced by the ladies, some of the men reorganized their old clubs in order to drop undesirables and make room for well-to-do newcomers, but as a whole the ladies on the hill had one set of standards and the politicians and business men had another, less rigid set. The men attended receptions given by wives of their friends even though the wives were not socially acceptable on Capitol Hill. Such wives included Baby Doe Tabor, the "Unsinkable" Mrs. Brown, and the Baroness Louise von Richthofen.

Racial tolerance among the men in the 1880's is proved by the election of genial Wolfe Londoner as mayor despite his Jewish blood. Londoner credited his election to a practical joke played by Eugene Field. In 1882, when Denver was having its growing pains, Field came to Denver to work on the *Tribune*. He thoroughly enjoyed recording the antics of the citizens; his facile pen matched Denver's exuberance. (Examples of his jokes and his writing will be found in Slice XII.)

Racial tolerance did not extend to the "Yellow Peril." A few Chinese had settled in Denver after finishing their work on the transcontinental railroad lines in 1870. "Chink Alley" was between Blake and Wazee above 16th Street. In 1880 there were 238 Chinese in Denver, mostly laundrymen. Their life was made miserable by boys and hoodlums who teased them, sometimes hurt them, all the while chanting "Chink, Chink, Chinaman" rhymes. This was not only local feeling. In the autumn of 1880 national political slogans included one which stated "The Chinese must go!" That seems to be the explanation for a riot in which Denver men hunted Chinese like rats and hanged one old man on 17th Street for no other reason than the color of his skin. The police made some attempt to quell the riot by using fire hoses. Finally, David J. Cook, the competent head of a local detective agency, organized the police and deputies and stopped the riot.

That the police alone were ineffectual surprised nobody in Denver. If the riot had not been so conspicuous, the police would have preferred to ignore it. Less obvious crimes flourished without interference from the law. From coast to coast Denver-town was known as wide-open. When, occasionally, laws were passed to close gambling joints and call-houses, owners of these places continued to operate, paying the police for protection, and, to the city government, handing fines instead of license fees. Contributions to campaign funds for the election of city officials came from gamblers like blue-eyed Ed Chase, or that artist of the shell game, Jefferson Randolph Smith, better known as "Soapy" Smith.

"Soapy" earned his nickname because, when not hunting bigger game, he stood on the corner of Larimer and 16th Street and sold pieces of soap. Right before the eyes of the crowd he wrapped the soap, first with a hundred dollar bill and then with blue paper, and offered to sell it for five dollars. When the buyer unwrapped the soap, somehow the greenback was not there.

"Soapy" Smith and his ilk streamed out of Denver after the panic of 1893 like rats leaving a sinking ship. This migration was not due to police action but to the lack of suckers with easy money in depressed Denver. "Soapy" went to Cripple Creek and then to Alaska where he was killed, but not by the law.[15]

The Slump
Denver preened itself throughout the 1880's, and 1890 was the peak year. Everything was silvery in Colorado, and the nation flourished. Then social unrest started, especially when farm crops failed. A third party formed in politics, the Populist Party. A purely local angle of the beginnings of that party concerns a homeopathic physician in early Denver, Dr. B. A. Wheeler.[16] Among his many interests was a farm ten miles east of Denver, watered, or supposed to be watered, by the High Line Canal. (The same British financiers who built this canal in 1882 also erected the Windsor Hotel. The history of the Windsor may be found in Slice VII).

The High Line Canal owners claimed "absolute ownership of the water and a charge was made of $10 to $30 an acre as royalty for the privilege of using the water carried in the canal,"[17] even when no water was delivered.

Dr. Wheeler, objecting to the royalty, was refused water. He led other farmers in a fight against the High Line company that ended in the Colorado Supreme Court. Its decision of January, 1888, was that a canal was a common carrier and that the canal owners did not own the water. The company could charge for

24

On December 1, 1868, for no special crime, Denver citizens lynched a distrusted character named Sanford S.C. Dougan. From a cottonwood branch on Cherry Street between 4th and 5th (present 12th Street between Walnut and Larimer), the body swung all night. The next morning two photographers, one of whom was a deaf-mute, fought for a scoop. That at least one of them snapped a picture is proved by the photograph on the left (from the *State Historical Society of Colorado.*) Obviously copying this photograph, the artist who sketched the scene shown on the right added the squabbling photographers and their cameras, as well as a policeman. The police had condoned the lynching. (Sketch from Cook's *Hands Up!* 1882, p. 122. *Denver Public Library.*)

Tree-lined Broadway was the "drag-strip" of Denver and driving was the universal "evening pleasure. . . . Driving is carried on to a great excess. Denver is noted for fine horses," wrote R. H. Constant in 1880. "The number of fine carriages, rigs of every description, excels anything of the kind I ever saw in any City." As early as 1863 the excellence of Colorado horses was observed by M. O. Morris, and attributed to the Civil War. Horse owners of the Midwest, fearing their mounts would be commandeered by the armies, brought or sent the best animals west. "Add to this that a large part of the horses to be seen in these latitudes have been 'jayhawked' at some period and brought out here in fear of recognition. And it is not to be supposed that the horse-lifters would select inferior stock." (Sketch probably from the *Colorado Exchange Journal*, 1888. *Denver Public Library*.)

Fine horses drew the hook and ladder wagon of Highlands Hose No. 1 along West 26th Avenue near the Highlands City Hall in June 1901. The City Hall at Federal Boulevard is still being used by the Denver Fire Department. Photo by Roy S. Kent, *Denver Public Library.*

Even the Street Cleaning Department had reason to be proud of its fine horses. These are crossing the Larimer Street bridge. (Photo from *Denver Public Library.*)

The streetcars on 15th Street near Lawrence were powered by an underground electric wire reached through a slot in the middle rail. Soon after July 31, 1886, its opening day, this system ran over the 15th Street bridge to Center Street. In October the company succeeded in sending a car up Colfax Hill to Kansas Avenue (Logan Street). But by November, 1887, the whole $200,000 project was abandoned. Despite the twenty horsepower dynamo at 15th and Tremont, the electricity was inadequate and spasmodic. Also, both citizens and mules objected to being shocked on rainy days when they stepped on the third rail. The inventor of this scheme was Sydney Howe Short, for five years professor at the University of Denver. He later had a brilliant career in the East, inventing workable electric gadgets. (Photo from Smiley's *History of Denver*, 1901, p. 858. *Denver Public Library.*)

The sketch shows the first ascent of Ivy Baldwin's war balloon, the "Santiago," on 1898. The twenty-four-man Signal Corps unit at Fort Logan helped Sergeant Ivy Baldwin make the balloon out of pongee and rub it with linseed oil and turpentine. They filled steel cylinders with compressed hydrogen obtained by burning wet iron filings and sulphuric acid. With this equipment they went to Cuba in the summer of 1898, where they were the entire air force of the United States Army. (Sketch from *Harper's Monthly Magazine,* June 1901, p. 42. *Denver Public Library.)*

The cornerstone of the Colorado Capitol was laid on the Fourth of July, 1890. During the long speeches, the ladies were glad they had parasols to protect them from the blistering sun. Note the derricks used to lift granite blocks into place after they had been fashioned from the almost 30,000 tons of rough Gunnison County granite. (Photo by F. M. Stiffler from *State Historical Society of Colorado*.)

Later the same year, 1890, the iron workers had their pictures taken on the Capitol tower. Note the two men at the very top. Above the golden dome today the Capitol is topped with an electric light globe, appropriate in 1908 when Denver was known as the "City of Lights." The decision to use the light in place of the proposed statue of a draped woman was made because too many mothers were clamoring to have their beautiful daughters serve as model. The round holes in the tower were filled with stained-glass portraits of Colorado pioneers. including one Indian, one Spanish-American and one woman, Frances Wisebart Jacobs, known as Denver's Mother of Charities. (Photo by U. S. Voice, from *Lester D. Galvin, State Historical Society of Colorado*.)

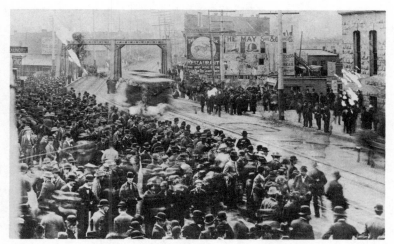

On March 15, 1894, derby-hatted Denver men awaited gunfire in the City Hall War. Would Governor Waite order the troops, who were at the scene, to fire gattling guns on the City Hall, or would the Fire and Police Boards, barricaded therein, toss out the fused dynamite with which they were armed? Note the Circle Railroad Station to the left of the Larimer Street bridge and the May Company's sign painted on the building to the right of the bridge. It advertises that derby hats could be bought at the May for three dollars. (*Denver Public Library.*)

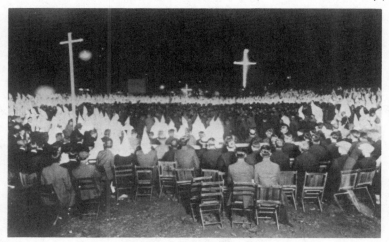

During its political reign in Colorado, the Ku Klux Klan met east of Golden on top of Table Mountain (spelled Kastle Mountain by the Klan). Though the fiery cross was burned on Kastle Mountain, the office of the Kleagle, Dr. Galen Locke, was at 1345 Glenarm Street, Denver. (Photo from Fuller's *The Maelstrom,* 1925, opp. p. 80. *Denver Public Library.*)

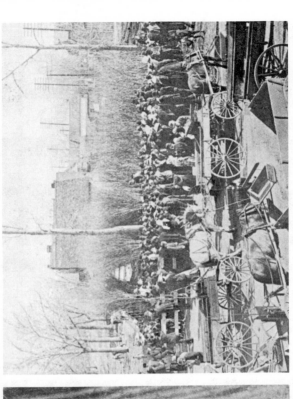

On the left, Mayor Robert W. Speer inspects trees to be given away to any citizen who wants to plant and water them; on the right, crowds come for the saplings. The older residential streets of Denver are now shaded by these fifty-year old trees (except where they have been sacrificed on the altar of four-lane highways). The trees are a living memorial to a mayor who did so much to help a desert town turn into a green city. (The photos are from *Denver Municipal Facts*, v. 1, p. 1, April 3, 1909, and v. 3, p. 30, Jan. 14, 1911. *Denver Public Library*.)

delivering water to the farmer, and that was all. This case was an epochal decision in the annals of irrigation law.

What has the High Line case to do with the Populist Party in Colorado? Dr. Wheeler and the farmers who organized to fight this case joined other farmers from eastern Colorado who were suffering from a periodic drought. These groups, along with the idle silver miners and other victims of the economic slump fast bogging down the nation, helped form the Populist Party.

The reason silver miners of Colorado were out of work was that the price of silver had dropped so low that owners closed the mines. Westerners were convinced that if the government would only start to mint silver again, the economy of the country (and certainly of Colorado) would recover. The nation, Westerners averred, was being "crucified on a cross of gold." This statement was made by the "young Nebraska lion," William Jennings Bryan. For the 1908 nomination for President of this "silver-tongued orator of the Platte," Denver completed its City Auditorium.

The Panic of 1893 hit Denver in July. Ten banks failed, real estate values collapsed, mortgages were foreclosed, and the town literally seethed with unemployed. Denver established a camp for them at the foot of 16th St. (Told in Slice IV, River Front Park.)

During the panic, the wisest of governors would have had trouble trying to control Colorado. To the unemployment problems were added labor strikes among the gold miners of Cripple Creek, coal strikes in southern Colorado, and a nation-wide Pullman strike. The Populist governor, Davis H. Waite, was certainly not endowed with the kind of wisdom that could deal with such emergencies. He was full of theories, unworkable. For instance, he wanted to ship silver to Mexico, have it coined into "Fandango dollars," and bring it back to Colorado to use as currency. Of this the legislature did not approve, but nevertheless earned the name of the "Freak Legislature." Perhaps this was because it passed one bill that was radical, even revolutionary. This bill allowed the people to vote on woman suffrage. In November 1893, women were franchised. On December 2, 1893, Governor Waite proclaimed that Colorado women henceforth could vote, and at the next election the women's vote defeated Governor Waite.

This man was not wise, but he was brave. He even tried to reform the notoriously corrupt city government of Denver. The result was the "City Hall War." During this fracas he ordered the First Regiment of Colorado Infantry and the Chaffee Light Artillery to train their guns on the City Hall at 14th and Larimer. Within sat two members of the Fire and Police Board whom the Governor wished to remove from office. These beleaguered men, accompanied by the city sheriff and entire police force (more than 200 in all) were supplied with the necessities of life and war by a grateful underworld, including "Soapy" Smith. Rather to the disappointment of the onlookers who crowded the streets and nearby windows, no shot was fired, no blood was shed.

Recovery from the Panic

Slowly Colorado, and therefore Denver, recovered from the silver panic. Gold, which had crucified Colorado, came to its rescue when the gold mines of Cripple Creek poured out their riches. This golden era is symbolized by the gleaming dome of the state capitol building. Originally covered with copper, it was sheathed in 1908, again in 1950, not with silver for the Silver State but with 200 ounces of pure, non-tarnishing gold leaf.

Agriculture gradually topped mining as the state's major source of income. This was made possible by the reservoirs built to catch the spring runoff from the snows high in the Rockies. The reservoir gates dole out water so that all year long Denver may drink and wash and raise lawns, and the farmers downstream on the Platte may produce rich crops. Their sugar beet crop is so large that the region is called the "sugar bowl of America."

In 1944—and this was before Western Slope water was diverted through tunnels to the South Platte River—an engineer stated: "About a million acre-feet of water flow off the eastern slope of the Rocky Mountains into the Platte River Basin. This water is being utilized and conserved to a degree exceeding any other similar enterprise in the entire world, unless we except some small areas in Spain."[18]

Cattle raising had flourished on the unfenced prairies until the middle 1880's. After barbed wire, farmers bred fine cattle and fattened them for market. Ranchers in the mountains raised

34

alfalfa on lovely uplands to winter-feed their white-faced cattle, turning them loose in the summer to feed on mountain greenery. The high ranges were so lucrative that, for their exclusive use, cattlemen warred—actually warred—on sheepmen.

Denver was the market for both cattle and sheep. It proudly became the big cowtown of the region, developing stockyards and packing houses. Along with the cattle the cowboys came to town. In October, 1887, at River Front Park (see Slice IV) a cowboy tournament was held. The events included "catching, saddling and riding a wild bronco . . . roping and hog-tying a wild steer . . . 'tailing' a steer . . . picking up twenty single potatoes by a rider going at a pace no slower than a lope . . ." Although the Humane Society quickly eliminated "tailing," it was from such tournaments (and this was one of the earliest big ones in the United States) that rodeos evolved.[19]

What is now called the National Western Stock Show and Rodeo is held every January in Denver. Ever since its beginning in 1905, Stock Show Week traditionally turns out to be the coldest week of the year. Cold or not, Denver people have always crowded the streetcars to see a performance of the Stock Show. Society night, Monday, used to be exciting when the new-fangled automobiles frightened the carriage horses. Denver men, proud of their fine mounts, entered in competition against Loula Long from Kansas City and other "foreign" exhibitors. Young Denver competed in the riding events, and the military from Fort Logan and Fort D. A. Russell (now Fort Warren) outside of Cheyenne gave exhibitions. To the old-timer, the rodeo, a rather recent innovation at the Stock Show, will never equal the thrill of watching a troop of U. S. Cavalry, with sabers drawn, charge across the tanbark.

Politics after the Turn of the Century
Politically, the tale of Colorado, and therefore Denver, during the early 1900's resembled the tale in other states. In New York, Governor Theodore Roosevelt had forced big business to relinquish political control and pay equitable taxes. Colorado struggled with the same problem. Mining men, turning their energies

into furnishing the State with electricity and water, with railroads and smelters, became politically all powerful. Many of them were not interested in preserving a democratic form of government. There was great inequality between labor and capital, "between privilege and the people,"[20] as Judge Ben Lindsey expressed it. "Colorado was considered by many reformers of the day as probably the worst governed state in the Union."[21] And the price Denver paid for being the state capital was that it was governed by the state legislature which in turn was controlled by vested interests.

After years of effort, Article XX of the Colorado Constitution gave Denver home rule, and she adopted a charter in 1904. Nearby towns like Valverde in the Platte Valley, Montclair on the plains, and Argo, the smelter town, were consolidated with Denver. The enlarged town was separated from Arapahoe County to become the City and County of Denver. The unification of city and county makes for a simpler government not enjoyed by cities such as Chicago in Cook County. It is unusual for the state capital to be located in the biggest city in the state. In 1950 the three largest of such dual-powered cities were Boston, Indianapolis, and Denver.

But home rule for Denver did not mean freedom from political machinations. In 1904, in an effort to prevent irregularities at the polls, the Colorado Supreme Court itself supervised the Denver elections.[22]

The first mayor elected under home rule was Robert W. Speer. He was one of the thousands who had come to Denver for his health. Holding city offices, mostly appointive, since 1880, he knew all the angles of city government. He was astute enough to retain the mayor's chair from 1904 to 1912, again from 1916 to his death in 1918.

Despite the non-democratic processes of his corrupt City Hall machine, the continued election of Mayor Speer was one of the best things that ever happened to Denver. He had a vision of the "city beautiful." When he visited Dusseldorf, to find out how the best-governed city in Europe was managed, "he looked like a painter seeing a paintable landscape . . . When he came home . . .

36

he was no longer merely good, he was wise. Mayor Speer set his city going in the direction you can see it taking now."[23]

Largely to Mayor Speer, Denver owes its Civic Center. He improved and created parks and, what is more important, he ordered all "Keep Off the Grass" signs removed from the lawns in these parks. He annually gave away thousands of elms and maples so that the city might have shade. "Mayor Bob" turned the eyesore that was the bed of Cherry Creek into a walled channel with a tree-lined avenue beside it, appropriately named Speer Boulevard.[24]

Perhaps the mayor's most controversial achievement was when he and his publicity director persuaded Mrs. William Cody that the body of her husband should be buried at the top of a foothill west of Denver.[25] (See Slice X for Buffalo Bill's connections with Denver before his burial on Lookout Mountain.)

Speer's enthusiasm for his town was infectious. Influenced by his motto, "Give while you live," Denver citizens gave lavishly—gateways to parks, Greek colonnades, statues, fountains, and the marble temple that crowns Cheesman Park. Speer's personal preference in the way of memorials was statuary, especially of children. The Children's Fountain at City Park, copied from one in Dusseldorf, was the choice of this childless man as well as the Lullaby Fountain in Washington Park. (See Slice XII which explains Denver's connection with this statue of Wynken, Blynken and Nod.)

For a statue to be erected in the Civic Center in memory of Robert W. Speer, a local gambling man named Vaso Chucovich left a sizable bequest in 1933, years after Speer's death. Competition for the commission between local and foreign sculptors became so heated that the city officials compromised. They used the money to erect the Robert W. Speer Memorial Building at the Denver General Hospital. Though this is not a statue, Speer would surely have approved because this building houses the children's wards.

Between World Wars
Denver did its part in World War I, like other American towns,

and its subsequent history followed the national trend. It gradually decontaminated its politics. "Big Business" relinquished its hold on votes, and the underworld no longer blatantly defied the law. Career men in city government started to replace less qualified political appointees. Like the nation, Denver went in and out of the Prohibition Era, 1916 to 1932 in Colorado. The depression following 1929 was partially alleviated by the Work Projects Administration, which accomplished such diverse things as the creation of Mountain View Park with its dramatic sundial silhouetted against the Rocky Mountains, and the construction of a model of Denver as it was in 1860 for the State Historical Museum.

Three events in Denver that followed the first World War should be listed. The only creditable one of the three happened in 1922. District Attorney Philip Van Cise rounded up thirty-four confidence men in the basement of the Universalist Church at East Colfax and Lafayette Street (razed in September, 1958). This place was used instead of the city jail because members of the underworld gang would have been "sprung" from the jail almost as soon as they were incarcerated. Van Cise's prisoners were headed by a pleasant elderly man named Lou Blonger. "From the late eighties until 1922 he held the Denver police department in his corrupt grasp."[26] As long as he did not bilk Denver citizens who might have embarrassed the police by complaints, Blonger was allowed to fleece Denver visitors and this he did from the time he took over the crown of the underworld from "Soapy" Smith. No one knows how many times Lou Blonger collected a downpayment on the 16th Street viaduct, from a tenderfoot.

Despite the money available to the gang, and despite the legal talent paid by this money, Van Cise managed to bring twenty men to trial. He secured convictions and Lou Blonger died in the penitentiary.

Two other noteworthy events of the 1920's were not so creditable. One was the reign of the Ku Klux Klan. It "had a rapid rise in Colorado. In 1924 it controlled the election of Governor, Senator and a majority of the state legislature. But its ascendency was short lived; it declined as rapidly as it had risen."[27] Few people, however, who saw the "fiery cross" burning on top of Castle Rock east of Golden will forget this era of intolerance.

The other unhappy event was the Denver tramway strike. Top wages in 1920 being thirty cents an hour, tramway workers asked for a raise. The management felt this was impossible. Mediation failing, the workers threatened to walk out. On June 29th, "Black Jack" Jerome and his scabs came to town—strike-breakers imported by the company from San Francisco. On August 1, 1920, the tramway workers—906 of them—refused to work. The mayor enrolled 2,000 volunteers to run the street cars, many of whom were young men recently home from the war.

There were clashes. Partisans of both viewpoints were hurt, seven people were killed. On one occasion, when four street cars were flipped over at Colfax and Logan Street, strike-breakers dramatically sought sanctuary before the altar of the Roman Catholic Cathedral. The *Denver Post* was raided and wrecked. One of the casualties there was the stuffed baby elephant prized by Publisher Tammen because it had been born in his Sells-Floto Circus. The hilarious crowd also seized a truck loaded with rolls of newsprint. The next day the city cleaning department was faced with the problem of picking up unrolled paper for blocks up Champa Street.[28]

The situation got so out of hand that martial law was declared (the first time since the Indian problems during the early sixties). United States troops came from Fort Logan, and General Leonard Wood brought troops from Camp Funstan in Kansas. The strike-breakers were disarmed, "Black Jack" Jerome left town. During the hot weeks from August 7 to September 8, 1920, a United States infantryman with gun rode every car, every trailer. All that seemed to result from the tramway strike was bitterness.[29]

Turning to pleasanter events of the 1920's, it should be noted that East, West, and South High Schools were all given new buildings before the crash of 1929. The between-war period developed Denver libraries, museums, the civic theater, and the symphony orchestra. This growth was no different from that in other towns, but the Red Rocks amphitheater where the orchestra plays in the summer is unique. (For John Brisben Walker's early ideas for the Red Rocks, see Slice IV.)

The population of these years grew slowly. Even with 325,000 in 1940, Denver was accused of being not a city but an overgrown cowtown. A bit smug in having a pleasant climate and interesting people, Denver did not bustle.

Since World War II

Today, Denver is part of the national rush toward urban living. In an effort to explain this migration locally, two recent waves into the Denver area are pointed out. During the second World War thousands of young men were trained in Denver and Colorado, many of whom returned after the war to make their homes.

The second wave of population comes from the establishment of Federal agencies here. Two of the largest of these are at either end of Sixth Avenue—the Federal Center (built for the Remington Small Arms Plant during the war) on the west and Lowry Air Force Base on the east. Because of these and many government bureaus, Denver is called "Little Washington." This would not have surprised William Gilpin, first governor of the Territory of Colorado. Back in the 1860's he held a geo-political theory that Colorado was perfectly suited to become the capital of the world![30]

The Federal thinking behind the establishment of government agencies in Colorado concerns, first, the climate (unlike Washington's) ; second, decentralization of government offices; and third, that Denver, being about as inland as a town can be, is somewhat safe from enemy attack. This theory, valid before the era of intercontinental missiles, still influences manufacturers of rocket parts and missile components to move near Denver, even though aware of water shortage and freight charges. Transportation bills are large because Denver is so many miles from everywhere.

Today, for the first time, manufacturing is the major source of income in Colorado, larger than agriculture despite cattle, wheat, and sugar beets; larger than mining despite zinc, molybdenum, and uranium; even larger than the tourist trade.

Is Denver Different?

Has Denver any characteristics that distinguish it from other overgrown American cities?

Perhaps there are two—neither of them man-made.

The first is climate. Many people like the Colorado climate with its vagaries. Storms seldom last. Because of Denver's altitude, a mile above the sea, it is hot in the sun and, supposedly, cool in the shade. Because of the mountain barrier to the west, the storms are unpredictable. One of the endless jokes about the local climate concerns the weatherman who asked to be transferred from his Denver post because the weather did not agree with him.

In Denver's earlier days, the dry, mile-high climate attracted health-seekers in droves (among them some of her best citizens). Consumptives became a major problem, especially when they were penniless. Unbelieveable tales of their hardships are literally true. The city tried to care for them. It is said that the half-open, half-closed cars of the Denver Tramway Company were devised because the tubercular needed fresh air. Many private sanatoriums were built, such as the one whose buildings now house the headquarters of Lowry Air Force Base. The world-famous National Jewish Hospital at Denver grew out of the early problems of coping with the emigrant sick. This institution has no religious barriers, but "none may enter who can pay and none may pay who enter."

Denver's second distinguishing characteristic may be its proximity to the Rocky Mountains which furnish Denver not only with water but with 150 miles of snow-capped view and a convenient playground.

True, one cannot always see the view because of smoke and skyscrapers. But neither of these problems is new. When Francis Parkman camped on Cherry Creek in 1846 he recorded: "Weather too smoky to see the mountains."[31] And in 1910, when Daniels and Fisher's tower was rising, Buffalo Bill complained: "I am not a sentimentalist, not at all; but when I come to Denver and every time I see the new massive steel frames of skyscrapers springing into the air, I cannot but think of the time when a view of the foothills could have been obtained—and a good one, too—from any point in the city east of Blake Street."[32]

Not content with a distant view, Denver people have always gone into the mountains for recreation. In the early days they

41

camped for weeks by fishing streams and, later, families returned to the same resorts summer after summer, or built mountain homes where they lived for three months every year. When the journeys were made by horseback or wagon, by stage or even bicycle, the vacation had to be longer than a week end. Short trips, or even one-day picnics, were made possible by the advent of the narrow-gauge railroads, though these companies made little profit because most Denver men held passes for themselves "and party"! Fishing trains up the Platte Canyon were crowded on week ends, and it is a wonder that any columbines were left in the mountains when excursionists, loaded with wild flowers, returned from trips to the Georgetown Loop or to the Boulder mountains via "The Switzerland Trail."

On Sundays trolley cars to Golden were thronged. From Golden one could ride funiculars to the top of Castle Rock or Lookout Mountain, or hike around the foothills. The Colorado Mountain Club, organized in Denver in 1912, persuaded the city of Denver to build the Beaver Brook Trail on the north slopes of Lookout Mountain. Mountaineers managed by use of trains and feet to climb mountains in every range of the Colorado Rockies. Some of these trips made before automobiles were common had the excitement of being first ascents.

"Wheelmen" made prodigious trips into the mountains. To act as brakes on the rough road down the west side of Berthoud Pass, they fastened young trees to their bicycles. When automobiles came to stay, motorists drove on old wagon roads without waiting for paved highways. The narrower and steeper the road, the more the driver enjoyed the trip. His pleasure was not always shared by guests from the flatlands.

A newspaper man who found Denver stimulating in 1914 wrote: "While Denver partisans hate one another's opinions and plans with fury not lessened by the high altitude, almost all are bound by a deep appreciation of one of the magnificently beautiful regions of the world."[33]

With the advent of the automobile, farsighted men persuaded Denver taxpayers to buy land in the mountains for public enjoyment.[34] As more and more land is fenced by private owners, these city-owned parks are increasingly appreciated. When George Cranmer directed the Parks Department of the city he started a great ski area—Winter Park beyond the Moffat Tunnel—which is owned and operated by Denver and used by thousands.

The road to the top of Mount Evans, 14,260 feet above sea level, was a Denver project. This is said to be one of the highest automobile roads in the world. Whether or not that boast is true, it surely must be true that there are few other cities of over half a million people from which a citizen can drive to the top of a major mountain in less than two hours.

Could this be Denver's real claim to distinction—that from it, escape is easy?

NOTES

(Throughout the Sources in this book, *RMN* has been used as an abbreviation for *Rocky Mountain News*.)

[1]Bell, J. R. *Journal of Captain John R. Bell . . .1820;* ed. by H. M. Fuller and L. R. Hafen. Glendale, Calif., Arthur H. Clark Co., 1957. p. 146.

[2]Du Bois, J. V. *Campaigns in the West, 1858-1861.* Tucson, Arizona Pioneers Historical Society, 1949. p. 117.

[3]Smiley, J. C. *History of Denver.* Denver, Times-Sun, 1901. p. 70.

[4]The emigrants must have torn up these guidebooks, or worn them out, for how else can one explain the scarcity of copies remaining today of the hundreds that were printed in 1858-59? Nolie Mumey of Denver has recently issued photostatic copies of some of these guidebooks. See L. R. Hafen's *Pike's Peak Gold Rush Guidebooks of 1859 by Luke Tierney, William B. Parsons and Summaries of the Other Fifteen.* Glendale, Calif., Arthur H. Clark Co., 1941.

[5]Smiley, op. cit. p. 241.

[6]Nathaniel P. Hill's letters from Colorado in 1864 and 1865 were published in the *Colorado Magazine,* October 1956 through June 1957.

[7]H. Martyn Hart, later Dean of St. John's in the Wilderness Cathedral (Episcopal) in Denver, went around the world in 1872. This quotation is from his diary. Arps, L. W., ed. "Dean Hart Pre-Views his Wilderness." In *Colorado Magazine,* v. 36, p. 32. Jan. 1959.

[8]From a photostatic copy of a letter written by Isabella Bird from Colorado on October 23, 1873. The copy is in the Denver Public

Library. Miss Bird's book *A Lady's Life in the Rocky Mountains* (London, Murray, 1879) is based on her letters.

[9]Vickers, W. B. *History of the City of Denver.* Chicago, Baskins, 1880. p. 230.

[10]Cassidy, Belle "Recollections of Early Denver," In *Colorado Magazine* v. 29, p. 53, Jan. 1953.

[11]Vickers, op. cit. p. 240.

[12]Interview with E. S. Kassler, 1957.

[13]Smiley, op. cit. p. 465.

[14]Pictures of these mansions in words and photographs are in E. E. Kohl's *Denver's Historic Mansions.* Denver, Sage Books, 1957.

[15]Parkhill, Forbes *The Wildest of the West,* enlarged ed. Denver, Sage Books, 1957.

[16]For a biography of Dr. B. A. Wheeler, see A. F. Stone's *History of Colorado.* Chicago, Clarke, 1918. v. 3, p. 818.

[17]Steinel, A. T. and Working, D. W. *History of Agriculture in Colorado.* Fort Collins, State Agricultural College, 1928. p. 207.

[18]Bancroft, G. J. "Diversion of Water from the Western Slope." In *Colorado Magazine* v. 21, p. 178, Sept. 1944.

[19]*Denver Republican,* Oct. 14, 15, 16, 1887. Also of rodeo interest is a silver belt, exhibited in the Colorado State Historical Museum, which was offered as a prize, in 1901 at Denver's Festival of Mountain and Plain, to the best cowboy rider.

[20]Lindsey, B. B. and O'Higgins, H. J. *The Beast.* New York, Doubleday, 1910. Judge Lindsey is best known for his juvenile court and his theories about "companionate marriage."

[21]MacColl, E. K. "John Franklin Shafroth, Reform Governor of Colorado 1909-1913." In *Colorado Magazine* v. 29, p. 37, Jan. 1952.

[22]Thomas, C. S. "Fifty Years of Political History." In *History of Colorado* by J. H. Baker and L. R. Hafen. Denver, State Historical Society, 1927. v. 3, p. 935.

[23]Steffens, Lincoln *Autobiography.* New York, Harcourt Brace, 1931. p. 651.

[24]To publicize city problems and improvements, Denver issued an official magazine filled with photographs. Its names and dates are: *Denver Municipal Facts,* 1909-1912; *City of Denver,* 1912-1914; *Municipal Facts,* 1918-1931.

[25]After the mayor died, the City Council authorized E. C. McMechen to write a biography of Speer. It is called *Robert W. Speer, a City Builder.* Denver, Smith-Brooks, 1919.

[26]Parkhill, op. cit. District Attorney P. S. Van Cise wrote his own story in *Fighting the Underworld.* Boston, Houghton, 1936.

[27]Hafen, L. R. *Colorado, the Story of a Western Commonwealth.* Denver, Peerless, 1933. p. 288.

[28]Pierce, N. O. Interview, Sept. 1958.

[29]Denver Committee of Religious Forces *Denver Tramway Strike of 1920*. Denver, 1921.

[30]"As for the site upon which the city of Denver is founded . . . we are upon the isothermal axis, which is the trunk line (the thalwez) of intense and intelligent energy, where civilization has its largest field, its highest development, its inspired form." From William Gilpin's address to the Denver Board of Trade, February 1869, as quoted in Smiley op. cit. p. 438.

[31]Parkman, Francis *The Oregon Trail Journal*, ed. by Mason Wade. New York, Harper, 1947. v. 2, p. 471.

[32]Colonel Cody granted an interview to a reporter from the *Denver Times* on February 16, 1910.

[33]Chenery, W. L. *So It Seemed*. New York. Harcourt Brace, 1952.

[34]Bradley, S. B. "The Origin of the Denver Mountain Parks System." In *Colorado Magazine* v. 9, p. 29, Jan. 1932. In this article Bradley gives credit for the original mountain park idea, including the Red Rocks theater, to John Brisben Walker. Walker talked before the Denver Real Estate Exchange in 1910. The Exchange took the matter up, other organizations became interested and on May 12, 1921, the people of Denver voted to assess themselves one-half mill levy for five years in order to build a system of mountain parks. For further information about John Brisben Walker, see Slice IV, River Front Park on the South Platte.

Drinking Water

Prairie dogs don't need it but people do. That's why, on the Great American Desert, Indians and mountain men made camp by a stream. Cherry Creek, for instance. On August 15, 1846, Francis Parkman found drinking water at the site of Denver, filtered drinking water. His diary records that he arrived at the junction of Cherry Creek and the Platte River after a hot morning's march to see "cherries—plums—black currants—and gooseberries. No water in creek—dug holes and got some."[1]

The first residents of Auraria and Denver drank water directly from the creek and the river, they and their oxen, horses, mules, and companionable dogs. Soon, even in that septic age, the purity of the water was questioned. The more particular people indicated a willingness to buy drinking water secured from sources away from town and presumably pure, like Baker's spring, which was under the east end of present Colfax Viaduct.[2] W. S. Cheesman, druggist, advertised water on draught or in bottles at his store on the corner of Blake and F (Fifteenth) Street.

Water peddling became good business. Though no accounts have been found of tank wagons in earliest Denver, they must have conducted their trade in much the same manner as the water wagons that peddled artesian water in the 1880's. Then four water wagons appeared on the streets of town. The water boys charged a nickel to deliver a two-and-a-half gallon bucket to the first floor, but they figured carrying it to the second floor was worth a dime.[3]

Dust being a major nuisance, sprinkling the streets also became good business. The price was twenty-five cents a week for a twenty-five foot frontage—a cent a foot and well worth it to the housewife fighting a losing battle armed with a turkey duster.[4] The city government, much to the delight of barefoot children, continued this sprinkling until the streets were paved, and then had to wash them. The importance of water!

Buying household water by the gallon was adequate for men who stayed in town only until they could get to the gold-veined hills, but family men who meant to live in Denver needed a better supply. Most householders dug wells. The water was alkaline but plentiful. These wells were shallow, shallower in West Denver (former Auraria) because that section lay on the lower side of the Creek. Denver men had to dig somewhat deeper which may have improved the purity of the water but certainly increased the labor. As more wells were dug, the water table lowered so wells had to be deepened. This posed a problem for householders who had carefully dug their wells first and then erected their kitchens over them.[5] (Today water is tapped from the Denver Formation which lies between forty and sixty feet below ground.)

Surface wells and buckets of water did not solve the water problem of a town of over 12,000 people. Saloons, though numerous, were not the answer. What Denver needed, and started to get in 1872, was indoor plumbing. The first company to pipe water into houses was the Denver City Water Company. Its president was an affable man from northern Ireland by way of St. Louis, James Archer. He was interested in practically everything that went on in Denver, from railroads—he first apeared in Denver in 1869 asking for two million dollars to complete the Kansas Pacific—to sugar beets to the Mercantile Library to the Archery Club to concerts. Especially successful were his gas works that lighted houses and streets from January 1871. Even today, fancy chandeliers in some of Denver's older homes have gas jets as well as electric sockets.

Colonel James Archer was one of Denver's most prominent men in the 1870's. It seems quite unfair that, except for a street named Archer Place and an enormous statue of him over his grave in Riverside Cemetery, nothing is left to remind Denver of the president of the first water company.[6]

On the board of directors of this company were two men whose names are still known to Denver. Walter S. Cheesman is remembered by the Cheesman Memorial in Cheesman Park and by the great Cheesman Dam on the South Platte River. David Moffat's name is on the Moffat Filter Plant and on the Moffat Tunnel, which was his dream.

But the day water first flowed through the pipes of the Denver City Water Company in January, 1872, was a day that belonged to President James Archer. He gave a delightful reception in his rooms on Larimer Street, rooms as elegant as the vintage wines and aromatic cigars which he offered his guests. They afterwards descended to F (Fifteenth) Street where the tests of water power were to be made. Hoses were attached to fire hydrants, the pumping machinery was turned on, and water arched more than a hundred feet into the air.[7]

The system was a success. This pleased the city, it pleased Colonel Archer, and it pleased the representatives of the New York company who had installed the machinery. Their system was known as the Holly direct pumping system. The citizens of Denver always referred to the water that came through these first pipes as Holly water.

The source of the water was the underground flow of Cherry Creek. It filtered through sand into a sump thirteen feet deep. The *News* reporter stated that the sump, or well, was near the Platte River but corrected himself the next day to Cherry Creek. The surface of the well measured sixteen by seventeen feet and the sides were lined with peeled poles. A pumping station was located near present 15th and Bassett Streets in the railroad yards. Some of the original pipe still rusts underground.[8] In 1872 four miles of pipe were laid around town, but not deep enough. After nine days of zero weather in January, 1875, the pipes had to be dug up from the old level of three feet below the surface and relaid at five feet below, and that took many months to complete. Fortunately at that time, Denver was mainly included between Welton and Wazee Streets and Cherry Creek and 21st Street. As nearly every home had a well, little suffering from water shortage was felt.[9]

48

Almost immediately after the company started operating, they had to double the size of their sump. They urged their customers to use water for domestic purposes only, but if a man was willing to pay extra he could water his garden. An emergency arose on August 2, 1876. The superintendent of the water company issued an order allowing householders with special irrigation licenses "to use water at any hour of the day or night for three days from date, if necessary, on account of the grasshoppers."[10]

Two days were enough. After arriving "like a tornado" the grasshoppers ate up every green thing in the South Platte Valley in two days. When they flew south, nothing verdant was left in Denver except a few lawns which had been flooded with water.

When Colonel Archer first organized his Denver City Water Company in 1870, Denver had 4,759 people and a sump might have been adequate for their water supply. But Denver grew. It held seven times that many people in 1880. The water company had to expand. Reorganized under a new name, it moved south to build a "colossal" plant. This involved a spillway that drew water from the Platte River about three miles south of Denver where the water would always be pure, the company thought. A ditch carried water to a lake. This was a slight depression in which Titus Spring had bubbled up. A second ditch carried water from the lake to West 12th Avenue where a building housed two pumps. Hydraulically powered, these pumps forced water into the mains beneath the city streets, and it was still called Holly water.

The lake lay east of the river, north of Ellsworth Avenue and south of 8th Avenue. (See endpaper map.) It was named Lake Archer so that Denver would always remember its water pioneer. But the lake has dried up and who remembers Colonel James Archer? The ditches, where boys loved to swim, have been filled in. Only the building that housed the pumps still stands. Enlarged, this is now the Denver Water Board's West Side Storehouse and Yard at 12th and Shoshone.

When the enlarged company started pumping water from the Platte about 1878, this Holly water, even though settled in Lake Archer and filtered in sand, was not so pure as had been hoped.

49

Kitchen faucets were equipped with strainers to catch stray fish. The city officials worried about this water, and, of course, about the shallow wells still in use all over town. One man's well would often be just a few feet from his neighbor's outhouse. Then there was Cherry Creek. Though its wide bed was used as a dumping ground, even for garbage, some people drank its water. At the little irrigation ditches that lined the streets, dogs, horses, and careless human beings quenched their thirst. No wonder typhoid fever was an integral part of life in Colorado.

About sanitation there was much talk and little action. Finally Dr. Charles Denison made a map of the water supply of Denver, indicated on it possible places of contamination, and presented his report to a meeting of Denver physicians. He blasted both them and the city government for not doing something about contaminated water. Typhoid, he insisted, was not the only killer traceable to impure water.[11]

The city had considered for some years the constructing of a sewer system. After Dr. Denison's report, they actually started to build it. Progress was slow because property owners, objecting to assessments, carried their objections to court. Officials were impeded by tax payers and needled by doctors. By 1886, the city which held about 54,000 people had only 3,050 water closets and 3,226 kitchen sinks emptying into the sewer.[12]

Presumably pinning their faith to the folk-saying that water purifies itself in a hundred yards, the city officials allowed the sewers to empty into the Platte River at Wewatta near 27th Street. This ignorance, sometimes called indifference by the towns and farmers down the river, continued until the comparatively recent installation of a sewage disposal plant. Today there is the added problem of foam from detergents.

In 1883 Holly water in Denver acquired competition from an unexpected source. A man named McCormick bored a deep hole west of the river. He was probing for coal beds. Much to his disgust, he was forced to stop drilling because artesian water bubbled up. Though attempts had been previously made, this is the first well on record that tapped the pressured water in what geologists call the Laramie Formation in the Denver Basin. (McCormick's pioneer bore was drilled just south of the Bears' baseball stadium in present Denver.)

The news of this water strike spread like gold-fever. Whoever had money, and plenty of men had money in Denver in the early 1880's, drilled a deep well. Zang, the brewer, was among the first. His well was 666 feet deep. Messrs. Daniels and Fisher, the department store owners, struck water at 575 feet. By June, 1886, over 130 artesian wells had been sunk.[13] One of these was the Albany Hotel's well. Drilled about 800 feet down, this still furnishes pure, soft water for boilers and drinking. It is pumped through an eight inch casing which must be pulled up and inspected periodically. Many other artesian wells are still in use in downtown Denver.

The Windsor Hotel advertised that water from its two wells was pure and available to take home for a small fee. Better patronized, not only because it was free but because it had a vigorous flow long after other wells had to be pumped, was the well at the Arapahoe County Court House. This well was on the 16th Street side, between Tremont and Court Place. It was almost a thousand feet deep. From it citizens fetched water in jugs and pitchers and bottles and buckets. As late as the turn of the century, it was not unusual for a business man to stop at the Court House well on his way home from work in the evening. He would take a long drink and fill a bottle to carry home on the trolley car as a treat for his wife.

The newspapers were full of the benefits of artesian water as opposed to Holly water. Learned treatises were printed, discussing the mineral content of each well. The opinions of doctors were sought as to which well was best to cure which ailment. Finally an enterprising reporter asked "a noted liveryman of the city" to give his opinion on the efficacy of artesian water. The liveryman replied by pointing out the unusual number of runaway horses on the city streets. "In every instance," the liveryman stated, "the horses have been drinking artesian water which gave them new life, new spirit, new energy and new kidneys. . . . [If you] see a runaway you may bet your sweet life he's taken fright at being brought near a ditch of Holly water. Why, I haven't a horse in my stable that I can get to cross the Platte River."[14]

Artesian wells were successful, though expensive to drill and, when the pressure lessened, expensive to pump. Therefore, for the ordinary householder in the 1880's, a connection with a water company's pipes was more economical. Many water companies competed with Holly water for business. Eleven water companies in Denver rose and fell between Archer's initial plant and the acquisition of the waterworks by the City and County of Denver in 1918.[15]

Some of these companies were started by eastern men who thought all a water company had to do was to sink a pump in the bounteous river that Nature seemed always to lead through a city. They soon found out about water rights on the meager western rivers. With eleven companies all squabbling over rights in Cherry Creek and the Platte River, the dockets of the Colorado courts were packed with water cases. The companies fought among themselves. Once the rates were cut 25%, and once in an effort to break a small company, one of the larger firms furnished water free for two years. All sorts of methods were used to wangle franchises from the city. One by one the small companies were absorbed by the larger ones until one corporation was left. This, the powerful Denver Union Water Company, was managed by W. S. Cheesman, later by David Moffat, and then by Cheesman's son-in-law, John Evans.

Two things made the average Denver citizen realize that this one company had taken over. One was that all water company buildings were soon painted a light yellow, the paint favored by the Denver Union Water Company. The other was that the iron lids over manholes were initialed D.U.W.C. The paint and the initials may still be observed.

Recognizing the need for a reservoir to hold the runoff from the snow pack, W. S. Cheesman and his associates built Cheesman Dam on the South Fork of the South Platte River. In fact, he built two dams there. The first one, earth filled, was almost completed when one of the spring floods he sought to control washed it away. This was May 3, 1900. Mr. Cheesman immediately

52

started over again. By January, 1905, he had completed a new dam. This one was faced with granite blocks chiseled to fit the curve of the structure. The chief stonemason won a fifty dollar suit of clothes from the management when water rose behind the 212-foot dam but none leaked through the fitted rocks.

At Cheesman's death in 1907, David Moffat became the symbol of Denver water. In 1909 he remarked that he was the only man still living who had been financially interested in James Archer's original water company of 1872. A great industrialist, Moffat financed many of his projects with the millions he dug out of mines like the Amethyst at Creede or the Anaconda at Cripple Creek. His biggest, and last, deal was the building of the Denver & Salt Lake Railroad. Hard pressed for funds to carry this line toward Salt Lake, Moffat tried to sell his water company to the City of Denver. After his death John Evans tried to get a franchise for the Denver Union Water Company without success.

Denver wanted the water works but haggled over the price. Both sides hired competent appraisers and the matter finally was settled. In a dramatic meeting at midnight on November 1, 1918, after David Moffat had been in his grave for seven years, Edwin S. Kassler, president of the Denver Union Water Company, and other company and city officials who stayed up late for the occasion, signed the papers that gave the City of Denver its own water. Perhaps "gave" is the wrong word. The city floated $13,924,000 worth of bonds to pay for the system. Of this amount, $424 was left as working capital with which the Denver Board of Water Commissioners started business.

Since Cheesman's day, Denver has acquired or built more reservoirs on the South Platte watershed. In 1924 it paid $450,000 for the Antero Dam in flat South Park and for the right to use sixty-six per cent of the flood waters that pile up behind the dam. Wrapped up with the Antero package was the High Line Canal. This canal was a tremendous engineering project in 1882 in the pre-bulldozer age. It comes out of the Platte River near Kassler (sometimes called Waterton) through a 600-foot tunnel, and ends eighty sinuous miles later at a farm east of the Rocky Mountain Arsenal. (It is easily traced because of the cottonwood trees on its banks.) The High Line Canal would have made the plains blossom like a rose, as promised by the original company, except it was usually dry. The High Line has water right No. 111 in the River. This, a junior right, gives water to the High Line only during flood times and unusually wet years.

Even in dry years, Cheesman and Antero Reservoirs proved inadequate to hold the spring runoff. In 1930 the City of Denver, then with a population of 287,861 people, started to dam Eleven Mile Canyon, and now plans more projects in order to wring the last drop of unappropriated water from the South Platte River.

But Denver has over half a million people in it today. The South Platte is too small to supply the city with water as well as to irrigate farms below Denver. To supplement its flow, the Denver Water Commissioners looked with envious eyes across the Big Divide to a great river rolling to the Gulf of California. But how could Denver tap the waters of the Colorado River? The answer was—tunnels.

The first of these tunnels utilized by Denver was the pioneer bore of the Moffat Tunnel. The main purpose of the Moffat Tunnel was to put Denver on a transcontinental railroad route. In order to build the railroad tunnel, engineers built a pioneer bore and then dug the big tunnel, using the smaller one for access by means of cross cuts. The railroad tunnel was finished in 1928, materializing the dream of many Colorado pioneers, including David Moffat.

The Denver Water Board leased the pioneer bore and prepared it for carrying water. Western Slope water first flowed through this tunnel on June 10, 1936. Since then more trans-mountain projects have been completed or are in progress, involving tunnels, pipe lines, siphons, and reservoirs, all to augment Denver's water supply. Residents of the Western Slope are not completely happy about all this activity.

In any diversion of water, rights must be adjudicated before a shovel of earth is turned. Legal problems are as involved as engineering problems. It was only through the patient work of men like City Attorney Malcolm Lindsey that enough water rights were bought or traded to fill the Eleven Mile Canyon Reservoir. Lawyer Harold D. Roberts smoothed out the Blue River water troubles for a twenty-three mile tunnel now being built. In recognition of the importance of legal work in general and of his "diplomacy, wisdom and patient and skilled labor" in particular, this new tunnel was named the Harold D. Roberts Tunnel. Mr. Roberts died forty-eight hours after the official dedication of the tunnel, in July, 1956.[16]

The day water starts to flow through this bore will be a day on which history repeats itself. In 1860, placer miners on Hoosier Pass built the first ditch in Colorado to carry water from the western to the eastern slope.[17] This water ran from the Blue River to the South Platte, as will the water in the Harold D. Roberts Tunnel, a full century later.

NOTES

Water being of the first importance, all the standard reference books on Denver and Colorado history carry much information, notably Smiley, Vickers and Hall. The personnel of the Denver Water Department have been kind in furnishing information. Their publication, *Denver Water News*, carried a series of historical articles starting in January, 1940. Another valuable reference is C. L. King's *History of the Government of Denver with Special Reference to its Relation with Public Service Corporations*. Denver, Fisher, 1911.

[1]Parkman, Francis *The Oregon Trail Journal*, ed. by Mason Wade. New York, Harper, 1947. v. 2, p. 471.

[2]Sebben, L. M. "Life of Nathan A. Baker." In *Colorado Magazine* v. 12. p. 220, Nov. 1935. The famous statue of an unsaddled horse stands over the tomb of Nathan Baker at Riverside Cemetery.

[3]According to Frank C. Timson in *Denver Water News*, August 1943.

[4]Loc. cit. Another writer says that in 1880 there were eighteen sprinkling tanks carried around town on horse-drawn wagons. Each was filled and emptied twenty times a day. Constant, R. H. "Colorado as seen by a Visitor of 1880." In *Colorado Magazine*, v. 12, May 1935.

[5]Interview with Edwin S. Kassler, 1958.

[6]James Archer died August 26, 1882 at Wagon Wheel Gap. He was survived by a wife and eight children. Obituaries were carried on the front pages of Denver papers the next day.

[7]Hall, Frank *History of the State of Colorado* . . . Chicago, Blakely, 1889-1895. v. 2, p. 114.

[8]*Your Denver Municipal Water System.* Denver, Board of Water Commissioners, 1934.

[9]Baldwin, H. L. "The Denver High School, 1874-1875." In *Colorado Magazine* v. 15, p. 114, May 1938.

[10]Steinel, A. T. and Working, D. W. *History of Agriculture in Colorado.* Fort Collins, State Agricultural College, 1926. p. 75.

[11]*RMN*, Dec. 10, 1879, p. 5, col. 4.

[12]*Colorado, Some Answers to the Questions likely to be asked by the Members of the American Society of Engineers during their Visit to Denver.* Annual Convention July 2, 1886. Denver Society of Civil Engineers, 1886. Chapters discuss the water supply, sewerage system, and artesian wells of Denver, as well as the narrow-gauge railroads and mining operations of Colorado.

[13]Strong, W. C. *The Sanitary and Chemical Character of Some of the Artesian Wells of Denver.* A paper read before the Colorado Scientific Society of Denver, May 7, 1894, and published in its *Proceedings.*

[14]*RMN*, Sept. 7, 1883, p. 6, col. 3.

[15]*Your Denver Municipal Water System* op. cit. p. 4. This lists the companies by name and corporation date from 1870 to 1894.

[16]*RMN*, July 25, 1956.

[17]Bancroft, G. J. "Diversion of Water from the Western Slope." In *Colorado Magazine* v. 21, p. 178, Sept. 1944. A longer article is D. B. Cole's "Transmountain Water Diversion in Colorado." In *Colorado Magazine* v. 25, pp. 49-65 and 118-135, March and June 1948. The Hoosier Pass ditch, enlarged, is still in use. It is part of the Colorado Springs water system.

Drinking Water

The Union Artesian Water Company started in 1884 to deliver water to people not rich enough to have their own artesian wells and too particular to drink Holly water piped from Lake Archer. The picture, taken at West 6th Avenue and Galapago Street, shows three of the tank wagons. Frank C. Timson, proprietor of the company, stands at the left. He furnished the photo to the *Denver Water News*, v. 2, p. 3, Oct. 1943. (*Denver Public Library*.)

Constructed in 1887 but still in use, the Cherry Creek Infiltration Galleries are downstream from the present Iliff Avenue bridge. The sketch shows how they were made. A horizontal pipe was laid deep in the sand. The wells, in which water collected and which provided access to the lower pipes when necessary, were at both ends of the pipe. Today, part of the water that fills the three Capitol Hill reservoirs at 10th and Elizabeth comes from these same Cherry Creek Galleries. Of course, the wooden pipes have been replaced by concrete, and the water is pumped into a chlorination plant before entering the city conduits. (Sketch from *Engineering Journal*, Sept. 29, 1888, p. 241. *Denver Public Library*.)

The Lake Archer Pumping Station, shown in the picture, is now part of the Denver Water Department's West Side Storehouse at 12th and Shoshone. When this was built Lake Archer was so far out that the water was guaranteed to be pure. (*Denver Public Library.*)

The winter of 1876-77 was a hard one—thirty degrees below zero on Christmas Day—and the twenty-five stonecutters employed by Colonel James Archer on his new residence were grateful for employment. In May, when the stonework was finished, the affable Colonel gave a lunch to them and his friends. It was a fine house. In summer the lawn was watered by Holly water and the flowers, said a Denver writer in 1880, "dazzled my eyes." Before it was torn down in 1925, the house was used as the Denver Municipal Dispensary. Because Colonel Archer was a public spirited business man of the 1870's, it seems appropriate that on the site of his home, 1307 Welton, now stands the Denver Chamber of Commerce Building. (Photo given by Alex. Martin to the *State Historical Society of Colorado.*)

JAMES ARCHER

Born Belfast, Ireland 1820. Lived Denver 1870's. Died Wagon Wheel Gap, 1882. Buried Riverside Cemetery, Denver.

This statue on his grave and a street in West Denver named Archer Place are all that remind Denver of a genial Irish business man who gave the town its first gas lights in 1871 and its first piped water in January, 1872. (The portrait is from *Representative Men of Colorado*, 1902, p. 143. Photo of tombstone by Sally Davis. *State Historical Society of Colorado.*)

This Greek pavilion was given to the City of Denver in 1909 by the widow and daughter of Walter S. Cheesman. The name of Congress Park was changed to Cheesman Park to honor the memory of one of the men who provided water to make such parks possible. The pure white marble was quarried, fashioned, and shipped on thirty freight cars from the Yule Marble Company's works on the Crystal River near Aspen. The picture is undated except by the dresses of the ladies and the lack of shrubbery around the Memorial. (Colored postcard at the *Denver Public Library*.)

The City Ditch

In the country the City Ditch was, and is, lined with cottonwoods. The picture shows it near Orchard Place on June 9, 1901. (Photo by Roy S. Kent, *State Historical Society of Colorado*.)

In the city little laterals, branching from the City Ditch on Capitol Hill, watered trees and lawns and gardens. This water turned 14th Street into a tree-lined avenue. The picture below shows 14th and Arapahoe in 1884. From her home on the right, Mrs. John Evans could step on the bridge that spanned the ditch to enter her carriage, watched by students attending the University of Denver across the street. (Photo by W. H. Jackson. *Denver Public Library*.)

The boy in the derby hat is Robert Hanington, later to become vice-president of Hendrie & Bolthoff Company. In 1890 he built a canvas canoe and tested it in the willow-lined Big Ditch that ran, instead of an alley, behind his father's house, still standing at 1080 Grant Street. (from *Mrs. Orlando Ward. Denver Public Library.*)

The Denver-Palmer Lake Cycle Path was pleasant in 1898. The ten-foot wide path, sponsored by the Denver Wheel Club, was a favorite ride with the 25,000 wheelmen and "cyclennes" of the Queen City. Though the path was never completed to Palmer Lake, the first section ran south of Denver on the west side of Broadway, then along the City Ditch, first on one side and then on the other. Bridges and cattle-guards were specially designed for cycling comfort. (Photo in *Colorado Magazine*, v. 10, p. 215, Nov. 1933. *State Historical Society of Colorado.*)

Children played along the City Ditch in Washington Park in 1910. Today, the City Ditch, open to the sky, still runs through Washington Park, and children still play on its banks; but the willows and cottonwoods are more numerous and larger than they were in 1910. (Photo from *Denver Municipal Facts*, v. 2, p. 1, June 4, 1910. *Denver Public Library*.)

Looking south on the Marion Street Parkway toward Steele School in 1913. The City Ditch remained open here until 1933, when it was enclosed in a concrete conduit by the Work Projects Administration. (Photo from *City of Denver*, v. 1, p. 16, July 12, 1913. *Denver Public Library*.)

The City Ditch

When he heard of the Pikes Peak gold rush, "Noisy Tom" Pollock hitched up a team and came north from New Mexico armed with the knowledge of how to extract gold from the gold-seekers. He had been around the West for years and knew the essentials of life were more important than gold. What he considered the essentials may be surmised by three advertisements he inserted in the first edition of the *Rocky Mountain News,* April 23, 1859. One stated he was a blacksmith, one advertised two barrels of old Magnolia whiskey, and the third publicized his ability as carpenter and cabinet maker. This item ended with the words "I have in my employ a good undertaker."[1] (Was it for business reasons that "Noisy Tom" volunteered to be the town's first hangman?)[2]

In the same edition of the *News,* the editor, in gratitude to his best advertiser, gave Pollock a news item:

> DITCH COMPANY.——A company was formed to-day for the purpose of turning Cherry Creek and bringing water to the dry diggings just west of town. They will commence operations on Monday next and give employment to some fifty men. Thomas Pollock, President; A. J. Sagendorf, Secretary.[3]

The president knew how to turn a creek because he had lived in New Mexico where Pueblo Indians and Spaniards had made irrigation ditches for generations. However, no further mention of this ditch to the dry diggings has been found. Perhaps the idea was abandoned when the fifty men tore off to Gregory Gulch where placer gold in paying quantities was discovered.

The officers of this early ditch company, nevertheless, did not abandon the idea of a ditch. They were two of the incorporators of another company organized to bring water to Denver City, Auraria, and Highlands from either Cherry Creek or the South Platte River. The incorporation date of this company was so early that it filed its papers not with the State of Colorado, nor with the Territory of Jefferson, nor with the Territory of Colorado, but with the Territory of Kansas. This was February 21, 1860.[4]

Shining through the legal jargon of the incorporation papers is the fact that a large number of influential citizens headed by A. C. Hunt—he was later to be governor of Colorado Territory—had the sense to know that people needed potatoes and horses needed hay, and if any crops were to be raised in or near Denver, the land had to have water.

After incorporating, the company's next step was to secure water rights. On November 28, 1860, the ditch company acquired the second right to the water on the upper part of the South Platte River.[5] Later, when courts established the official order of water rights in Colorado, this company, known by then as the Platte Water Company, was awarded right No. 1 in District 8 of Division 1, a position it still holds today. This means that even during the driest years, the City Ditch may use the thirty second-feet of water it acquired in 1860.

The organizers of the company planned to take water from the South Platte. They built an intake on R. S. Little's farm, about half a mile above the present town of Littleton. "After spending $10,000 and any quantity of hope [the company] found by demonstration that their engineer, a recent graduate of Troy, had omitted to give any fall to his grade. The discouraged promoters dropped the scheme, and the engineer dropped his profession."[6]

In justice to the engineer it should be mentioned that this ditch, though not surveyed with enough fall line to take water to Denver, was capable of turning the wheel of the Rough and Ready Mill in Littleton.[7] In fact it was only a few years ago, when the hydraulic machinery was in need of repair, that the Rough and Ready Mill changed over from water power. (The City of Denver owns this mill.) [8]

The ditch company lay dormant for a year or two until a man named John W. Smith,[9] one of the competent business men of early Denver, agreed to build a new ditch for $10,000 and one half of the capital stock. He started much farther upstream than the emigrant engineer had done. Smith put his headgate six-and-a-half miles above present Littleton. The height of the source enabled the water to run by gravity to Brown's Bluff, east of Denver.

At one place along its surveyed course the sagacious Mr. Smith observed a natural depression on the prairie—perhaps a buffalo wallow. In and out of this basin Smith ran his ditch. From the resulting lake he harvested ice in the winter. Today this lake is officially known as Smith's Lake, but is better known as the north lake of Washington Park. By meandering to all points of the compass (see map on endpapers), the ditch arrived at Brown's Bluff above and to the east of the little town of Denver. Then it wandered off northeast. There was not a house in sight when it filled Dillon's Lake at 12th and Washington.[10] This may have been its destination under Smith's contract. As to the dates of its building, the source that seems the most reliable states that Smith started to construct the ditch in 1865 and finished in May 1867.

The part of the ditch that most interested the citizens of Denver was that which ran near the western edge of Brown's Bluff, later known as Capitol Hill. It was obvious that any branch from the ditch here would run downhill through Denver on the way to the river.

Denver needed water badly, especially in 1870. That spring the citizens decided that they could not stand their drab, dusty town another summer. They made a concerted effort to bring cottonwood saplings from the Platte bottoms and shrubs from Cherry Creek to plant in their yards. Lawns were seeded and flower gardens started by homesick women who had cherished seeds and roots all the dreary journey from "America."

It was easier to plant these efforts toward greenery than it was to make them grow. What to do for water! Buying water from the water wagons was expensive and well water had to be pumped. Even when Colonel Archer's Holly water started to flow through pipes, it was for domestic uses. So the City of Denver contracted with the Platte Water Company's chief stockholder, John W. Smith, to rent water from the ditch on the hill at $7,000 a year.

Presently an entrancing system of small streams flowed from the bluffs east of town. On the flat, the water was directed down each side of the streets toward the Platte River. One authority states there were 1,000 miles of lateral ditches watering what is now downtown Denver. Thirsty dogs and horses were delighted. Trees grew, gardens flourished, and lawns were praised for their greenness all summer long, as they are in Denver today.

The officials were satisfied with the system but unhappy about the rent. The mayor decided it would be cheaper in the long run to buy the ditch. He submitted a bill to the people that provided for the issue of $60,000 worth of bonds to pay the price John W. Smith demanded. Though defeated at the first election, at a special election the bill won by a majority of fourteen votes.

Whereupon some quibbler found a statutory law that forbade city officials to pay more than $50,000 for anything. About 1875 an agreement was made with Mr. Smith to pay $10,000 a year and ten per cent interest on the balance. This went on until the spring of 1882 when Robert Morris was mayor of Denver.[11] At a meeting of city and company officials, "after much useless palaver" the city paid a final $12,500 to the company and John W. Smith signed over his ditch to Denver.[12] Officially renamed the City Ditch, it was called by most Denverites the Big Ditch to distinguish it from the smaller streams that ran from it to water the trees along the streets.

These small streams brought trouble as well as water. Mothers scolded small boys who waded in them on hot summer days despite the broken glass. The boys loved to make water wheels and would sometimes divert the streams to private projects not appreciated by property owners farther down the street. Drinking water being scarce, some grown people drank ditch water and swelled the ranks of typhoid patients. This despite the fact that the streams were often choked with litter. The newspapers occa-

68

sionally asked that fetid matter cleaned from the ditches should not be left in piles along the streets to contaminate the air.

These and other problems forced the city to hire water policemen. In 1882 Sidney Roberts was the commissioner in charge of thirty men. They tried hard to control the use of the laterals and to keep them reasonably clean, but it was an impossible job. By the late 1880's, physicians had persuaded the city authorities to fill up some of the ditches. They were mourned by old-timers such as this articulate man who wrote in 1893: "Ditches have been banished from many parts. . . . There are portions of the city, however, where a visitor may see the irrigation ditches in all their pristine, purling beauty, and listen to the silvery twitter as they chase themselves down the light decline. We, who for so many years have listened to their chippering voices, miss them as one of the lost domesticities of our earlier Colorado civilization."[13] By 1898 the little street ditches were all gone. Trees on the downtown streets rapidly followed them into oblivion.

Though Denver no longer had its little ditches, the Big Ditch remained. In fact it still furnishes water to farmers south of Denver, fills both lakes at Washington Park, and meanders around till it flows, by gravity, into City Park Lake. It is hard to persuade a man driving from Washington Park uphill to City Park that water can do this!

Back in the 1880's, when mansions started to rise on Capitol Hill, the original line of the ditch was somewhat straightened. Between Grant and Logan north of 8th Avenue it took the place of an alley. Almost every house had a vacant lot nearby, so boys could put planks across the ditch and use the shrubbery on the opposite side as pirate hideouts.[14] Youngsters built boats, both toy and boy-size. That the ditch was their playground pleased the boys more than their mothers, for more than one child has drowned in the City Ditch.

Bridges were built across the ditch as needed. There was a diagonal one at 11th near Logan.[15] It was a convenience when a bridge spanned the ditch at 16th and Humboldt. This enabled the herd boy who rounded up the cows kept by residents north of present Cheesman Park to take his charges dry-footed to pasture in what is now City Park.[16]

To the City Ditch, Denver owes its City Park. After Arbor Day of 1884, when school children of Denver stuck sticks in holes and patted earth around them, the water from City Ditch was let loose to soak the prairie and some of the sticks may now be seen as the oldest trees in City Park.[17]

When streets were laid out east from Capitol Hill, culverts were supplied where the street crossed the ditch. Presently the ditch was enclosed and covered over in yards, and even in some vacant lots. About 1902, complaints were made that fetid material in the City Ditch was endangering the children of Emerson School, so it was covered at 14th and Ogden. By the 1920's, it was visible in only a few places, like 7th and Downing where it ran between the north sidewalk and the street. Perhaps the last open part of the ditch near a street was on the Marion Street Parkway where it was used as a landscape asset. (See picture, p. 64.)

About 1935, when the Work Projects Administration was active in Denver, the City Ditch was confined in a thirty-inch concrete conduit, except in Washington Park where it still flows open to the sky. (It is also open in places before it reaches the city limits.) This concrete pipe was buried beneath the streets and lots, but you may see the flume as it crosses Cherry Creek. It hangs below the western balustrade of the Downing Street bridge. From there the water flows to Corona Street. The ditch no longer meanders west to Capitol Hill but flows straight up Corona hill to 14th Avenue. This apparent disregard of gravity is made possible by an inverted siphon. (The old and new routes of the City Ditch are indicated on the map on the endpapers.)

There are two laterals from the ditch. One runs through the grounds of the Colorado State Children's Home. It's dangerous. The Denver Country Club pays for water that runs through the other lateral. This branch fills the Club's new lake south of Cherry Creek, then crosses the Creek at University Boulevard to water some of the golf links.

The main duty of City Ditch today is to fill Washington and City Park lakes, provide water for the colorful electric fountain in the middle of City Park lake, and water the trees and grass. Signs are nailed to the trees in the parks which read "Water unsafe for drinking." These words are a link with the 1880's when water policemen must have used them when they caught thirsty citizens drinking from the street ditches.

Anyone in search of an authentic link with early Denver need only walk along the open ditch in Washington Park. Large willows and old cottonwoods will give the searcher shade. This is the same ditch that has enabled parts of Denver to have trees and lawns since 1867 when water first started to flow in Smith's ditch from the South Platte River.

NOTES

[1]*RMN,* April 23, 1859, p. 3, col. 6.

[2]"The first murder trial to come before the People's Court was that of John Stofel, for shooting his brother-in-law . . . April 7th, 1859 . . . The condemned man was placed in a wagon, taken to Tenth Street on the west side and there hanged, the executioner being 'Noisy Tom,' a well-known frontiersman." Hall, Frank *History of the State of Colorado.* Chicago, Blakely, 1889-1895. v. 3, pp. 267-268.

[3]*RMN,* April 23, 1859, p. 3, col. 1.

[4]The act creating the Capitol Hydraulic Company, which started to construct the Platte Water Company's ditch, is given in full by W. F. Stone in his *History of Colorado.* Chicago, Clarke, 1918. v. 1, pp. 497-498. The incorporators were A. C. Hunt, Charles H. Gratiot, John A. Clark, Thomas Pollock, Henry Allen, William M. Slaughter, Richard Sopris, A. P. Vasquez, A. Sagendorf, W. N. Byers, H. H. Scoville, Jr., J. A. McDonnel, F. Z. Salomon, John H. Wing, and their legal associates. A true copy of the incorporation papers, on file at the Denver Public Library, states that the ditch is to be built in "Arrapahoe County, Kansas Territory."

[5]Irrigation records are in the Colorado State Engineer's office. A note there explains that the very first water right went to S. P. Epperson, May 1, 1860. It was for a small amount of water, 2.25 second-feet. When the Work Projects Administration moved the channel of the South Platte River in the 1930's, the state engineer installed a pump for the Epperson water right. Later, permission was granted to the owner (Rex B. Fuller in 1957) to use rain water from Sanderson Gulch, north of Ruby Hill, and no record is kept of the amount. So

actually the Epperson right antedates the City Ditch, but since Platte River water is not now pumped to the land, the City Ditch is called No. 1.

[6]*Colorado, Some Answers to Questions likely to be asked by the Members of the American Society of Civil Engineers during their visit to Denver on the occasion of their Annual Convention, July 2, 1886.* Denver Society of Civil Engineers, 1886. p. 126.

[7]An article about the City Ditch in the *Municipal Facts,* June 12, 1921, seems to be the best source. This has been used as the basis for this chapter. It differs in figures and dates from other authorities, such as Smiley, who dates the completion of the ditch in 1865, and Vickers, who says the laterals started running in 1872.

[8]This is but one of the many bits of interesting information given me by Robert Riley of the Denver Water Department, who is chiefly concerned with the City Ditch, the High Line Canal, and the Farmers' and Gardeners' Ditch, which ran north to the old Denver Poor Farm.

[9]Like James Archer, John W. Smith seems to have been eclipsed by the silver kings of the 1880's, though he was one of Denver's most important earlier business men. He was born in Pennsylvania in 1815. As a young man he came to Kansas, and on June 3, 1860, brought a wagon train loaded with machinery into Denver City. He brought in the first mill burrs, and built numerous mills—planing, quartz, and flour—over the state. J. K. Mullen bought his Excelsior Mill. Smith was also one of the directors of the Denver Woolen Mills. In 1868 he built the American House, a famous hostelry, and was connected with the Interocean Hotel (which still stands). Smith's Chapel, with its stone spire, remains in use at 900 Galapago. This he financed in 1882 for the United Brethren, and Mr. Smith also donated liberally to the Roman Catholic Church. Smith started a Colorado Savings Bank in 1871 but closed it because too few people were saving money. A promoter of the Denver Pacific Railroad, he was later president of the Denver, South Park and Pacific. In 1880 he organized the Denver City Steam Heat Company. Inheriting this business, the Public Service Company of Colorado still pumps steam into downtown buildings. Smith is said to have brought an organ across the plains in 1861, and he started a cracker factory. A man of varied interests! The gentler side of this stern Welsh-Irish executive may be remembered on Pearl Street which he named after his son Albert's daughter, according to Mrs. James Waring, one of Smith's granddaughters. John W. Smith left Denver for his health in 1883, dying in Oakland, California, twelve years later. His Denver interests were carried on by his sons and sons-in-law, especially by Charles H. Smith, who built and lived in the Charline Apartments, and Henry M. Porter. The best of many

sources for the biography of John W. Smith seems to be an article in *The Trail*, v. 4, no. 5, p. 5–8, January 1912.

[10]Spalding, W. M. *Early Reminiscences of Denver*. Denver, privately printed, 1937. p. 4.

[11]Perhaps Mayor Morris's interest in acquiring the ditch was linked with his attempts to start a city park east of Capitol Hill, so far out on the prairies that even his friends called him a visionary. City Park is now in the heart of Denver.

At one time the City Ditch ran beyond City Park. Rollandet's map of Denver of 1895 ends it at 36th and Madison. Another man said it went to 40th and York where stood the Union Pacific Hospital. It took four sinuous miles for it to go from 17th and Colorado Boulevard to that point. It is also said that water from the City Ditch was pumped to irrigate the grass and trees on Montview and 17th Avenue Parkways when they were first landscaped.

[12]*RMN*, May 26, 1882.

[13]Stone, W. G. M. *The Colorado Hand-book: Denver and its Outings*. Denver, Barkhausen and Lester, 1893. p. 87.

[14]Interview with Henry Hanington, 1956. As a boy he played pirate behind his home at 1080 Grant Street.

[15]Interview with E. S. Kassler, 1958.

[16]Letter from J. S. Barrows in *RMN* Mar. 2, 1955.

[17]Fallis, E. H. *When Denver and I Were Young*. Denver, Big Mountain Press, 1956.

Cherry Creek

Why is it called Cherry Creek? The men who were boys when Denver was young could have told you. They remembered "Cherry Creek cherries were just a little more plentiful, just a little more juicy and altogether more alluring . . . than those found in other localities."[1] If wild cherries tasted so good to the well-fed boys of Denver in the 1870's, how succulent they must have seemed to the fruit-starved men who crossed the plains in the pre-gold-rush days. Colonel Dodge and his U. S. Dragoons in 1835 found "cherries very plentiful" when they camped "on a dry creek entering the Platte that the traders usually ascend in passing from that river to the Arkansas."[2]

Who first called it Cherry Creek? Evidently not Colonel Dodge or he would have called it by name. It was labeled Cherry Creek on Abert's map of explorations in 1845.[3] Years before that, the Indians probably called it the equivalent of Cherry Creek in their own languages. Cherries were important to Indians. One can hear the matriarch of a band of Arapahoes saying to her warrior husband on a June day, "Go chase the Utes around the hills if you want to, but remember, in the late summer you braves must hunt buffalo along Cherry Creek so we homemakers may pick fruit to pound into our pemmican." Today, though Cherry Creek, except for ornamental cherry trees, runs cherry-less through Denver, above the big dam located southeast of the city wild cherries are still picked by thrifty housewives who boil them into jelly.

A geography lesson shows why insignificant Cherry Creek is important to local history. The eastern plains of Colorado are drained by two big rivers—the Platte on the north and the Arkansas on the south. Between them is a high plateau which is called the Divide, as it divides the two drainage basins. It is also called Cherry Creek Divide because Cherry Creek rises on it, at an elevation of about 7,500 feet, and flows north-northwest. At the end of fifty miles the Creek empties into the South Platte River in the middle of Denver.

In fur trapping days a mountain man who wanted to go from Fort Laramie on the Platte to Bent's Fort on the Arkansas had to cross the Divide. He usually, as Colonel Dodge pointed out, ascended Cherry Creek. His feet followed an Indian trail which wagon wheels soon widened into a road. This was used by gold-rushers who came west this way to the Arkansas River and over the Divide. In 1858 the Russell brothers of Georgia and their hundred companions found flecks of gold in Cherry Creek. Not many, but enough to encourage them to look farther.

The proof that the Russells paused on Cherry Creek is found on today's maps. Four miles above Franktown lies Russellville Gulch. The gulch makes a nice Sunday afternoon walk, but what about the "ville"? Of it there is no trace. In 1931 a trained historian had a hard time finding even its site.[4] Reminiscences in print, however, prove the existence of Russellville.[5]

To help us imagine what Russellville on Cherry Creek looked like a hundred years ago, let us read the diary of a woman whose husband brought her down the east side of Cherry Creek in the summer of 1859, a year after the Russell brothers traveled the same route:[6] "[June] 25, [1859] Started at moon rise and traveled 15 miles before breakfast, to a pine forest—very beautiful and sad from the number of graves here—8 are in view of persons who have frozen to death,[7] one as late as June third, '59. The changes are so sudden even in the summer that from being very warm it will be so cold as to benumb the body before fire can be made to warm it. . . . When the cattle were driven up to start again they were nearly frantic with the stings of a large horse fly, patches as large as both my hands were black with them and blood streamed from the biten part for an hour while passing through the pines.... We camped in a beautifully undulating valley. The mountains to the left and lofty pine-clad hills on every side. A beautifull clear spring and abundance of grass for our accommodation.

"26. Started again at moonrise. Stopped for breakfast at 7½, in two hours started again and traveled till 4, crossing Cherry Creek. We saw miners' cots near the crossing and some digging two miles beyond. Found a steam mill in full blast and a little town called Russelville sprung up around it. Nine log houses were in process of creation and three were inhabited. The country here is handsome and the soil looks good."

To these nine houses presently were added "an immense barn, a stockade, and a corral for horses, and a log tavern. But there was no saloon."[8]

It was not the lack of a saloon that doomed Russellville. It was logic. Men in a hurry to make a fortune reasoned that a straight line was the shortest distance between the Missouri River and the gold fields. Why come up the Arkansas and angle north over the Divide when they could come almost straight west on the Smoky Hill routes, thus avoiding the Divide (and deserting Russellville)? Thereafter many eastern trails led directly into Cherry Creek Valley at different places and different dates. The thing to remember is that all the emigrants were glad when they reached the Valley and could follow, more or less, the present Parker road into Denver. From present Colorado Boulevard they angled across the prairie to Colfax and Broadway (the Pioneer Monument) and then turned down 15th Street to Blake or Larimer.[9]

We do not need dates and details to fill the Parker road with the ghosts of covered wagons pulled by tired oxen, or men riding horses or mules, or plodding along on foot pushing wheelbarrows, or carrying their supplies suspended from their persons. All of them scattered to the roadside when the Concord stages raced by.

There were three stage lines, one from Santa Fe, two from the Missouri River. The first to arrive in Denver were two coaches—they always traveled in pairs because of Indians or accidents—that belonged to the Leavenworth and Pikes Peak Express Company. The stage arrived in Denver on May 7, 1859, after six days and nights on the road. Fare $100. The returning coach caused a furor in Leavenworth on May 21st when word spread that it carried $3,500 worth of Pikes Peak gold.[10]

The hardships of the Middle Smoky Hill route (called the Starvation Trail by its intimates) were too much! The Leavenworth and Pikes Peak line "in six weeks . . . abandoned its original route into Denver, by way of Cherry Creek, past the desolate first cemetery . . . and its coaches were coming in by the Julesburg route." Following the Platte River was longer but not dry. Presently the company had fifty-two Concord coaches and the "best draft mules money could buy."[11]

Many eager emigrants, however, continued to use the various Smoky Hill routes and in 1865 the Butterfield Overland Dispatch Company drove stages over the Smoky Hill South which was not only dry but infested with Indians.

All this traffic made the banks of Cherry Creek very busy. The equivalent of modern filling stations and motels sprang up along the highway. The stage companies established a series of stations at certain intervals, called "mile-houses," the Twelve-Mile House, for instance, being twelve miles from Colfax and Broadway. At some of these houses passengers were fed, though not well, while tired mules or horses were exchanged for fresh ones. At the "swing stops" passengers were not allowed to escape from the stuffy coach while the horses were changed in record time. The stage drivers were the overlords of the country, obeyed by all men and worshipped by small boys.

Some of these mile-houses still stand today. The Twenty-Mile House may be seen at Parker. For the Seventeen-Mile House see the picture on p. 89. At the site of the Twelve-Mile House nothing reminds today of yesterday's hotel, the largest on the route. It was here that Johnnie Melvin's four handsome white horses were hitched to the stage so that its entrance into, and exit from, Denver would be dramatic.[12]

The Four-Mile House was where the dusty traveler "spruced up" for his entry into Denver. This house still stands where Forest Street runs into Cherry Creek from the north. A two-story house made of logs but later covered with clapboards, it has been continuously occupied all the years since its erection.

One might think that Auraria, being the original town, would have been the terminus for the Leavenworth and Pikes Peak stage line. But "the rivalry between the sorry little metropolises standing here in the winter loneliness of the great plains"[13] was so intense that bribery was used. By a generous gift of town lots, the officials of Denver City persuaded the stage company to come to rest on the east side of Cherry Creek. "Anchoring the Leavenworth and Pikes Peak stage line . . . was the conclusive factor in making Denver the Pikes Peak metropolis of 1859."[14]

Not that Auraria was above using bribes! Though they lost the stage station, they snagged the *Rocky Mountain News,* by influence of real estate—two city lots. Editor Byers issued the first edition of his paper from the attic of Uncle Dick Wootton's log store. (This would carry the address of 1413 11th Street if it still stood today.) Byers chose Auraria as his initial base, but he was too canny to limit his paper in any way to an embryo town with an uncertain future. His first all-embracing masthead reads: "Rocky Mountain News, The Mines and Miners of Kansas and Nebraska. Cherry Creek, K. T., Saturday, April 23, 1859."

Later Byers erected his own buildings, one after the other, to house his paper. With the fourth one he was still hedging. He perched the building for his press and office on low piles sunk in the sands of the bed of Cherry Creek. This was at the foot of McGaa Street (present Market Street). Slightly nearer the west bank, it was technically in West Denver (former Auraria) but actually on neutral ground since both towns claimed the creek bed.

That his office stood where the creek had obviously run at many previous dates bothered Byers no more than it did other people who built offices, stores, the Methodist Church and the city jail in or near the creek bed. The editor had probably been told by the "pioneers"—men who had been in Denver almost a year—that Cherry Creek had dried up and disappeared in the fall of 1858.

These pioneers of 1858 and 1859 considered, in general, that they had discovered the West. The mountain men were ignored. The gold-rushers renamed places that had carried names for thirty years. Vasquez Creek, for instance. On this stream Louis

Vasquez had collected beaver since the heyday of the beaver-hat fashion and had, in 1832, built a log shelter at the mouth of his creek. The gold-rushers renamed this Clear Creek and then proceeded to dump mine tailings into it so that it is seldom clear.

Some of the mountain men, like Louis Vasquez, told the emigrants of 1858-59 to beware of the insignificant streams which could (and did) become powerful torrents without warning. As the mountain men "were assumed to be romancers of rare ability, little heed was given to their stories in Denver."[15] Even the Indians told Byers that Cherry Creek could suddenly become "Heap big water so-o-o-o high!"[16] Byers looked at the Indians with their hands stretched above their heads, then looked at little Cherry Creek meandering no bigger than an eastern branch, and "built his house upon the sand."

He learned. At 2 a.m. on May 20, 1864, Cherry Creek roared between the two towns with a wall of water which did not start to recede until seven o'clock the same morning. With no effort, it swept the *Rocky Mountain News* building off its piles and almost drowned five men who were asleep in the building. Later, pieces of the power press were taken off a sandbar in the Platte River opposite 20th Street, and seven years later, when Colonel Archer was sinking a well for the first waterworks of Denver, his workmen found part of the old *News* hand press twelve feet below the surface of the sand.

Other buildings were wrecked as "the mighty volume of impetuous water . . . rolled, with maddened momentum directly toward the Larimer Street bridge . . . the large Methodist church and the adjoining buildings, all of which it wrested from their foundations and engulfed in the jaws of bellowing billows as they broke over the McGaa Street bridge. . . . The now over-shadowing flood upheaved the bridge and the two buildings by it, Messrs. Charles and Hunt's law offices, in the latter of which C. Bruce Haynes was sleeping, whom, with the velocity of a cataract, it launched asleep and naked on the watery ocean of eternity. . . ."[17]

The journalist responsible for this graphic description was able to see the events because "the moon would occasionally shed her rays on the surges of muddy waves," and because curious citizens lighted bonfires along the banks the better to see the flood. Thus early was established the two-fold pattern of behavior of Denver people whenever Cherry Creek flooded. Those who were not desperately striving to extricate themselves and their possessions from the flood waters hastened to the swollen Creek to see the excitement.

A third, smaller group, were the heroes. They tried to warn people away from the torrent and rescued many from its power. Among the heroes of the 1864 flood were the Union soldiers from Camp Weld (near 8th Avenue and Vallejo Street). They contrived "valiant skiffs" and manned them efficiently, while the officers' ladies at Camp Weld drove in to see "the awful sight."

Because of the newness of the town and the changing population, no accurate record was possible concerning the number of people drowned. At least twenty, probably more. Many people made miraculous escapes. When the Denver jail collapsed, one frightened Negro prisoner grabbed a passing cottonwood tree. He was fished out of the Platte miles below town. One presumes he was not re-jailed since there was neither jail nor city hall. The safe from the city hall has never been found.

Mixed with the debris of buildings were animals. "Messrs. Reed, Palmer and Barnes lost, collectively, over 4,000 sheep off their ranches up Cherry Creek."[18] Some of these were rescued in Denver and below. During the early part of the summer, the Platte Valley was noisome with the stench that rose from the unrescued.

West Denver, which had been Auraria, was more submerged than Denver because it was lower. Many West Denver merchants, instead of rebuilding in the mud drying over their former building sites, started business anew on the east side of Cherry Creek, greatly diminishing the rivalry between the two sections of town.

After 1864, Cherry Creek rested eleven years. In the middle of July, 1875, six and a half inches of rain fell in twenty-four hours in Denver as well as on the Cherry Creek watershed. The Creek again flooded West Denver and the lower part of Denver. No buildings were carried downstream—even Mr. Byers had learned not to build in the creek bed. This flood, like the first one, had its literary chronicler who started his account in the *Rocky Mountain News* of July 20, 1875, thus: "There is a tide in the affairs of Cherry Creek which taken at the flood (like that last evening) leads on to fortune below Omaha." He called Cherry Creek "that incorrigible old dame," a name which city officials probably repeated in 1878 when she again swept away the bridges that spanned her bed.

One thing is sure about Cherry Creek—she follows no pattern. May 20th is the earliest she has flooded, as in 1864, but June, July, as late as the 27th of August, all seem equally effective dates for a flood. "That incorrigible old dame" sometimes rests three years between floods, sometimes three days, sometimes nine years, or seven or eleven.[19] The two main floods of the twentieth century, in 1912 and 1933, had a span of twenty-one years between them, and it has now been a quarter of a century since the last big flood.

The reason for the floods is, of course, that Cherry Creek drains an enormous watershed—fifty miles long by at least five miles wide—and when a cloud bursts over it as clouds do in desert country, or even when a long steady rain falls, all the water runs into Cherry Creek and Denver has a freshet.

In 1890 another item of danger was added to Cherry Creek. A private company threw a dam across West Cherry Creek. Castlewood Dam was 70 feet high and 630 feet along the top. The promoters promised that water from Castlewood Lake would turn Cherry Creek Valley into the garden spot of Colorado. The Arapahoe Ditch was built, ending south of Montclair, and a few farms received water. At one time this project was called the Clark Colony, after Rufus H. (Potato) Clark who owned the land. (See Slice IX for the story of Clark's potatoes.)

Various companies tried various promotion schemes, none of them successful, to make the colony flourish. A sugar beet factory was proposed, in fact a brickyard started to make bricks for the factory walls. Acreages were sold to business men for their retirement years. Almost 900 acres of cherry trees were planted which somehow were never watered, and the dry sticks stuck out of the ground for years.

Castlewood Lake, only thirty miles from Denver, was to be a

81

pleasure resort. W. E. Alexander, one of the original owners, built a unique cottage of fancy boulders, moss-covered rock, and petrified wood, hoping to inspire others to build along the lake shore. Perhaps some other cottages were built and occupied, but the only permanent resident was the caretaker of Castlewood Dam.[20]

The engineers of the city of Denver always suspected the safety of Castlewood Dam. From 1890 onward, every time Cherry Creek flooded, a rumor spread that Castlewood Dam was breaking. Paul Reveres galloped along the banks, shouting for people to get out of bed—the Creek always seemed to rise at night—and go to higher ground. "Castlewood dam is breaking!" they called. First these Reveres came on horseback, then in Model T Fords, then on motorcycles, and later the nightmares of children who lived near Cherry Creek had to do with the banshee wails of the official police cars or motorcycles as they drove up and down Speer Boulevard warning people that Castlewood Dam might break. Whole families would rise, dress, and following their usual pattern of curious behavior, go toward the Creek to see the flood.

Denver was really frightened on July 14, 1912, when the "incorrigible old dame" again let loose her waters. This time many people who lived between the Denver Country Club and Broadway went to Cheesman Park where coffee was served all night long. Lower down the Creek, 500 refugees took shelter in the City Auditorium and ate their breakfast there. The police matron had a busy night caring for twenty-five children who had become separated from their parents. The next day, after parents were found, housing had to be secured for the homeless. In the flood of 1912 some lives were lost, and the property damage, especially in the warehouse district, was tremendous.

During the flood of 1912, the curiosity seekers had an interest not present during previous floods. The Speer Administration had recently finished the high cement walls retaining Cherry Creek. From Downing to Larimer Street the walls were in place and Speer Boulevard was emerging along the bank. In the 1912 flood, sections of the walls toppled into the water and had to be rebuilt.

The weeks that followed the flood of July 14, 1912, were paradise for children who lived near the Creek. They found the sand in the unpaved streets more interesting because of cottonwood snags or rusty nails or even dead pigs.

But Castlewood Dam did not break in 1912.

It broke August 3, 1933. About five o'clock in the morning, after due warning because of the heroism of the caretaker at the dam and the telephone operator at Parker and policemen whose cars raced ahead of the crest of the flood, the water from Castlewood Reservoir moved into Denver. Basements of houses in the Country Club district were again filled with mud and many people repaired to the homes of their friends in Park Hill, or once more from Cheesman Park watched the dawn move down the western mountains. Downstream, the wholesale district was under muddy water.

Though the damage was severe, the night Castlewood Dam broke was somewhat of an anti-climax to Denver people who had dreaded the event for more than thirty years. In the first place, radios announced the impending water from about midnight on, and no matter how urgent an announcer's voice, he could not be as dramatic as the warning wail of a police siren. In the second place, the anticipated flood was so well publicized that the curious, who came from all over town, got tired and went home to bed before the height of the flood reached Denver after sunrise.

After every Denver flood, citizens concocted schemes that were guaranteed to control Cherry Creek. In 1875 it was recommended that a channel be cut through West Denver so that Cherry Creek would empty into the Platte above the lowlands. Later a scheme was considered that would divert the Creek into Sand Creek, to the east of town.[21] By 1901 the historian, J. C. Smiley, was discouraged about Cherry Creek. He said it was "a nuisance, a blight and an abomination but it is not now probable that any remedy will soon be applied."[22]

Sooner than Smiley expected, in 1904, Mayor Speer faced the problem of Cherry Creek and turned it into beautiful Speer Boulevard. His first move was to define its channel and in order to keep it within the channel he bordered it with high cement walls. As we have seen, sections of the wall did not withstand the flood of 1912, but the creek was confined at least during normal years.

After the flood of 1933, the city officials decided they had better build a flood control dam on Cherry Creek. This they started in 1935, on the site of an embryo town named Kenwood, not far from Sullivan (near the present Iliff Street bridge over Cherry Creek). It was a dirt-and-rock filled dam, the rock coming from quarries near Morrison. Kenwood Dam was 4,000 feet long with a capacity of 10,000 acre-feet, and was considered adequate by local engineers.

A few years later the Engineer Corps of the U. S. Army put their minds, their men and federal money into the problem of taming Cherry Creek.[23] Their dam was built a thousand feet upstream from the Kenwood Dam, of which nothing now remains but some concrete spillways. The dirt and riprap from the Kenwood Dam was incorporated in the Army's dam, but was as nothing compared to the tons of rock the Army brought from North Table Mountain near Golden. Completed in 1950,[24] the Army dam irritates some local people who think it uselessly big.

The capacity of the present Cherry Creek Dam is large enough to handle a flood similar to that in the Republican River in 1935. Had the clouds dropped their rain twelve miles farther west, this water might have come into Cherry Creek. The Army engineers computed the 1935 flood and built their dam high enough to control 85,000 acre-feet of flood water. To make doubly sure, because when lives are at stake an inadequate dam is worse than no dam, the Army engineers cut a great spillway to Sand Creek.

Though the Cherry Creek Dam is not an irrigation project, it might turn into one some day, if, for instance, more water rights could be secured in the Blue River. This Western Slope water, coming through a tunnel to the South Platte River, could be carried east from the end of Platte Canyon to the Cherry Creek reservoir. For this purpose the old High Line Canal might be utilized, with the help of a pump at the dam. Lands that were to be irrigated east and north of Denver by the original promoters of the High Line back in the 1880's may yet be productive farms.

When the Cherry Creek Dam was completed it was for flood control only. There was to be no lake, no boating, no fishing. Today a lake, surrounded by a recreation area, perhaps a state park, is being strongly promoted. The dam would make a fine lake if its total height (140 feet) and its three miles of length could be used to back up water. But the purpose of the dam would be defeated if the lake was already full when a flood descended. Across the dam is one of the most beautiful drives near Denver, beautiful especially of an evening when

> The moon's a sand lily petal floating down
> Behind the blue wall of the Rocky Mountains.[25]

Since 1950 when the dam was completed, indeed since 1933 when Castlewood Dam broke, no big flood has flashed down Cherry Creek. Someday it will—"Heap big water so-o-o- high!" Old-timers in Denver are looking forward to the summer when a cloudburst on the Divide will pile water behind Cherry Creek Dam. Only then can it be proved whether the U. S. Army engineers have at last succeeded in taming the "incorrigible old dame" that is Cherry Creek.

NOTES

[1]Sanford, A. B. "The 'Big Flood' in Cherry Creek, 1864." In *Colorado Magazine*, v. 4, p. 100, May 1927. George Kelly, Denver horticulturalist, says this cherry was the Western Chokecherry (Prunus melanocarpa).

[2]*Journal of the March of a Detachment of Dragoons, under the Command of Colonel Dodge, during the Summer of 1835.* In Report of the Secretary of War . . . Feb. 27, 1836. Sen. Ex. Doc. 209, Serial 281. Washington, Gales & Seaton, 1836.

[3]*Map Showing the Route Pursued by the Exploring Expedition to New Mexico and the Southern Rocky Mountains . . . conducted by Lieut. J. W. Abert . . . during the year 1845.* Sen. Doc. 438, Serial 477. Washington, 1846.

[4]Sanford, A B. "The Cherokee Trail and the First Discovery of Gold on Cherry Creek." In *Colorado Magazine*, v. 8, pp. 30-34, Jan. 1931.

[5]Russellville is not to be confused with Russell Gulch, the town south of Central City in Gilpin County where the same Russell brothers from Georgia found their fortune in gold in 1859.

[6]"Diary of Mrs. A. C. Hunt, 1859." In *Colorado Magazine*, v. 21, p. 168, Sept. 1944. A. Cameron Hunt was to be governor of the Territory of Colorado in 1867-69.

[7]One of these graves on West Kiowa Creek can still be found. It is that of a soldier named Fagan who died in the blizzard of early May, 1858, while serving with troops who carried supplies to General Johnston in Utah. Two of the best accounts of this blizzard are in Du Bois, J. V., *Campaigns in the West, 1858-1861*. Tucson, Arizona Pioneers Historical Society, 1949; and Marcy, R. B., *Thirty Years of Army Life on the Border* . . . New York, Harper, 1866.

[8]Long, Dr. Margaret *The Smoky Hill Trail.* Denver, Kistler's, 1943, p. 139.

[9]Dr. Margaret Long, a Denver physician, found time to locate and log the various prairie trails and publish books about them. In her *The Smoky Hill Trail* she includes the Trapper's Trail (east of Cherry Creek), the Jimmy Camp Trail (east of that), and the Cherokee Trail west of West Cherry Creek. This had been used by Cherokee Indians en route to the California gold rush, and later was the route of the West Cherry Creek stage line to Santa Fe. Dr. Long also logs the three Smoky Hill trails, the route of the Leavenworth and Pikes Peak Express Company's stages, and the branches of the Overland Trail and the Santa Fe Trail that entered Denver. Her book *The Smoky Hill Trail* should be standard equipment for any automobile that travels the Parker road.

[10]Smiley, J. C. *History of Denver.* Denver, Times-Sun, 1901, p. 353. An impecunious journalist from Cincinnati, Henry Villard, later to become president of the Great Northern Railroad, was on the first coach into Denver. He wrote *The Past and Present of the Pike's Peak Gold Regions.* St. Louis, Mo., Sutherland & McEroy, 1860. Two other newsmen came over the same stage line in June. Albert D. Richardson wrote *Beyond the Mississippi.* Hartford, 1867. His famous companion, Horace Greeley, gathered the letters he wrote back to his *New York Tribune* into a book called *An Overland Journey, from New York to San Francisco, in the Summer of 1859.* New York, Sexton, Barker, 1860.

[11]Smiley, op. cit. p. 329. The cemetery was where Cheesman Park is today.

[12]Long, op. cit. p. 45.

[13]Smiley, op. cit. p. 235.

[14]Smiley, op. cit. p. 479.

[15]Smiley, op. cit. p. 371.

[16]Sanford, "The 'Big Flood' in Cherry Creek, 1864". op. cit. p. 100.

[17]O. J. Goldrick wrote the classic description of the flood of 1864 in

the Denver paper, *The Commonwealth*, May 25, 1864. The sentences are too long to quote in full. The first sentence contains 136 words.

[18]Goldrick, op. cit.

[19]After the flood of 1912, A. Lincoln Fellows, engineer, compiled flood statistics as chairman of the Cherry Creek Flood Commission. The report was printed in May 1913.

[20]Among the articles that have appeared in the Denver newspapers concerning Castlewood Dam and its various owners and promoters, three of the best are *Denver Times,* March 22, 1890; *Denver Post,* May 12, 1901; *Rocky Mountain News,* August 4, 1933.

[21]In 1949 the U. S. Army dug a spillway from their Cherry Creek Dam in order to direct a possible overflow into Sand Creek. Another scheme for Cherry Creek proposed years ago is being considered in 1959. This is to cover the creek bed entirely and use it for building sites or a mall.

[22]Smiley, op. cit. p. 463.

[23]Information about these dams came chiefly from Edward A. Smith, retired engineer for Denver, and S. A. Miller, present engineer for the U. S. Army project.

[24]*Denver Post,* Jan. 19, 1950.

[25]Ferril, T. H., "Waltz against the Mountains." In *Westering.* New Haven, Yale University Press, 1934, p. 52.

River Front Park on the South Platte

Here he was, a riverman, stranded in the middle of the Great American Desert, over 600 miles from home—the 600 miles he had just walked. And for what? Gold—but there was no gold! With his back turned to the collection of log huts that called itself Denver City, he stood on the bank of the South Platte River. What did he care if yonder he could see where the stream issued from the Rocky Mountains? The water was flowing to the River —his River—the Missouri River. Suddenly he decided. He was not going to walk back 600 miles over the Starvation Trail on sore feet sticking out of worn boots, cursing his oxen with every step. He would sell his cattle, build a scow, and float down the South Platte River like the riverman he was.

This typical character—this John Doe from the River—was not the only one in Denver to make a nautical decision in the spring of 1859, during the lull before gold seekers swarmed to the hills. The first edition of the *Rocky Mountain News* notes: "Within the last three days several small boats left here laden with returning emigrants bound for the States. May they have a prosperous voyage down the turbulent Platte.

"P. S. Since writing the above we learn that two of the above boats have been upset, their freight lost and their passengers returned to try their fortunes in the mines again."[1]

Shipping news continued in later issues of the paper. "Boat departure: Sailed on 14th, Clipper Pittsburg, Capt. J. Steiner. 8 passengers and baggage to St. Louis."[2] The scows "Ute" and "Cheyenne" left for the mouth of the Platte and the "Arapahoe"

The Seventeen-Mile House in Cherry Creek Valley southeast of Denver was built, probably in the late 1860's, of squared logs. Later it was covered with clapboards and painted white. The house today looks much as it did in 1889 when this picture was taken, except that it is surrounded by the fields of an 800-acre farm made green by wells sunk in the sands of Cherry Creek. The road shown in the picture is the old road over which came stages from the Smoky Hill or Cherry Creek routes. The length of the road shown in the picture would not have been long enough to accommodate a wagon-train. (Photo by Charles L. Hinke, 1889 from *Mrs. Charles Race. State Historical Society of Colorado.*)

Larimer Street after the Cherry Creek flood of 1864. The historic bridge on which the two towns had celebrated their union in the moonlight, April 5, 1860, was completely swept away. Professor Goldrick's rhetorical account of the flood had to be printed on the *Commonwealth* newspaper presses (building at left of picture) because the *Rocky Mountain News* office had ridden the waves toward the Platte River. (Photo by George D. Wakely. *Denver Public Library*.)

The flood of 1878 took out the middle of the wooden Larimer Street bridge. It was replaced by a single-span iron bridge. The large building on the right-hand side of Larimer Street toward the foothills, labeled West Lindell [Hotel] in the picture, still stands at 11th and Larimer, though the penthouse has been removed. (Photo by W. G. Chamberlain. *Denver Public Library*.)

Cherry Creek flowing under the Larimer Street bridge during the flood of 1885. The Denver City Hall (1881-1946) at 14th and Larimer is seen at the right of the picture. (Photo by H. L. Aulls. *Denver Public Library*.)

The flood of 1933 filled the parking lot in front of the Denver Union Depot. Incoming passengers were perched on luggage carts and pushed by wading redcaps to 17th Street, where they boarded seagoing taxi-cabs, as shown in the picture. (Photo from *Denver Public Library*.)

To take this picture of Cherry Creek in 1897 the photographer stood on the Broadway bridge and shot upstream. Previous shots had been fired near this site. In 1859, before 200 spectators, Mr. Whitsitt plugged (not fatally) a fiery Southerner named McClure who had challenged him to a duel with Colts at ten paces. Today along Speer Boulevard, the Creek bed has been walled and lined with trees. The Denver Buick Company occupies the corner of 7th and Broadway, some of the houses shown still stand on Sherman Street, and the Jacques Brothers, Monuments, have moved south across the creek. (Photo by Hile High Photo Co., in *Denver Municipal Facts*, Jan. 14, 1911, p. 25. *Denver Public Library*.)

In January, 1888, when John Brisben Walker ran a toboggan slide from the top of the grandstand in River Front Park, he advertised that horsecars would wait in the Park to take customers home. The newspaper reporter noted how small the horsecars looked from the top of the slide. Such a horsecar on its tracks is shown in the picture. For the benefit of illiterates, the cars on each route were painted a different color. The "unvestibuled" driver stood in the front of the car in all kinds of weather, his feet deep in straw in the winter. The slot through which the passenger handed his fare shows in the picture. The driver handed back change in a sealed envelope. (Photo from *Denver Public Library*.)

The Castle of Culture and Commerce, better known as Walker's Castle, stood north of the 16th Street Viaduct. It was surrounded by the trees of pleasant River Front Park. To its left may be seen part of the half-mile race track. The streetcar on the viaduct is a cable car with trailer. The gripman stood in the center. With his instrument he reached through a slot in the third rail to grip the endless, moving cable. When he wanted to stop, he released the grip. The Union Depot (which was always called *Dee' po,* never Station) stretches behind the Castle. In the center background is the Windsor Hotel. (Photo by W. H. Jackson. *Denver Public Library.*)

The relief camp at River Front Park, June, 1893. Very small letters imposed on the picture mean A—Surgeon's Tent; B—Headquarters; C—Mess Tents; and D—Tents for "Inmates." (Illustration from *Harper's Weekly,* Aug. 18, 1893, p. 788. *Denver Public Library.*)

Denver gave planks to some of the unemployed who were camping at River Front Park (note grandstand to the right). They built boats to float down the Platte. The signs on the boats read: "Vote the People's Party ticket straight," "American financial system good enough for US," and "A fine job for willing workers." (*Denver Public Library.*)

for New Orleans.[3] One boat, wrecked thirty miles out, lost botanical and geological specimens to the value of $1,000.[4]

The odds were not favorable to safe voyaging. Sporting men of Denver City and Auraria amused themselves by betting on whether or not the boats would be wrecked, or how long would it take them to reach the River. Much money was at stake when Salisbury, Payne & Company built a boat with sleeping and cooking quarters, so there need be no disembarking en route. With a large sail and a rapid current they expected to get to Plattsmouth in six days, a time that would beat the stage company's Express. Wagers were never settled because the paper was unable to learn "the fate of this good ship."[5]

A few years later the editor of the *Rocky Mountain News* summed up the river travel of 1859 thus: "In the insane rush back . . . hundreds embarked on rudely constructed boats and entrusted their lives and future to the swift and treacherous waters of the Platte. Many were drowned, more yet were wrecked, or their boats swamped, and they were picked up by returning teams, whilst a large number made the voyage in safety. Some were carried to the mouth of the Platte in seven days."[6]

By 1866 local residents knew a thing or two about navigating the Platte. Relating the news that two deserters from the 18th Infantry were shipwrecked at the mouth of Clear Creek, the editor inferred that anyone should know that "the Platte will not be navigable until the June rise."[7]

But H. M. Stanley (later to be known by "Dr. Livingstone, I presume?") did not wait for the June rise. In Denver in May of 1866, with fifty dollars (borrowed) , he and a friend "bought some planking and tools and, in a few hours, constructed a flat-bottomed boat. Having furnished it with provisions and arms against the Indians, toward evening [they] floated down the Platte River. After twice upsetting and many adventures and narrow escapes, [they] reached the Missouri River."[8]

More important to early Denver than the scows that left town by water were ferry boats that plied from one bank of the Platte to the other. The first one docked at the foot of present 11th Street, which Aurarians naturally called Ferry Street. The usual fare was a dollar a wagon. Business was good when the rush to the mountains started in the summer of 1859—no one could get to the hills without crossing the River—and continued good until a bridge was built. After the bridge collapsed in the flood of 1864, the ferry was again in business until another bridge was built.

The 1859 ferry looked like any ferry across any stream back in the States—long, flat, and strung on heavy ropes. It was propelled by the current. Before the ferry, however, the Indians had devised a unique means of crossing the rivers of the West. They bent willows into a frame shaped like a tub and covered it with buffalo hides. They vigorously paddled these bull-boats across the current, landing on the other side some yards downstream.

The South Platte River rises in South Park in the Colorado Rockies, emerges from the mountains a few miles southwest of Littleton, flows north through Denver where it acquires water from Cherry Creek, is augmented by many larger streams like the St. Vrain and Cache La Poudre, takes a turn near Greeley, and leaves the state in the northeast corner near Julesburg. The North Platte also rises in Colorado, in North Park, but immediately flows into Wyoming. At North Platte, Nebraska, the two branches join and together flow to the Missouri River at Plattsmouth, which is below Omaha.

In French the word *plate* means *shallow*. Voyageurs from Canada or Creoles from St. Louis may have christened the River. This was before the Lewis and Clark expedition in 1804. Years later, the Oregon Trail followed the Platte and North Platte. It was neither an easy trail nor a trustworthy river, and very early the saying started that the Platte had less water and more mischief than any other western stream.

Compared with the main Platte of the Oregon Trail, the South Platte is historically insignificant, but important to Colorado. It furnishes Denver with water and irrigates thousands of acres of fine farms below Denver. Therefore Coloradans must be forgiven if they drop South from its name when referring to their Platte River.

Before irrigation laws could be established for the Platte in

Colorado, courts had to decide whether or not it was navigable. After much discussion, the final decree was negative, but that does not deter an occasional motor boat from trying its waters today. The Colorado White Water Association members paddle on the Platte in canoes, foldboats, and rubber rafts. In 1948 occurred a tragedy. Three men and a girl were drowned after their rubber raft upset near Waterton.[9] A much publicized voyage started on February 1, 1957, when four men embarked at the foot of 23rd Street, Denver, in two sixteen-foot canoes. Six months later they reached Old Town, Maine, proud of their whiskers and that they had paddled their canoes 5,000 miles.[10]

From bull-boat to fiber-glass canoe, the South Platte has floated various kinds of craft, but none more amazing than the side-wheel paddler of 1887.[11] On this pleasure craft, for the reasonable price of fifty cents each, a man could take his family to Brighton and back. The steamship sailed at three p.m. from the wharf at the foot of 16th Street in River Front Park. So said the advertisement, but the length of the voyage was almost immediately shortened when the craft was shoaled on a sand bar far upstream from Brighton.

The owners of the ship thereupon dammed the South Platte River at 19th Street. The water backed up to 15th Street. On this lake the side-wheel paddler puffed. Of a summer evening families took the watery air from its deck while the band's music floated to the fine houses on the North Denver bluffs.

One summer the boat was actually a showboat—just like the Mississippi crafts. It was converted into the *H. M. S. Pinafore,* and on its deck a traveling company rollicked through Gilbert and Sullivan's nautical opera every evening except Sunday. And on one Sunday! That evening the police courteously waited until after the performance (they probably wanted to see the show) to board the ship. They arrested the manager and treasurer and "all hands were piped off to the police station," where a fine was imposed for breaking the Sunday blue law.[12]

The steamship was part of the entertainment offered in the River Front Park by its owner, John Brisben Walker.[13] He was a man who made himself prominent in the East as well as in Colorado. In New York his most successful venture started in 1889 when he bought the moribund little magazine named the *Cosmopolitan*. After spicing its contents and reducing its price to ten cents a copy, he sold it to William Randolph Hearst in 1905 for, some say, a million and a half dollars.

His next eastern venture was less perspicacious. He took up the new fad of motorcars, but, believing that the gasoline engine was not feasible and Edison's electric battery impossible, he invested in the Stanley Steamer.

In Colorado his successes and failures were equally assorted. Walker turned up in Denver about 1876 saying that the U. S. Secretary of Agriculture had asked him to find out whether alfalfa was a good crop to grow in the rarefied air of the West. This he easily proved on the 1,600 acres of land he bought near present Berkeley Park. His success was not surprising to Colorado men who had been growing alfalfa for years.[14]

Walker disposed of his farm land at a handsome profit. Some of the land, however, he gavè away—to the Roman Catholic Church 50 acres in 1887, for Regis College. In 1909, however, Denver paid him for Inspiration Point.

Near Morrison, Mr. Walker then bought some red sandstone rocks and planned to "turn the Garden of the Angels into a Coney Island for Colorado."[15] Between the two biggest rocks a green field sloped down to a sandstone platform. On this, one day in 1910, Mary Garden stood and sang. Her voice easily filled the natural amphitheater, proving what Walker had been telling the citizens of Denver—that the acoustics of the place were perfect. His idea materialized eventually into the present theater at Red Rocks Park.

Years before this Morrison project and much nearer Denver, John Brisben Walker promoted an amusement park. The year was 1887 and the park was the River Front Park. It ran along the east bank of the South Platte River from 16th to 19th Avenue. The land, now vacant, is easily seen from the 16th Street Viaduct. Rising from the bottom-land, a gray stone building with a square tower and slit windows was befittingly called Walker's Castle. In the fall of 1887 it was called the Castle of Culture and Commerce.[16] That year during the Exhibition (something like a state fair), the castle held displays. In the commercial side were minerals from various mines and the biggest potatoes, the finest sugar beets, and the best wild raspberry jam. In the cultural side was an art gallery with oil paintings,[17] and also embroidered cozies and cams made by Colorado needlewomen. One exhibit reported by the newspaper combined both culture and commerce. This was the "Rocky Mountain Canary" made of soap in the exhibit of the Denver Soap Company.[18]

The cowboy tournament held in connection with the Exhibition at River Front Park in October, 1887, is said to have been one of the earliest rodeos in the West.[19] The hero of the affair was a cowboy from Arizona who rode under the nom de plume of Dull Knife. Years later Charles Siringo, cowboy author, admitted he had used the name during the show.[20]

In both 1887 and 1888 professional baseball games were played at River Front Park.[21] During one of the games between the Chicago White Stockings and the All-Americans, a fielder made a "bandstand" play.[22] He jumped up the steps of the bandstand to catch the ball. Once when John Brisben Walker's favorite team won a game he ran into the Castle of Culture and Commerce and returned with nine pies, presenting a pie to each member of the team. In baseball's early days in Denver, members of the Denver Athletic Club not only encouraged their team by placing a keg of beer at each base, but threw twenty-dollar gold pieces to players who stole a base or made a home run. A local amateur player thought it unfair that such incentives were offered to the professionals, especially when they played the East High School team, which was so good in the late 1880's that it held its own against any opponents, professional or amateur.[23]

The bandstand, noted above, on which the ball player leaped, was unusual in that it was movable. It was made in 1888 especially for the incomparable Gilmore and his fifty-five-piece band. For all three of Gilmore's concerts the price was only four dollars. Horsecars carried patrons across the railroad tracks directly to the entrance of River Front Park and waited right there until after

101

the performance to carry them back again. Carriages drove into the Park.

The performance of Gilmore's band may not have been "the greatest musical event in the history of Colorado," as stated in the advance publicity, but it certainly must have been one of the loudest. Augmented by 500 local singers, the first concert opened with a rendition of the Star Spangled Banner which called for the discharge of cannon. The band was equipped with six pieces of artillery and real anvils for clanking during the *Il Trovatore* number. Of course they played the *William Tell Overture*. The least noisy item was "Come Where My Love Lies Dreaming," done by four French horns. The music critic on one of the Denver papers, although shocked that Gilmore had arranged the *Hungarian Rhapsody No. 2* for band, which everyone knew had been written for piano, reluctantly admitted the performance was effective.[24]

John Brisben Walker fancied himself a judge of horses and provided a quarter-mile race track at River Front Park. The races were between trotting horses hitched to sulkies, but that does not mean that the excitement of the betting was any less than if jockeys had been riding running horses, as today. In 1892, after an afternoon of sulky events, two chariots raced. Chariot A won the race but the charioteer of Chariot B, leaning back on the reins with all his strength, could not stop his horses. The team—two grays and two blacks—circled the track four times, making much better time than during the race.[25]

In 1889 Walker booked a fireworks specialist, the famous Pain of New York and London, to stage a series of spectacles at River Front Park.[26] Being fireworks, they were night events. On the opposite, or west, side of the Platte River the scenery—12,000 square yards of canvas—was hung on an iron structure. The program was varied but every night the audience was urged to keep their seats until after the final bouquet of 500 rockets fired simultaneously. One night Denver people heard Nero fiddle while they watched Rome burn; one night they saw Pompeii destroyed. In this show, after Vesuvius had exploded with a terrific scattering of stones, lava poured down the bluffs across the river, "while

102

hundreds of actors and actresses . . . gaily and correctly garbed . . . were poems of motion on the great stage," and gondolas carried others up and down the river.

Denver's favorite show was the *Siege of Sebastopol*. The pageant opened with Russian troops encamped on the river bank. A spy was discovered and captured after he had made a leap for life "over thirty guns which were discharged while making the leap." Soon the allies appeared on horseback, and the Charge of the Light Brigade was re-enacted. The reason Denver preferred this show was that a local man played the bugle that sent the Light Brigade to death and glory. This same man with the same bugle in real life had stood at Lord Cardigan's side at Balaklava to bugle for the 11th Hussars. The bugler's name was Alexander Sutherland. As a private in the First Colorado Regiment in 1862, he played his historic bugle at Glorieta Pass, New Mexico. This was where "Gilpin's Pet Lambs" (Colorado troops) stopped the Confederates from taking over the Rocky Mountain West and the gold therein.[27]

Summer was a busy time at River Front Park with fireworks, racing, band concerts, baseball games, and pleasure cruises. John Brisben Walker hated to waste the winters. Knowing that January in Denver was often open and very cold, he built a toboggan slide, like those used in Canada. Some of the young Denver belles who rode it wore toboggan caps and even genuine toboggan suits, just like Canadiennes.

The slide towered fourteen feet higher than the grandstand. You walked up a flight of stairs. From the top you saw ten electric lights on the slide itself and bonfires that illuminated the Park. Far off twinkled the lights of the city. From such a height the horsecars looked small.

Ten feet wide, the slide was covered with felt. Every midnight the felt was soaked with water, which froze. Presumably the ice lasted until the next night. There were three tracks and three toboggans side by side. The young men tucked the fairer sex into the front seats, then sat protectively behind them. The guide threw himself upon his stomach on a back platform and the

103

attendant pulled a lever. "With merry cries of 'Now for a race' the toboggans sped downward."[28]

Perhaps a chinook ruined the toboggan business, or for some other reason the restive Walker lost interest in River Front Park. The papers reported that he sold the Park in 1891,[29] and again in 1903,[30] this time for a million dollars. Whatever the date, the Northwestern Terminal Company did acquire the land and still owns it.

Since Walker's time the land has been used by circuses, like Ringling Brothers', and roadshows like Dr. W. F. Carver's. In 1897 Sells Brothers' Roman Hippodrome played at River Front Park.[31] Revivalists, also, have pitched their tents on this land by the River.[32]

In 1898 and for a few years thereafter the Woman's Club of Denver gave the children in the lower part of town a place to play in the summer by running a day camp, complete with kindergarten, lemonade, and a school of domestic science. In the Castle they hung Perry prints. Each child was allowed to choose one to take home for a week. At first the ladies let all the children into the Castle at once, but soon learned it was better to allow one child to come alone into the art room.[33] On the last day of one summer Governor Adams sent sixteen and a half gallons of ice cream for the ladies to give the children.[34]

Walker's Castle was used for many things in its sixty-odd years of life. In 1893 the Ramblers (bicycle) Club held their smokers there,[35] but presently it was housing the laundry for Pullman car linen, and then was a washroom for the men who worked on the Moffat Road. In it the Denver & Rio Grande Railroad stored many records. They were there, along with tons of hay, in November, 1951, when the Castle burned.[36] The fire was so hot that bits of rock popped from the gray stone, reminding old-timers of the *Eruption of Vesuvius* as portrayed by Pain. The wreckage left by the fire was removed in 1952. Now all that remains of the Castle of Culture and Commerce is a small pile of rubble below and a little to the north of the 16th Street Viaduct.

For a final story of River Front Park in the old days there is the tale of an armada on the River Platte.[37] The date—1893. The time—summer. The reason—the silver panic had hit Colorado. Mine owners found it unprofitable to run their mines. Miners in David Moffat's Maid of Erin, for example, refused to take a fifty-cent cut in wages just because the price of silver tumbled. When Moffat closed his Leadville mine and let the water in,[38] the miners came down to Denver. Workers from the Arkansas Valley smelter came up from Pueblo. Daily, other unemployed drifted into the capital city.

Here they found no jobs. On the street corners they joined Denver men who had lost their jobs in stores and hotels. The papers reported holdups by hungry men, and suicides. Denver was frightened.

The city decided to establish a refugee camp. Applicants were screened by Parson Tom Uzzell and Dean H. Martyn Hart. John Brisben Walker contributed the land at River Front Park. The National Guard furnished tents for almost 400 men, another 200 slept in the grandstand. The city fed between 500 and 1,000 each day for over two weeks, starting July 27, 1893.

At the same time, the city fathers were making strenuous efforts to get the destitute men out of town. Railroads reduced fare to six dollars to the Missouri River, and then to nothing. Trains pulled out of the Union Depot with standing-room-only—passenger coaches, not cattle cars.

Among the unhappy men at River Front Park who watched the waters of the Platte flow toward the Missouri River were those who knew about boats—rivermen. They wanted to float downstream. The City of Denver furnished them with lumber from which they constructed rude flatboats and the armada pushed off. (See picture on p. 96.) Many were wrecked, some of the sailors were drowned but some of the boats reached Plattsmouth. Here some of the men joined Coxey's Army. This was the army of unemployed who marched on Washington in 1894. Demanding relief from the President, they even camped on the White House lawn.

These were turbulent times in the country, and in Denver, just as they had been in 1859 when men stranded in the middle of the

Great American Desert were desperate enough to try boating on the shallow waters of that non-navigable river, the South Platte.

NOTES

[1]*RMN*, April 23, 1859.
[2]*RMN*, Sept. 17, 1859.
[3]*RMN*, Sept. 9, 1859.
[4]Villard, Henry "Letter to the Cincinnati Daily Commercial," June 3, 1859. In *Colorado Magazine*. v. 8, p. 236, Nov. 1931.
[5]*RMN*, June 21, 1862.
[6]*RMN*, April 23, 1867, p. 1, col. 3.
[7]*RMN*, May 18, 1866, p. 4, col. 2.
[8]Stanley, H. M. *Autobiography*. Boston, Houghton Mifflin, 1909, p. 222. After Stanley became famous, Central City men remembered that he had been the bookkeeper in a smelter owned by J. E. Lyon in 1865. *Denver Republican*, June 17, 1890.
[9]*Denver Post*, May 23, 1948.
[10]*Denver Post*, Nov. 30, 1957.
[11]Advertisements for this boat trip are in the newspapers for the summer of 1887.
[12]*Denver Times*, April 1, 1891, and "50 Years Ago!" In *RMN*, July 7, 1940.
[13]Walker had 14 children by his first 2 wives and assorted grandchildren, but few family memoirs are available. We must be content with short articles about him like those in the *Dictionary of American Biography*, the *Rocky Mountain News* for June 13, 1948, and the *Empire Magazine*, Sept. 8, 1946, and May 21, 1950.
[14]Steinel, A. T. and Working, D. W. *History of Agriculture in Colorado*. Fort Collins, State Agricultural College, 1926, p. 411. This book credits the first alfalfa raised in Colorado to Major Jacob Downing. He planted alfalfa seeds from Mexico in front of his law office at 12th and Holladay Streets in 1862, later growing an extensive crop near Green Mountain, south of Golden.
[15]*Denver Post*, May 14, 1906, p. 12, col. 7. The *Central City Register-Call* for June 28, 1895, credits Governor John Evans with naming the Garden of the Angels (present Red Rocks) during the time that the Denver, South Park & Pacific Railroad ran to Morrison.
[16]*Denver Times*, Sept. 13, 1887 and days following.
[17]John D. Howland, Denver artist, supervised the Art Department. Howland's best known work is the statue of the Union Soldier that stands in front of the State Capitol Building. McMechen, E. C. "Art,

Drama and Music." In Hafen, L. R. *Colorado and its People.* New York, Lewis, 1948. v. 2, p. 427.

[18]*Denver Evening Times,* Sept. 18, 1887, p. 4, col. 3.

[19]Westermeier, C. P. "Seventy-five Years of Rodeo in Colorado." In *Colorado Magazine.* v. 28, p. 16, Jan. 1951.

[20]Siringo, C. A. *A Cowboy Detective.* Chicago, Conkey, 1912, p. 45.

[21]*RMN,* April 22, 1934. Sports sec., p. 3. This article says that professional baseball in Denver was first played at 31st and Larimer about 1883, at River Front Park in 1887 and 1888, and then at Broadway Park.

[22]*RMN,* April 23, 1934.

[23]Henry Hanington, who was captain of the East High baseball team when he was fifteen years old, remembered the pies, the beer, and the gold pieces.

[24]*RMN,* June 13, 1888, p. 5, col. 7 and days following.

[25]*RMN,* May 27, 1892, p. 3, col. 1.

[26]Augmenting the newspaper accounts of Pain's spectacles is a program for June and July, 1889, in the Western History Department of the Denver Public Library. Its first page is reproduced on page 93.

[27]According to his obituary in the *Denver Post,* Nov. 8, 1904, p. 2, col. 3, Sutherland died at 624 27th Street, fifty years after Balaklava.

[28]*Denver Republican,* Jan. 4, 1888, p. 3, col. 8.

[29]*Denver Times,* April 29, 1891.

[30]*Denver Post,* Feb. 9, 1903.

[31]*Denver Times,* June 30, 1891.

[32]*Denver Post,* Sept. 3, 1899.

[33]*Denver Times,* May 16, 1899 and days following.

[34]*RMN,* Sept. 3, 1898, p. 10.

[35]*RMN,* May 31, 1893, p. 3, col. 2.

[36]*RMN,* Nov. 18, 1951.

[37]Smiley, J. C. *History of Denver.* Denver, Times-Sun, 1901. p. 917; *Denver Times,* Aug. 9, 1893.

[38]Platte, W. A. "The Destitute in Denver." In *Harper's Weekly,* Aug. 19, 1893. *RMN,* July 27, 1893 and days following.

SLICE V

Gold Coins in Denver Mints

The gray fortress at West Colfax and Delaware, just west of the City and County Building, is the Denver Branch of the United States Mint. This building celebrated its fiftieth birthday in February, 1956, which means that for over half a century coins have been coming from its machinery for Americans to jingle in their pockets.

Up to 1934, this jingle had the unmistakable ring of gold. In 1906, its first year of minting, the Denver mint turned out almost two million pieces of gold. These coins, like all coins minted in Denver, carried D as their mint mark, so if you see a gold coin marked D, dated between 1906 and 1933,[1] you may know it was fashioned at the Denver mint.

The story of gold in Denver goes back more than fifty years. It goes back to the beginning of the discovery of gold in the mountains west of Denver. If it weren't for the "gold in them thar hills" there might never have been a Denver.

Let's follow the story of gold by telling the tale of an early day prospector. We'll call him Jim.

Jim came to the mountains during the Pikes Peak gold rush, in the spring of 1860, and worked his way up North Clear Creek to a hill near Black Hawk in the Gregory District of present Gilpin County, Colorado. On the hill he partially filled his iron pan with dirt, went down to North Clear Creek, and filled the pan to the rim with water. This he swished around and around, thumbing out the big rocks as they came to the surface on the lower side of the slightly tipped pan. He disregarded his cold thumbs—

rheumatism was a small price to pay for possible riches—and finally all he had in the bottom of the pan was the heaviest. If he was lucky, this sediment included gold.

Jim picked out the nuggets, then the shot. He tried to sort out some of the scale from the black sediment, but he ignored the glittering dust that was too fine to pick up with his clumsy fingers. The dust was recoverable by amalgamation with quicksilver, but Jim was the impatient prospector, not the scientific miner.

Jim carefully poured his gold into his poke, which was a pouch made of raw buckskin. Then he rushed back up the hill for more pay dirt. When he had filled his poke, he soaked it in the stream, and dried it in the mountain sun. The raw buckskin shrank into a compact parcel of gold. After a few weeks of this, Jim got tired and ran out of grub, so he sold his claim for more gold pokes and headed down hill to the plains and over the plains to dusty Denver sprawled in the August heat where Cherry Creek runs into the South Platte River.

The first thing Jim did in Denver was to drop in to Uncle Dick Wootton's saloon to buy a drink of "Taos lightnin'." This so-called whiskey cost a quarter a shot, but Jim had long since spent the last two-bit piece he had brought from the States. He paid for his drink by opening his gold pouch and offering it to the bartender. The bartender took a pinch of gold between his thumb and forefinger. One pinch was considered worth two-bits, no matter what size the thumb or how long the fingernails.

Then Jim went to the general store to buy some grub. That was expensive, not to be paid for in pinches. The grocer put a weight on the pan that swung at the end of one arm of the scales on the counter, and Jim tipped his poke until enough gold had poured into the other pan to balance the weight. However, if Jim did not trust the merchant, he whipped from his pocket his own small scales and his own set of weights to weigh his own gold.

Gold dust being, at times, as fine as flour, this method of barter involved much waste. The gold would spill on the floor and sift between the cracks. Reminiscences of early Denver are not complete without a tale of how much gold was recovered from floor sweepings in saloons or beneath the ticket windows of theaters.[2]

Jim did not care to waste the profits of his busy summer thus. Besides, now that he had sold his claim, he had too many pokes to carry around on his person in a town as tough as Denver.

After looking the town over for a bank, he chose to enter one on McGaa³ and G Streets (Market at 16th) labeled Clark, Gruber & Company. The teller emptied Jim's gold pokes on to scales and paid him according to the market price of gold in the States the last time anyone had heard from the States. (Two years later, in 1862, the price was $17 an ounce; today, gold has been pegged at $35 a troy ounce.) The teller paid Jim in gold coins. These closely resembled standard United States gold pieces, but when Jim examined his wealth minutely, he found they were stamped not only with the bank's name but were labeled Pikes Peak. Jim, being a Pikes Peaker, was delighted.

The bank had been started by three bankers from Leavenworth, Kansas, the brothers Clark and E. H. Gruber. Leavenworth was one of the supply towns for the gold-rushers so the bankers talked to many men who had been West. From what they told them, the bankers estimated the problems they would encounter if they were to establish a bank in Denver. The first problem was transportation. The nuggets and gold dust they bought from prospectors would have to be packed in a strong box. This they would padlock and ship, under armed guard, on the stage line that ran to the River, and from the States they would have to import United States coins to pay for the dust. The Clarks and Mr. Gruber considered the waste in this method, with cracks in the boxes and Indians on the plains. They resented what they considered exorbitant freight charges—five per cent of the value of any shipment, each way.

They further noted that bankers and merchants had the aggravating problem of the slick customer who early devised ways of substituting brass filings for gold flecks, and of manufacturing "retort nuggets" out of base metals which he veneered with gold. To ascertain just what the customer was selling, bankers had to refine the gold, or a sample of it. Clark, Gruber & Company figured that as long as they had to refine gold anyway, they might as well go one step further and mint coins that could be used as legal tender, thus avoiding the expense and waste of shipping raw gold to "America."

So the firm decided to establish a bank and mint in Denver. One of the Clarks went east to buy the latest money-making machines which he freighted by railroad to the Missouri River, by ox-team across the plains.[4] On McGaa and G Streets the other two partners supervised the erection of a two-story brick building above a large basement. In this basement they set up machinery, adding an engine room and an acid room. Opening for business on July 20, 1860, they formally minted the first of their gold coins in the presence of invited guests. The first coin, of the ten dollar variety, was slightly imperfect. Nevertheless it was presented to William Byers,[5] editor, who expressed his gratitude by giving the firm publicity in his *Rocky Mountain News*.

In the two years they operated their mint, 1860 and 1861, Clark-Gruber coined about $600,000 worth of gold coins. Surprisingly few of these are left today.[6] Western numismatists eagerly collect these Denver coins along with the even rarer pieces from other private mints of early Colorado, such as the Conway coins made in Georgia Gulch not far from Breckenridge, and the Parsons coins minted in the Tarryall country of South Park.

Clark, Gruber & Company minted four denominations of coins in each of the two years they were in the minting business— double-eagle, eagle, half-eagle and quarter-eagle.[7] Locally, the 1860 double-eagle and eagle of the Clark-Gruber mintage are the most interesting, for on them was printed a picture of a mountain, obviously intended to represent Pikes Peak, since the inscription circling the mountain reads *Pikes Peak Gold*. (See illustration on page 116.)

The two larger coins of 1860, the double-eagle and eagle, had another distinction beside the portrait of Pikes Peak. Their color is yellower than that of the later coins, indicating greater content of pure gold. The gold-rushers complained that these coins were too soft, they dented and wore. Thereafter the company used more alloy. Even so, the Clark-Gruber coins were made of purer gold and weighed more than the United States gold

111

pieces. This was done deliberately to forestall any complaint of not receiving full value.

Clark, Gruber & Company were not breaking the law when they minted gold coins in Denver. Before they set up their mint, they consulted lawyers who found no law in 1860 which said the privilege of minting coins belonged exclusively to Uncle Sam. Such a law was not passed until June, 1864.

After two years of minting coins, the brothers Clark and E. H. Gruber decided, except for making small ingots, that they wanted to get out of the minting business. They asked Hiram Bennett, delegate to Congress from the Territory of Colorado, to urge Congress to buy their Denver setup and establish a Federal coinage mint. Other citizens of Denver, eager to have minting continued locally, added their urgings. One man took a poke of gold dust to Congress, another sent the Speaker of the House a gold snuffbox.[8] Such lobbying was effective. The United States Government paid $25,000 to Clark, Gruber & Company for their building and machinery and took possession in April of 1863. The government immediately enlarged the building, but imagine the rage of the man who had contributed the gold snuffbox to the Speaker of the House when Congress changed its mind about minting money in Denver. The Denver Branch of the United States Mint, from 1863 through 1905, accepted raw gold and refined it into ingots which they neatly piled in boxes and shipped to Philadelphia to be coined. The Denver mint was really just an assay office, though it was also used as a Depository of Public Funds. Later the depository business was acquired by the First National Bank of Denver, heir to all the banking business of Clark, Gruber & Company.

The ingots refined by the United States Mint in Denver were brick-shaped, though never as large as a conventional brick. They varied from 100 ounce bars (worth $2,000 at that time) to 1,200 ounce bars. They were pretty things, smooth and shiny. No wonder people tried to steal them, despite the mint marks stamped upon them.

Theft of bars from the Denver mint has been tried twice, once in 1864,[9] again in 1920. In 1864, a young gentleman from Pennsylvania named James D. Clarke held a job as a pay clerk in the

The Clark, Gruber & Company's building at 16th and McGaa Street is labeled *Bank*. The date, 1862, was after the company had stopped minting Pikes Peak gold coins and before the United States Mint had taken over its building and the First National Bank of Denver had acquired its banking business. (Section from Dillingham's sketch of *Denver in 1862. Denver Public Library.*)

Denver in 1864 with the road to Boulder leading to the right horizon. The Denver Branch of the United States Mint had enlarged the Clark-Gruber Building. Diagonally across the street are six shedlike buildings, in one of which Miss Ring taught school. On their site H.C. Brown erected a three-story brick building in 1868. It still stands, though barely. For its picture see p. 248. (Photo probably by W. G. Chamberlain. *Denver Public Library.*)

About 1893. In the right foreground are the powerhouse for the cable cars and the fire station for Denver Hose No. 1. (Photo from *Municipal Facts,* May, 1923, p. 4.)

About 1904. The Denver mint (A-3½) moved to its new building. Other buildings, some of which may be located in the other pictures on these pages, are:

A-2½ St. Leo's Church.

B-4 La Veta Place, stylish terraces built by Tabor.

C-3 The present Zook Building was built by the Continental Oil Company just in time for the panic of 1893. W.H. Jackson had a sky-lighted studio on the top floor. The building was later used as a warehouse by Scholtz Drug Company

E-2 Sloan's Lake, with Manhattan Beach on N.W. side.

E-6 After the cable cars stopped running, A.D. Wilson, real-estate man, turned the powerhouse into a store building.

F-3 Longfellow School, later Opportunity School.

F½-2½ St. Elizabeth's Church.

F½-3½ Hotel L'Impériale. Here Tabor boarded (dining room on top floor) and Richthofen died. It is the present United Fund Building.

J-3 Denver Athletic Club, opened December, 1890.

J-5 Bates Triangle had three homes on it.

M-6 Fire House No. 1.

Colfax and Broadway from about 1893 to 1913

About 1911. La Veta Terrace has been torn down and the Denver Public Library (1909-1956) erected. This building now houses the Denver Water Department. One of the homes on Bates Triangle has been replaced by an automobile company, and the Fire Station No. 1 has given way to the base of the Pioneer Monument. (Photo by L. C. McClure.)

About 1913. The buildings from Bannock to Broadway were torn down in 1912 and the lawn planted for the Civic Center the next year. The plot remained as shown in the picture until Mayor Speer's last term of office, 1916-1918. Soon the Greek theater encroached on 14th Avenue to the left and, in 1921, Voorhies Memorial Gateway rose on the Bates Triangle. The closing of Colfax Avenue between this and the library put a kink in Colfax which otherwise is said to run straight from Kansas to the Rocky Mountains. (Photo by George L. Beam. All photos from *Denver Public Library*.)

The eastern die maker who designed this pattern for a gold coin thought Pikes Peak looked like an equilateral triangle. Clark, Gruber & Company looked out of their window at the broad mass of Pikes Peak south of Denver and rejected the pattern.

But they accepted this revised triangle. The sketch shows one of the double-eagles, or twenty dollar gold pieces, minted by Clark, Gruber & Company in 1860 in Denver. One of these gold pieces, now collectors' items, sold recently for $1500.00.

A company named the Denver City Assay Office got as far in their plans to mint tokens as to have $5 and $20 trial tokens made in copper by Cord Brothers, jewelers.

DENVER COINS 1860
(Sketched by Gertrude Pierce)

Denver mint. On Saturday night, February 13, 1864, at about nine o'clock, young Clarke "stole from the safe of that institution in gold bars and in treasury notes a sum amounting to $37,000 and absconded. This theft astounded the city both by its magnitude and the previous good character and standing in society of the absconding clerk . . . a young man of fine appearance and very pleasing address and manners. Eastern connections of the highest respectability had recommended him for the situation he possessed, and no meeting or social gathering in the city, either religious or secular, seemed perfect without his presence."[10] Young Clarke's salary at the mint was $1,800 a year, a sum so large that it led him into the gambling dens and wineries (which his boss shunned so was unaware of his habits) and into the clutches of "a gay and crafty milliner of Larimer Street."[11]

With some of the notes, Clarke bought a sorrel horse, which had "a tolerable long tail" and was nearly blind in the left eye.[12] He also bought a saddle, saddlebags, spurs, two navy pistols, and a revolver. Most of the treasury notes he stuffed "like a rat's nest" into a saddlebag and then sewed it up. A few notes he used for shinplasters under his underwear, which, along with his black beaver coat, may have helped to keep him warm those February nights.

Thus equipped, he turned his horse's one good eye toward Cherry Creek and rode out of Denver, fast but unsuspected. A little southeast of town he threw away the gold ingot he had included in his loot. This bar, weighing about ten pounds, was awkward to carry.

Six days later three men, including the son of his boss, caught up with him twenty-five miles south of Colorado City. This was not difficult as Clarke had lost his horse. (The newspapers were derisive when they heard the greenhorn had lost his horse!) He had managed to save his saddlebags, still sewed up. With them, he was brought back to Denver. All but $4,419.90 of his "take" was recovered, including a bag of one dollar gold pieces. With one of these little tidbits he had made a futile gesture toward Lady Luck. The official report reads: "Found in searching Clarke at the Mint in gold $1.00 in his boots."[13]

117

Weeks later, an indifferent jailer casually reported that Clarke had escaped. What Clarke did after this escape, as he told a reporter later, was to sojourn in the Denver neighborhood for ten or eleven days "part of the time occupying a shady couch under the stage of the Denver Theatre, and part of the time inhabiting the groves near Beckworth's Ranch up the Platte [near present Overland Park]. While hereabouts, he says he had a good time, living on cooked grub, cocktails and clothing, which were kindly furnished him by friends in town, whose names he has no better sense than to disclose."[14] Clarke finally took a pack and headed north, on foot—no more horses for him—and got a job as stock tender near La Porte, where a deputy marshal arrested him and brought him back to Denver. Clarke was tried and told to leave the Territory.

So much for the genteel Clarke. But what about the ingot he threw away near present Cheesman Park? On the Sunday morning after the Saturday night robbery two young men were strolling over the hill east of Denver. They found the ingot. Quickly returning to their cabin, they sawed the brick in half and pounded out the mint marks. One of them took his half to Central City where the Kountze Brothers' bank bought it. After the bank became suspicious, he was arrested and implicated his friend who still had the other chunk of gold.

In 1864 Denver was really too busy to bother with the "puerile perpetrations . . . and abnormal imbecilities"[15] of a juvenile delinquent like Jim Clarke. Because of the Civil War and Indians, the town was full of soldiers from Camp Weld. Denver had the first of her famous flash floods and her worst Indian scare. This was set off when the bodies of the Hungate family, who had been killed by the Indians on Running Creek, were exhibited in Denver. During the first week in June rumors started that the Indians were massing to descend on Denver. "There was not in point of fact any Indian near the city, and no danger menaced the people, yet they rushed hither and thither through the darkness of the night for places of safety, while alarm bells rang out wildly . . ."[16] Some of the women and children were packed into non-frame buildings, like the Lindell Hotel, which still stands at 11th and Larimer, and the U. S. Mint. In daylight the panic died down. Denver was never attacked by the Indians.

Being brick, the mint might have adequately protected the women and children against an Indian raid, but it was not a very attractive building. As time went on citizens started to complain about its looks. In 1889 one wrote that the mint "is on Holladay Street at the corner of Sixteenth and is the only one of the public buildings which is not a credit to the city or the Government."[17] It continued to be used until 1904 when its personnel moved over to the unfinished new building.

The old building, on being vacated, found itself in the vegetable business. The large basement proved an ideal place to store potatoes and onions. It was, however, not vegetables that A. M. Donaldson was looking for when he bought the dirt from the floor of the basement, to wash it for gold in the South Platte River.

Charles Boettcher bought the old mint for $31,000, the quit-claim being dated August 11, 1909. When the building was razed, the wreckers found that the vault had a patch over a hole in its side. Everyone conjectured as to the nefarious uses of this hole, but the mystery was solved when a former employee of the mint remembered that in 1877 the lock of the vault had stuck. In order to get into the vault, the hole was officially made and officially patched.

The building that now stands at 16th and Market (1410 16th is the address) bears no resemblance to the old mint but it commemorates the historical importance of the site by its name— The Mint Block.

In February, 1906, coining machines in the new mint building on Colfax and Delaware Street started to stamp out money, the first that had been made in Denver since Clark, Gruber & Company stopped minting gold coins in 1861. During 1906 the new mint manufactured silver coins and almost two million pieces of gold coins worth five, ten, and twenty dollars each. (The first $2.50 pieces with the D mark (for Denver) were minted in 1911.)[18]

At one point during the process of refining gold to turn into coins, anodes of pure gold measuring seven by three and a half

119

inches were produced. These were so valuable that door guards were especially alerted to watch for their possible theft. Nevertheless, over a period of months in 1920, an employee managed to carry out $80,000 worth of these gold anodes. This man, named Orville Harrington, had attended the Colorado School of Mines and owned a gold mine in Victor. He planned to mix his mint gold with his mine gold and thus avoid detection (and probably start a stampede to the Victor region!).

Harrington had an artificial leg. When the story of the robbery broke, journalists wrote that the man had secreted gold bars in his wooden leg. The papers even published an artist's sketch of the leg with a hollowed-out hiding place in which reposed a gold ingot.[19] The headlines referred to the crime as the "Wooden Leg Robbery."

We have the word, however, of Rowland Goddard,[20] Denver's able supervisor of U. S. Secret Service, that Harrington carried the gold out of the mint in his vest pocket. His artificial leg caused him to walk with a limp. His slump made his coat hang loosely over the left side of his vest, and it was in the left vest pocket that he carried out the gold anodes.

Mr. Goddard should know. He it was who received a tip from one of Harrington's fellow employees, watched the man closely, hid among the weeds in the vacant lot near his home, saw him bury gold under the back walk, arrested him, and recovered all the gold from beneath the back walk and from behind the cement walls of the basement of the house at 1485 South University Boulevard.[21]

Another robbery happened in front of the mint in 1922. This one put Denver on the unsolved-crime map of the nation. On December 18, 1922, a Federal Reserve Bank truck drew up in front of the mint, parking on West Colfax Avenue. The guards, as was their usual practice, started to carry packages of crisp, new, five dollar bills into the mint for safe keeping. From a nearby car bandits leaped, grabbed $200,000 worth of bills, dashed back to their car and sped away. The gun play between the robbers, the Federal Reserve guards, and the guards at the mint entrance left bullet holes in the walls of the building. One of the Federal

Reserve guards was killed and weeks later the body of one of the bandits was found in a car in a rented garage on Capitol Hill.

The criminals were never apprehended for this crime, but some of them, in prison for other crimes, later confessed their participation. The money was peddled in St. Paul for fifty per cent of its value. Some of it is in general circulation, but Secret Service Supervisor Goddard of Denver recovered $80,000 in St. Paul.

Officials of the Denver mint point out that this robbery had nothing to do with the mint. Proud of their record of no loss since the Clarke affair in 1864, they resent that the 1922 robbery is known as the Denver Mint Robbery. They prefer to have it called the Robbery of the Federal Reserve Bank truck in front of the Denver Branch of the U. S. Mint.[22]

The Denver mint today is America's next-to-best gold hoarder, surpassed only by Fort Knox, Kentucky. The great reserves of gold bullion so neatly stacked and carefully guarded in the Denver mint started piling up after March 6, 1933. That was when President Franklin D. Roosevelt signed the law that stopped the minting of gold. The law demanded that all gold coins (except collectors' items) be sold to the U. S. mints where they were melted into bars. Each bar weighs thirty-two pounds and is worth about $14,000.

Before World War II, the center portion of the Denver mint was entirely remade into a building within a building in order to safeguard the gold bullion. It is four stories, and angled mirrors enable guards on upper levels to check the intricate underground passageways at a glance.

So large a building might not have been necessary if, in the fall of 1934, the Government had not transferred two and one-half billion dollars worth of gold bullion (and over another billion later) from San Francisco to Denver for the greater security offered by an inland location. The gold came by parcel post, on seventy-five railroad mail cars, divided into twenty-five trains. At the Denver depot, the gold bricks were transferred into mail trucks. Denverites were fascinated by the lines of mail trucks running to the mint with sirens sounding in police cars fore-and-aft. Exactly the same amount of gold arrived at the Denver mint as had left San Francisco.

How much gold is stored in the vaults of the Denver mint? Officials announce its value every now and then, but the figure is too large to mean much. Besides, the amount increases every week. Gold is still dug from the earth of Colorado and other mining states and shipped to Denver where it is refined and re-buried at the mint. "Back to the earth again."

NOTES

Note: Much of the information concerning the early mint came from Nolie Mumey's *Clark, Gruber & Company (1860-1865), a Pioneer Denver Mint; History of their Operation and Coinage,* Denver, Art-craft Press, 1950. From the photographs in that book, sketches were made of the 1860 twenty-dollar gold pieces, with permission of Dr. Mumey. (See picture on p. 116.)

The sketch of the Denver City Assay Office coin was made from a photograph in the State Historical Society's Library. Information about this coin came from P. W. Whiteley's "Colorado Specie." In the *Numismatist,* v. 71, p. 785 ff. July 1958.

[1]Warning to collectors: U. S. gold coins marked D but dated from 1858 to 1861 were made in Dahlonega, Lumpkin County, Georgia. The gold for these coins could have been mined by Georgians (like John Gregory) before they came to Colorado in the gold rush of 1858.

[2]A modern tale of gold dust tells that in 1936, when the floors of part of the Denver Branch of the U. S. Mint were dismantled, $67,000 worth of gold was recovered. This and other facts are found in a pamphlet called *The Story of the U. S. Mint, Denver* (prepared through the Denver Convention and Visitors Bureau by Miller-Stock-man Supply Company, n.d.).

[3]McGaa Street was named for a trapper who was living at the mouth of Cherry Creek when the gold-rushers came. In 1866 the name was switched to honor the transportation king, Ben Holladay, but by 1899 the holiday spirit on the street had become so rampant that moral citizens changed its name to Market Street.

[4]This original machinery is now on exhibit at the Colorado State Historical Museum in Denver, where it was deposited by the Government in 1898.

[5]Smiley, J. C. *History of Denver*. Denver, Times-Sun, 1901. p. 810. Mumey, op. cit., wrote that in 1950 the first coin was owned by C. Y. McClure, the son of the original melter at the Clark-Gruber mint.

[6]A complete set of Clark, Gruber & Company coins is worth well over $3,000. Various coin collectors have sets as has, of course, the First National Bank of Denver. The Colorado State Historical Museum has not only a fine collection of Clark, Gruber & Company coins in its safe, but also a gold ingot stamped with early mint marks.

[7]For the benefit of people too young to remember the days when money could be shiny gold, the term *eagle* should be defined. It was a gold coin decorated on the reverse side with the likeness of an eagle, the emblem of our country. The single eagle was the ten-dollar coin; the weight was doubled for twenty dollars (the double-eagle) ; halved for five dollars (the half-eagle) ; and the quarter-eagle was $2.50.

[8]Smiley, op. cit., p. 810.

[9]Copies of the official letters concerning this robbery are in the files of the Denver Branch of the U. S. Mint. Based on these records is an article by Forbes Parkhill called "Pioneer Denver Mint Robbery." In *Denver Westerners Monthly Roundup*, v. 13, July and August, 1957.

[10]Wharton, J. E. *History of the City of Denver*. Denver, Byers & Dailey, 1866. p. 115.

[11]This sentence is quoted from an article, probably clipped from a magazine called *Inter-Ocean*, pasted in the Dawson Scrapbook, no. 23, p. 301, at the Colorado State Historical Society Library.

[12]A bulletin published in the *Rocky Mountain News*, February 15, 1864, offered a reward of $1,000 for the recovery of thief and money. The description of the horse leads one to hope that Jim Clarke did not pay much of his stolen money for it. As for Clarke, the bulletin describes him as "21 years old, smooth face, light hair, cut pretty short, spare built, of genteel address, boyish look, about 5 feet 6 inches high."

[13]From the official records at the mint as quoted by F. Parkhill, op. cit.

[14]*RMN*, July 18, 1864, p. 3, col. 3. The issues of the paper in the last part of February, 1864, are full of the Clarke robbery.

[15]Ibid. The reason Editor Byers almost bankrupted his vocabulary on young Jim Clarke was that Byers had been fooled by Clarke's "genteel address"—in fact Byers had given him his first job in Denver.

[16]Vickers, W. B. *History of the City of Denver*. Chicago, Baskin, 1880. p. 211.

[17]Twenty-Sixth Grand International Convention of the Brotherhood of Locomotive Engineers at Denver, Colorado, Oct. 16th, 1889. *Program*.

[18]Information about rare gold coins may be found in various numismatic books such as R. S. Yeoman's *A Guide Book of United States Coins* (Racine, Wis., Whitman, 1956).

[19]The *Denver Post* on Feb. 5, 1920, p. 3, published a sketch of the wooden leg.

[20]Some of the interviews with Rowland Goddard concerning the Harrington affair, which he considered his most spectacular case, appeared in the following papers: *Denver Post,* Aug. 13, 1933, and Aug. 19, 1945; *Rocky Mountain News,* Aug. 21, 1945 and Oct. 22, 1946.

[21]To save treasure hunters a useless trip to 1485 South University, it should be noted that every one of the gold bricks stolen from the mint was recovered and that the house was razed when a highway was built at that location.

[22]"Just as though that would fit into a two-column head" was newspaperman Lee Casey's remark about the correct title. His masterly account of the 1922 robbery appears in his introduction to *Denver Murders*. New York, Duell, Sloan and Pearce, 1946.

Tabor Ghosts in Denver

Where in Denver shall we look for the ghosts of Horace A. W. Tabor and his two wives? The first place to look is in the telephone book. One of the Denver exchanges is called Tabor, and every time we dial TA 5 we invoke the ghost of the Silver King. This name for a Denver exchange is historically fitting because of Tabor's connections with the early telephones. He financed the first Leadville telephones and, in December, 1879, the long distance line from that town to Denver. From 1881 to 1890 the Denver switchboards for the "galvanic muttering machines" were housed in the attic of his Tabor Building at 16th and Larimer.

If we are to sleuth the Tabors around Denver, we must brief ourselves on their looks. Photographs of practical Augusta and alluring Baby Doe reveal their characters well enough, but somehow Tabor's black moustache comes between our clean-shaven age and the man. Let him be pictured for us by Eugene Field in the *Denver Tribune* of January 29, 1883:

"Senator H. A. W. Tabor, 53 years; 5'10"; weight about 165 pounds; stoop shouldered; ambling gait; awkward with hands; black hair; inclined to baldness; large head; rugged features; big black moustache, which spreads at ends; dresses in black; magnificent cuff buttons of diamonds and onyx; large diamond ring; rather drawling in speech; stove-pipe or black felt hat; has habit of nervously pulling moustache; temperate; no public speaker; earnest in conversation; generous and charitable; fond of the theatre; capital poker player; on the street carries his hands in overcoat pockets; worth $8,000,000."

125

Tabor's awkward hands had been trained to the stonemason trade in Maine, where he married the boss's brunette daughter, Augusta. He brought her to a homestead in Kansas, in what is now called Tabor Valley. For ready cash, Tabor helped fashion the stone walls of nearby Fort Riley, where Augusta sold butter and eggs to the Army wives. In April, 1859, they added their ox-drawn wagon, followed by two milk cows, to the long parade of gold-seekers snaking across the plains to the Cherry Creek settlements.

They camped for two weeks near Denver City or Auraria, waiting for the hoofs of their oxen to heal. Under what cottonwood tree they camped, only the South Platte River knows. Then they moved west. Tabor worked a mine claim near Idaho Springs and Augusta baked bread to sell. They came back to Denver in the late fall to a room over a store. No one seems to know over what store, so we cannot locate Mrs. Tabor's ghost cooking bread for the hungry emigrants. In February, 1860, Mr. Tabor lifted his frail wife and their sickly son, Maxcy, into a wagon and set off for the Arkansas Valley.

Eighteen years later, Lieutenant-Governor Horace A. W. Tabor came to Denver to preside over the state legislature. He was newly and vastly rich from the Leadville silver mines. When the *Leadville Democrat* remarked that "the City of the Plains had an electric shock when Tabor came to town,"[2] it referred, not to Tabor's scandalous private life, but to the money he poured into public buildings.

In 1879 Tabor built Denver's first skyscraper, five stories high, on 16th and Larimer. The Tabor Block still stands, though one of its subsequent owners changed its name to Nassau. Tabor, a stonemason, sent for the gray stone all the way to Ohio, where it was cut and each block numbered in the order in which it should be laid. The railroad must have collected a good share of the $200,000 the building is said to have cost. It can be most easily recognized by the pediment over the corner door, on which is carved *Dies Faustus,* which means (and some one had to translate it for Tabor) Lucky Day.

We will find Augusta's ghost uptown, unhappily roaming the site of the Mile High Building, for it was where this building stands on 17th Avenue, between Broadway and Lincoln, that Tabor bought a red brick mansion[3] in which he expected his wife to live in the grand manner. Augusta did not like the twenty-room house nor the servants needed to run it, nor the pretentious furnishings, nor the silver cuspidors,[4] and sharply said as much, especially when she found herself living in it without her husband. Tabor, with unlimited silver pouring through his fingers, sought the gay life. In January, 1881, he moved to the Windsor Hotel. Later Augusta reluctantly divorced him.

After the Brown Palace Hotel was built in 1892, Augusta moved across Broadway to it, so you may catch a glimpse of her unhappy ghost peering from a balcony in the rotunda of the Brown. About the time the Silver King was slipping into penury, Augusta went to California, where she died in Pasadena in February, 1895. She left an estate of over half a million. She specified in her will that she left nothing to her "beloved husband."

Her son Maxcy brought her body back from California to bury it at Riverside Cemetery, northeast of Denver. Even there, under a flat headstone carved with her name and dates, Augusta is lonely, for Maxcy's body[5] lies in Fairmount Cemetery and that of her "beloved husband" beside his second wife at Mount Olivet.

When Tabor met the woman who was to be the second Mrs. Tabor, she was Mrs. Elizabeth McCourt Doe, divorcee. From Oshkosh, Wisconsin, she had come to Gilpin County with her husband, Harvey Doe. After her baby died and Harvey had proved completely luckless in making money in the mines, Lizzie divorced him. She was beautiful, with pink and white skin, red-gold hair that curled, "small pearls for teeth," and intensely blue eyes. No wonder the men of Gilpin County called this plump divorcee "Baby"—she became known as Baby Doe.

One of these men took her to Leadville, where she met Tycoon Tabor earnestly trying to be a playboy. Gradually she eliminated his other girls. When Tabor moved to Denver, he brought her down to the Windsor Hotel. Even he understood, when he moved to the Windsor from Augusta's house, that he had better establish Lizzie elsewhere, especially if he expected to be appointed senator by the Colorado legislature. He moved her to a house, which displeased her, and then to another hotel.

During Tabor's one month in Washington as fill-in senator, he married Baby Doe at the Willard Hotel—she in white brocade and maribou, he with his habitual black suit enlived by a white velvet waistcoat.

They returned to Denver and the Windsor bridal suite, with its second-floor corner balcony. A legend tells that the bridegroom amused his lovely "Baby" by throwing silver dollars from the balcony. The bride liked to watch the passers-by scramble for Tabor's silver.

Mrs. Senator H. A. W. Tabor thought hotel life was for the unmarried. She longed for domesticity; so they soon moved to a two-story house at 1645 Welton Street[6] where they lived while Tabor searched for a setting worthy of his showpiece wife. He found it on 13th Avenue, a house on a three-acre plot between Sherman and Grant. The house, built in 1879, was "probably the finest residence in the State, with spacious grounds adorned with the various articles of *vertu* which a refined taste can suggest and unlimited wealth supply."[7] For all this, Tabor paid $54,000 in December, 1886.

Mrs. Tabor selected more "articles of *vertu*." Surely the fountain shooting water in the living room was a Baby Doe touch. She dotted the garden with iron deer and marble statues. ("Nüde!" gasped the fashionable ladies of Capitol Hill!)

Though the land was bounded on the north by 13th Avenue, the address was 1260 Sherman Street. The stables faced Grant Street. These stables were so large that after the turn of the century the horses belonging to a troop of Denver military men were all stabled there. When Tabor owned the place, the stables held at least six horses and three carriages, with coachmen and footmen, of course. One way that idle Lizzie Tabor amused herself was to order the carriage that best suited the costumes she had chosen for herself and her two daughters for the day. The most striking ensemble was the black carriage with white upholstery drawn by jet black horses, but Baby Doe preferred the bright blue carriage that matched her eyes.

Mrs. Tabor entertained lavishly. She wanted so badly to be accepted socially in order to help her husband in his political ambitions and to make a place for her two daughters. Her receptions for visiting celebrities were attended by theatrical troupes, politicians, men-about-town, but no female foot belonging to one of Denver's social elite ever stepped across her threshold.

The Tabors lived at 1260 Sherman for about ten years—until Tabor lost all his money. During the last months, because of unpaid bills, they had neither lights nor water. They had to fetch water from the well on the north side of the Court House. Upon their ejection from Capitol Hill, the Tabors moved to "a humble cottage in West Denver"—too unspecific a location for ghost hunters. Then they stayed some months at the Eclipse Mine near Ward, Colorado. In 1898, Baby Doe took the girls to New York where she lived a year, incognito and in squalid poverty, upheld by the eccentric notion that she might sell a curio—a petrified bone—for a fortune.

During these months, back in Denver Tabor roomed where he could, though the city directory lists him as boarding at the Hotel L'Impériale. This is the present Mile High United Fund Building at 314 14th Street. The old dining room was on the top floor, so this is a likely place to look for the stoop-shouldered ghost of Mr. Tabor. In January, 1898, Tabor was appointed postmaster of Denver. Hearing of his appointment, Tabor remarked that he was "pretty well known and, I believe, well liked by the common and middle class people all over the state."[8] Tabor served as postmaster conscientiously, but one wonders if he missed Augusta, who had helped him when he was postmaster of Buckskin Joe, Oro City, and Leadville before the silver from his lucky mines dug a gulch between them that neither was able to cross.

The Denver Post Office where Tabor served, now called the Old Customs Building, still stands on 16th and Arapahoe. It was built on land that Tabor sold to the United States Government. The building itself was (and is) "conspicuously inconvenient, ill-arranged, cramped, dark and inadequate."[9] (See picture on p. 136.) As such it is exactly the right setting in which to look for Tabor's ghost. Perhaps we can see him sitting lonely in his office around Christmas time in 1898, when his beloved wife and little daughters, Lillie and Silver Dollar, were in New York.

When Tabor was ill with appendicitis, his family returned from New York. They all stayed at the Windsor Hotel in Rooms 302 and 304—not the bridal suite and not furnished with frail gold chairs. There Tabor died on April 10, 1899.

Because he had been Lieutenant-Governor and Senator, his body lay in state at the Capitol, with flags at half-mast. The military escorted his body to the Sacred Heart Church at 28th and Larimer for final services. (Tabor had become a Roman Catholic shortly before his death.) Then a slow procession with bands playing the funeral march proceeded to Mount Calvary Cemetery (now a vacant lot east of Cheesman Park). After the cortege disbanded, Mrs. Tabor sat alone all afternoon by the grave. There she is an easily pictured ghost on an April evening as the sun goes down behind the mountains.

From the Windsor, Mrs. Tabor took her two girls to live in a four-room cottage at 833 Broadway. Today this site, a vacant lot below the street level, is marked by two billboards. After two years the Tabors moved to 1215 Pearl Street, an address to which the Denver water board has never made a connection. There is no such address today. After 1902 the Denver directory lists her name no more.

All Widow Tabor had to cling to was the advice her husband gave her on his deathbed: "Hold on to the Matchless Mine." So she took her two girls to Leadville, where her daughters soon left her to her eccentricities.

In a shack at the Matchless Mine, outside of Leadville, Mrs. Tabor existed among her silver dreams. Occasionally she thought of a new scheme to recover some of the money Tabor had lent or invested in far-flung businesses. Then she would journey down to Denver and shuffle along 17th Street on small feet now clad in miners' boots, calling on lawyer after patient lawyer who found none of her schemes workable.

On March 7, 1935, her frozen body was found stretched on the floor of the Matchless cabin and was brought to Denver for burial at Mount Olivet Cemetery. Afterward, the body of Tabor was moved across town to lie beside her. Some years later a marker was erected over the graves by the Mile High Optimists and a generous stonemason, and surely Tabor would have appreciated his act of professional courtesy.

Let us end our search for Tabor's ghost with a happy return to the heyday of his career. In 1881, on 16th and Curtis, Tabor hustled among architects, stonemasons, and carpenters as they constructed the finest opera house in the nation. On a rainy night of September of that year, the great singer Emma Abbot opened the Tabor Grand Opera House with the mad scene from *Lucia*. Then the curtain was lowered, the curtain inscribed with the prophetic lines:

> So fleet the works of men,
> > Back to the earth again
> Ancient and holy things
> > Fade like a dream.

When the curtain was raised again, it revealed a man by a small table in the middle of the stage. He asked for Mr. Tabor. From the wings, Mr. Tabor appeared and was presented with a book signed by the firms that had constructed the $800,000 opera house. Then Tabor was given a ponderous watch fob, a token of gratitude from one hundred citizens (at five dollars each) for what the millionaire had done for Denver. On the fob a Latin inscription read "Labor omnia vincit," which might have elicited a cynical "Whose labor?" from Augusta had she seen the fob.

But Augusta was not at the opening of the Tabor Grand Opera House even though she had written to Horace begging to attend with him. Mrs. Elizabeth McCourt Doe, heavily veiled, was there. She watched from the parquet as Mr. Tabor, in tails, drawled an awkward but short speech of acceptance. The Tabor box was empty.

Everyone knew which was the Tabor box because it was labeled. A plaque engraved with the word TABOR hung on the rail of the box. The plaque was made of silver from the Matchless Mine. After their marriage, if Lizzie planned to attend the theater, Tabor always had the box banked with white lilies. Sometimes, when Governor and Mrs. Tabor were conspicuously occupying their box, with their two babies running around it as in a sixteen-foot playpen, Augusta stood outside the theater, sobbing.

In 1921 the theater was remodeled for motion pictures. Today it takes effort to imagine the theater as it looked when it was opened. But we do not have to imagine the watch fob, for Baby Doe held on to it through all the thirty-six years of her poverty-stricken widowhood. After her death, deep inside a ball of rags that might easily have been discarded as junk, was the watch fob. She also saved two pieces of stone from the home Mr. Tabor bought for her at 1260 Sherman Street.[10] These and other mementos of the Tabor family were acquired by the State Historical Society of Colorado. The ghost hunter may see many Tabor items at the Society's museum on 14th and Sherman, such as Baby Doe's wedding dress trimmed in maribou.

From the museum the ghost hunter may walk one block south to the site of the Tabor Mansion. He will see today along 13th Avenue a row of stores and a filling station, with apartment houses lining the Grant and Sherman Street sides of the original Tabor grounds. How historically pleasing it is that one of these apartments is called Camellia House, a flower so fitted to the blond beauty of Baby Doe!

NOTES

[1]The story of Tabor is one of the few local tales known outside Colorado. The thin slice presented here has been whittled from the many printed sources of Tabor material. Caroline Bancroft, Denver writer, is the authority on the Tabors. She has written these pamphlets about them: *Silver Queen* (1950); *Photo Story of the Matchless Mine* (1953); and *Augusta Tabor* (1955), all printed by the Golden Press at Denver. One chapter of her book *Gulch of Gold* (Denver, Sage Books, 1958) concerns Baby Doe in Central City.

The first teller of the Tabor tale in extended form was G. F. Willison in *Here They Dug the Gold* (New York, Brentano, 1931). To David Karsner's *Silver Dollar* (New York, Covici, Friede, 1932) may be traced the modern nickname HAW for H. A. W. Tabor. Mr. Tabor's contemporaries called him Mister, Governor, Senator or

For his wife, Augusta, H.A.W. Tabor bought (and remodeled) this house on 17th and Broadway. It had been built in 1875-76 by H. C. Brown. On this site now stand the Denver U. S. National Bank and the Mile High Building. (*Denver Public Library*.)

For Denver, Tabor built its first skyscraper, the five-story Tabor Building. Over the doorway he had carved *Dies Faustus,* meaning Lucky Day, and symbols of the miners' trade including a gold pan crossed with drill and shovel. Though Tabor's Lucky Day was short, the building, with pediment, still stands at 16th and Larimer Streets. (Photo by Harry Smith, 1956. *Denver Public Library*.)

For Baby Doe, his second wife, Tabor bought 1260 Sherman Street. The picture shows the house when it was newly built in 1879 by J.W. Bailey. The Tabors and their two daughters, Lillie and Rose Mary Echo Silver Dollar, lived here until after Tabor lost his money and the utilities were turned off because of unpaid bills. On its site today stand apartment houses and stores. (Sketch from Vicker's *History of Denver,* 1880, p. 126. *Denver Public Library*.)

The interior of the Tabor Grand Opera House before the chandelier was hung. The painting over the stage, the cherry wood columns from Japan, the tiers of boxes, and the gallery all disappeared when the theater was changed to a movie house. (Photo by Joseph Collier. *Denver Public Library*.)

The picture on the opposite page was taken in February, 1900. Hacks were waiting for fares on 16th Street near Curtis. It was a cold night. To the left of the entrance of the Tabor Grand the Rocky Mountain Fuel Company advertised Ruby Anthracite coal; to the right the Opera House Bar also dealt in warmth. (Photo by Roy S. Kent, *Denver Public Library*.)

The U. S. Post Office Building (now the Customs House) still stands on 16th and Arapahoe. H.A.W. Tabor, who had sold the site to the government and had built the Tabor Grand Opera House across the alley, spent the last months of his life in this building as postmaster. The H.H. Tammen trademark shows to the right. Beyond, the statue of the miner tops the red sandstone Mining Exchange Building. Note the horseless carriage on 16th Street. (Photo by J. C. McClure. *Denver Public Library*.)

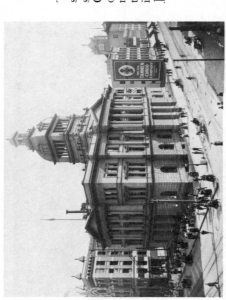

If you are looking for the Tabor ghosts in Denver, look for brunette Augusta, black-suited Horace, and blonde Baby Doe. (Photos from *Denver Public Library*.)

The Windsor Hotel

The new Windsor Hotel, opened in June, 1880, dominated the downtown district. The spire to the left of the Windsor was the German M.E. Church; to the left of it were the great walls of the Central Presbyterian Church; and the cupola to the left of that topped the Arapahoe Street School. The Windsor, without its tower, still stands. (Photo probably by W. H. Jackson. *Denver Public Library*.)

The Windsor parlors, said an old pamphlet, are on the second floor, 18th Street side. They are "three apartments *en suite*, decorated in blue, terra cotta, and olive, respectively . . . The colors are subdued, the heavy lace curtains and trimming contrasting beautifully with the rich hue of Wilton carpets and Axminster rugs . . . The furniture is of that elegant pattern and finish that pleases the senses without offending the sight . . . The conversation chairs of new and novel design . . ," doubtless pleased any young couple who dared sit out a dance at the Rho Zeta Club's affairs. (Sketch from pamphlet printed by Collier & Cleveland, Denver, n.d. *Denver Public Library*.)

The Drawing Room.

The Windsor lobby was noted for its skylights, gas-jetted chandelier, solid walnut staircase leading off right, and the safe embedded high in the wall above the cashier's desk. The gentleman on the right is heading for the elevator and the man sitting under the clock may soon step around the corner to the bar. Mother and daughter face the Ladies' Entrance. (Sketch from advertisement in *Kings and Queens of the Range*, v. 2, April-May, 1898. *Denver Public Library*.)

Noisy Larimer Street in the 1880's was frequented by men and horses, no women. You can see an omnibus with four white horses, a horsecar, tracks, and a hack turning into 16th Street. "Soapy" Smith was not operating on his corner the day this picture was taken, but across the street you can see the Tabor Building with its *Dies Faustus* pediment over the corner doorway. The Windsor Hotel stands in the distance. Note the top-heavy telephone poles. After any wind, inspectors climbed the poles to shake the lines loose one from another and received a shock if some one happened to be cranking a signal to Central. (Photo probably by W. G. Chamberlain. *Denver Public Library*.)

Horace. *The Tabors, a Footnote to Western History* (New York, Press of the Pioneers, 1934) was accurate according to the sources available to its author, L. C. Gandy.

The curator of the Colorado State Historical Museum, E. C. Mc-Mechen, was made executor of Baby Doe's estate. Thus he had access to the innumerable letters left in her trunks in Leadville and Denver. His long awaited work based on these sources was published as a pamphlet called *The Tabors* (Denver, State Historical Society of Colorado, 1952).

In 1956, an opera based on the life of Tabor was produced at Central City, Colorado and again in 1959. For this *Ballad of Baby Doe*, Douglas Moore composed the music and John LaTouche wrote the libretto. In April, 1958, it was produced by the New York City Opera Company at New York City Center. It was favorably reviewed.

[2]*Leadville Democrat,* Jan. 1, 1881.

[3]Tabor bought this house from its builder, H. C. Brown.

[4]Some of Augusta Tabor's belongings were auctioned. *RMN,* July 13, 1932.

[5]Maxcy Tabor lived at 1120 Grant Street where his only daughter, Persis, was married in 1914 to Captain Paul La Fargue of the French Army. They had four children.

[6]On this site now stands the First National Bank Building with its twenty-eight story tower built in 1958 by the Murchison Brothers of Texas.

[7]Vickers, W. B. *History of the City of Denver.* Chicago, Baskin, 1880. p. 324.

[8]*RMN,* Jan. 14, 1898.

[9]Smiley, J. C. *History of Denver.* Denver, Times-Sun, 1901. p. 967.

[10]*Denver Post,* Mar. 25, 1935. Mrs. Tabor stored trunks at St. Vincent's Hospital in Leadville and in Denver at Bekins Storage Company where the storage was paid by Willard McCourt.

The Windsor Hotel

James Duff of Scotland thought up the Windsor Hotel. At least, he suggested the idea of building a comfortable, family hotel in Denver, Colorado, U. S. A., to the English Company, the popular name for the British investment company he represented in Denver. What Duff originally planned, however, and what the Windsor turned out to be were two different things.

When James Duff came to town in the late 1870's, Denver was crackling because of the silver mines at Leadville—Denver being the point of departure for supplies and people. For a house to live in, Duff unsuccessfully combed the town. He found the crowded hotels over-priced and under-equipped. Leadville's Tabor was not helping the Denver room situation by pulling down the Broadwell Hotel to erect his office building at 16th and Larimer. Finally the Duff family, including the beautiful daughter, settled in three hotel rooms (the bowl-and-pitcher type) at a price that hurt. The Scotsman wrote his company in London that what Denver needed was a reasonable hotel for a civilized family, estimating such an investment would earn at least fifteen per cent.[1]

So the Denver Mansions Company was incorporated in London in February, 1879,[2] the word *mansions* implying a brownstone front with café attached. As the plans for the mansions materialized, James Duff's conservative suggestion was transfigured into a plush hostelry with such modern conveniences as three elevators, hot and cold running water on all five floors, and—this was not merely taken for granted—adequate sewerage. Even the name became palatial—The Windsor Hotel.

There were nearly 36,000 people in Denver in 1880, but the population trebled in the next ten years. Denver was busy, much too busy in 1879 when the Windsor Hotel started construction, to furnish much help to the English Company. Many of the artisans and even some of the work gangs were shipped from Chicago, where both the architect and construction company had headquarters. The only important local contribution to the building was the stone used for the outside walls. It was gray stone from the quarries near Castle Rock, trimmed with red sandstone from near Fort Collins.

If the English Company actually spent the reputed $100,000 for nine lots and $350,000 to build the Windsor, it was doubtless glad to turn over the expense of furnishing and running the hotel to a Colorado firm named Tabor, Bush and Hall. The timing was perfect. Horace Tabor was fresh from Leadville, where he owned or partly owned everything including the Clarendon Hotel. In Denver, Tabor felt he must buy into a hotel where he could live the kind of life he felt appropriate to the Silver King.

It cost $200,000 to put the Windsor into running order. Some of this money was invested by Charles Hall of Leadville silver and South Park salt. Almost immediately Hall sold his interest in the Windsor to Augusta. Tabor's wife thereby acquired the right to keep an eye on what went on at the Windsor where her husband was leading the gayer half of his double life. Maxcy Tabor, their son, about twenty-two years old, was hired as cashier of the hotel. It was a family affair, made even more so when Tabor installed blond Baby Doe in a lavishly furnished suite. Such family goings-on had not been what James Duff had in mind for a family hotel.

The middle member of the firm of Tabor, Bush and Hall was William Bush, hotel man, one of the best. Bush always managed to have his current hotel in the heart of the busiest place in changeable Colorado. He ran the Teller House in Central City when Gilpin County was golden, the Clarendon Hotel in silver Leadville, and the Windsor on Larimer Street when Larimer was the best business street in Denver. Hardly had he opened the

Windsor when he felt the uptown trend. Jumping up to 17th and Broadway, he helped build the Metropole, the kind of family hotel James Duff had wanted.[3] In 1892, Bush opened the Brown Palace which surpassed the Windsor in elegance. But there was nothing finer than the Windsor when Mr. Bush and Governor Tabor went to Chicago to order massive black walnut bedroom sets that were exactly alike for all five floors, and ingenious patented platform rockers.

Mr. Bush considered that a local department store named Daniels and Fisher was capable of furnishing the "Little Windsor" with walnut furniture and Brussels carpets. The "Little Windsor," a twenty-nine-room building directly across the alley from the northern part of the big hotel, housed the female help. For them the management generously provided a bathroom on each floor. A tunnel from the basement of the hotel gave direct access to this annex, enabling the hotel maids to avoid walking on Holladay Street (now Market Street) which was beginning to have an unsavory reputation.

Besides this tunnel, which definitely existed though it has been filled in since,[4] there are tales of other tunnels—to the Windsor carriage house on Lawrence, to the horse car barns up Larimer, to the Union Depot, and under 18th Street to the basement of the Barclay Block. This last tunnel was supposed to facilitate access from the Windsor to the steam baths in the Barclay Block,[5] which supplanted the original baths in the basement of the Windsor.

Today, anyone poking around the wrecked baths in the basement of the Barclay Block observes an opening leading toward the Windsor Hotel.[6] Some people *know* this tunnel was solely occupied by a large pipe carrying steam from the Windsor's boilers[7] to the Barclay baths. Other people *know* this was a pedestrian tunnel, and relate its uses.

The stories of the uses of the tunnel may be divided into two classes, north-bound and south-bound. North-bound tales say that members of the Colorado State Legislature, which met in the Barclay Block while the Capitol was nearing completion, walked through the tunnel when in need of inspiration obtainable at the Windsor Bar, unobserved by the critical eyes of Larimer Street.

144

South-bound stories concern men who drank too much at the Windsor Bar, confident that they could stagger through the tunnel to soak themselves sober in the Sudsatorium, the Frigidorium, the Lavatorium, or in the marble swimming pool.

As for the other tunnels that may or may not have emanated from the Windsor cellar, let us leave ourselves open to conviction, and return to June, 1880,[8] when Bill Bush was ready to open his new hotel. Being publicity-minded, he gave the newsmen a preview from tower to artesian wells, so that every newspaper in Denver carried long stories about the new hotel on the opening day.

In the 1880's the height of elegance was measured by the height of ceilings so all the reporters admired the high ceilings (graduating from nineteen feet on the ground floor to eleven and a half feet on the fifth floor).[9] The exquisite proportions of the rooms achieved by the Windsor architect remained unnoted in the papers, but are certainly notable today.

The newsmen admired the plumbing—hot and cold running water and sixty bath tubs.[10] They noted gadgets, many and modern. A time clock kept track of the night watchman, and an annunciator in each room connected with the office desk. The passenger elevator had a shelf slung beneath it to carry luggage, and there were three chairs in front of every elevator door. Even the second floor ballroom, with its alternating maple and walnut floor boards, was a gadget. This floor was (and is) suspended on cables to give resilience to the dance.

In the cavernous cellar, along with the artesian wells and generators to create electricity for the elevators, were the wine room (lavishly stocked), the cigar room (damp), and more gadgets, like two rotating steam washing machines and an ironer designed to take the place of twenty workers. There was also a steam-powered ice cream freezer.

Fire was the nightmare of the Nineteenth Century and the Windsor Hotel was protected against fire by gadgets. A "mercurial alarm," set in the ceiling of each room, notified the desk clerk if the temperature soared above 120 degrees. Employees could then rush to the fire equipment on each floor, unwind sufficient hose and pour water from an iron tank housed on the roof.[11]

Maybe these gadgets guarded the Windsor or maybe it was just luck that the nearest approach to a major fire was in 1939,[12] when firemen (seven companies strong!) carried aged and infirm residents to the lobby to spend the night.

Despite the heavy walls advertised as fireproof, when the Windsor was new the fire hazard was terrific. The hotel was lighted by gas and, though steam-heated, many rooms had wood-burning fireplaces. Tom, the Flying Dutchman, was "supervisor of woodwork." This could mean either that he carried firewood, or polished the woodwork of the fifty-foot bar and the handsome black walnut staircases.

These staircases, though they are hardwood on the first floor only,[13] are of interest. The Larimer Street stairs were skillfully engineered without visible means of support; the staircase next to the alley on 18th Street earned the title of "suicide stair" during the Windsor's depressed years. In the hotel there were suicides, murders, and uninvestigated accidents—such as the fatal fall over the third floor banister of a man clutching a pair of trousers, an extra pair.[14]

In its happier years, where but at the Windsor should Governor and Mrs. Pitkin hold their levee, on February 1, 1881?[15] The guest list was diplomatically headed by the Governor's defeated opponent, W. A. H. Loveland. Also present were three ex-governors (Gilpin, Evans, and McCook) and one bishop (Spalding). Two thousand guests streamed through the three parlors on the second floor, 18th Street side. These parlors were charming, connected by arches and decorated in blue, terra cotta, and olive, respectively. (See picture on p. 138.)

At the levee, the ladies' gowns were gay, but their brilliance was dimmed promptly at nine o'clock by the entrance of the gaudy military—the Chaffee Light Artillery, the Governor's Guards, and the Loveland Guards. Kaufman's orchestra played from a station near the ladies' dining room, and promptly at ten o'clock the doors of the Club Room across the hall from the parlors were opened for the collation.

For more than a decade, Denver's social season was opened at the Windsor by the annual Charity Ball,[16] though the word *ball*

146

was frowned on by the churchly Episcopal ladies who preferred to call the affair "The Reception." The proceeds helped support little St. Luke's Hospital, on the Boulevard in the Highlands. (See heelpiece picture.) The reception held October 18, 1882, was "an affair of brilliancy and splendor rarely witnessed in the West." Nor did the brilliance flash from costume jewelry. Society columns, pages long, noted pearls on Mrs. Judge LeFevre; Mrs. Doctor Rogers wore pearls in coiffure and white ostrich plumes; while Mrs. Senator Hill exhibited magnificent diamonds.

Fifty odd years later, in 1938, the Cactus Club of Denver held a "bal poudre" at the Windsor in memory of such receptions.[17] Many descendants of pioneer society came dressed like their forbears. Beautiful Mrs. Robert L. Stearns, for example, represented her grandmother, Mrs. Governor Pitkin. Why one of Denver's socialites chose to dress as Marie Antoinette is historically confusing, but the appearance of Captain the Honorable Lyulph Ogilvy was authentic. He looked even more distinguished in his white tie and tails than he had looked half a century before at the original functions.

As a young blade, this Captain Ogilvy knew the Windsor well. He and his sister, Lady Maude, came to Colorado in 1881 with their father, the Earl of Airlie, who, quite unexpectedly, died at the Windsor. In October, 1886, Lady Maude and her husband came to the Windsor to spend their honeymoon, she arriving in a "gray casamir travelling dress with polonaise neatly draped." Somehow that neat polonaise seems to haunt the Windsor lobby, but if you are looking for the ghost of Captain Ogilvy, better check the bar. Young Ogilvy was one of Colorado's boisterous characters and the practical jokes he played at the Windsor have added to its legends. After the Captain's marriage in 1902 he never touched liquor, always refusing a proffered drink with the courteous explanation "I have had my share." From his farm near Greeley he came to Denver to live. For decades after 1909 he wrote an agricultural column for the *Denver Post,* signing it Lord Ogilvy, a title generously bestowed on him by the newspaper.[18]

To return to Larimer Street in the 1880's—the dining room of the Windsor became the mecca for gourmets. Manager Bush had learned in Central City and Leadville that the best food, served with finesse, attracted men of the world hoping to make millions in Colorado mines or cattle, as well as unpolished millionaires aping men of the world. Bill Bush set his tables with fine linen, monogrammed Haviland china, Reed and Barton silver, and ringing crystal. Most of the thirty-two waiters, all white, and the cooks and their numerous helpers were imported from Chicago, though the head steward, J. W. Renard, came down from the Silver Queen Café in Georgetown, Colorado.[19]

The clientele immediately included Europeans who appreciated this touch of civilization halfway between two oceans. When Baron von Richthofen wished to impress the residents of Montclair with his schemes for developing their village, he gave them a dinner at the Windsor. James Duff entertained at the Windsor. On St. Valentine's Day of 1881 the menu for his dinner party was printed on gold satin and hand-painted with flowers.[20] Despite this dainty touch and the sentimental day, the dinner was a stag affair. The fifty-two guests represented the wealth of Denver. Wouldn't you like to know what scheme was discussed over the brandy to justify such expenditure by Scotsman Duff?

The menu included fresh oysters (1700 miles from the Atlantic and no dry ice!) and exotic guava jelly; also local prairie chicken. The hotel employed hunters to bring in wild fowl as well as venison and elk meat, sometimes bear, and fishermen brought tubs of trout from icy mountain streams. Not hired hunters, but enterprising youngsters sold frog legs to the leading cuisines of Denver. They caught the frogs in Smith's Lake (now Washington Park's north lake).[21]

The skid-road locale of the Windsor today makes it hard to realize that, when it opened, the Victorian mammas of Denver allowed their daughters to attend dances there. In fact, in 1891, the daughter of Governor Job Cooper announced her engagement to Ed Kassler at the Rho Zeta dancing party at the Windsor.[22] This club, organized in 1887 by forty young beaux, danced four or five evenings each winter on the Windsor's suspended ballroom floor. Denver's best orchestra, the Koenigsberg, played for them from eight to midnight. Before the dancing started, each young man busied himself filling in his partner's dance card, easy to do if the girl was popular. The daring belle who sat out a dance with her beau in one of the parlors risked her reputation. At midnight the young men escorted their ladies home in hired cabs. Usually, for economy's sake, two couples shared a cab.

After the sobering panic of 1893 a less frivolous club met at the Windsor. Started on December 20, 1894, by April the Candlelight Club had 457 members. It was a dinner club, men only, and "to dress" was customary. It was called the Candlelight Club because of its place cards—silver candlesticks about ten inches high engraved with the members' names. The fees were fifty cents for candles, five dollars for dues, and "$2.00 for every dinner eat." The sole entrance requirement was that the candidate be "a genial and tolerant fellow."[23] A civic-minded organization, it heard debates on current questions like strikes, bi-metallism, municipal mismanagement, and "What Standards of Morality Can be Maintained in a Modern City?" Even the first Ladies' Night of the Candlelight Club, May 2, 1895, had a serious discussion on "Woman's Broader Sphere and Its Influence on the Home." The broader sphere referred to the recent enfranchisement of women. Men were apprehensive of its baleful influence on the home.

A less formal gathering, strictly masculine, consisted of patrons of the Windsor bar. The head bartender, from Baltimore, who admitted he was the world's best bartender, was H. H. Tammen. At the Windsor, Tammen watched prospectors exhibit chunks of ore to their neighbors at the bar, and soon acquired enough specimens of his own to fill a mineral cabinet. This he expanded into a curio shop in one of the stores on the ground floor of the Windsor. Graduated from bartending and bored with available curios, Tammen started to manufacture tourist items; the H. H. Tammen Company of Denver still wholesales curios to the West.

After Tammen became half-owner of the *Denver Post,* he collected larger curios, like elephants for his circus. When his

Sells-Floto Circus wintered in Denver in the 1910's, its human performers, including the freaks, lived at the Windsor Hotel. To this circus Tammen lured the aging Buffalo Bill. The Great Scout, bending an elbow with the freaks at the Windsor Bar, must have remembered the days of his own Wild West show when he and Johnny Baker and Little Annie Oakley and the Indians stayed at the Windsor. In those well-heeled days, Colonel Cody always gave a farewell dinner in the plush dining room before his show hit the road again.

But H. A. W. Tabor is the Windsor's favorite character. After he invested in the hotel, he lived there for about three years in his (and its) most opulent days. Mr. Tabor let no one forget he practically owned the place. He had a special room for his private poker games, and a whole floor for his campaign headquarters when he was angling for a seat in the U. S. Senate.

When word leaked back to Denver about Tabor's wedding in Washington, the Windsor staff was piqued. The room clerk complained that Tabor had not told any of the help about his marriage plans.[24] Nor did Senator Tabor wire before coming home. He just walked into the Windsor lobby with his bride on his arm, followed by her brother Peter McCourt.[25] They breakfasted in the bridal suite, second floor corner, with Maxcy, Baby Doe's new stepson.

Sixteen years and a number of million dollars later, Tabor died at the Windsor Hotel in a small room on the third floor with a view of the Rocky Mountains.

That the hard-up Tabor family could stay at the hotel in 1899 shows that the Windsor prices had been reduced. Two dollars per day, two dollars and fifty cents with bath. As Denver moved uptown, Larimer Street fell into disrepute. Surrounded by pawn and grog shops, the hotel struggled through the years to keep respectable and solvent. It was reduced to advertising for "tourists . . . traveling men . . . mining men . . . Texans and Southern Tourists . . . It is the most popular house in Denver with southern visitors on account of its low rates and superior accommodations."[26]

In 1902 a roof garden with summer cafe was advertised. The

penthouse was about ten and a half feet square.[27] In 1903 the New Windsor Hotel Company lured travelers with free omnibus rides from the Union Depot and charged two dollars American plan.[28] The downward slide was not halted when the Denver police made an effort to close the dives of Market Street in 1915. During prohibition, from 1916 to 1932, the hotel was soaked in bootleg, some of it flowing through the tunnel which is said to have afforded a get-away to the north in case of raids. Sixty deputies—the large number constituted a distinction—were required to raid the Windsor for gambling in 1922.[29] That May the district attorney threatened to board up the hotel as a common nuisance. This almost ruined the Windsor's boast that since 1880 it had never closed its doors to the public.

As a flop house during the great depression of the 1930's, it achieved the rating of a "constructive demonstration for homeless men."[30] This meant that rooms were rented for a nominal sum and two meals a day furnished for twenty-five cents. The roomers contributed labor to keep the place cleanish.

About 1937 the first of a series of women leasers or owners took on the Windsor. These women had romantic and historic vision coupled with tremendous energy. They tried to restore the Windsor, their most important tool being the scrubbing brush. One of the managers had the Denver artist Herndon Davis paint murals of men and women who had stayed at the Windsor.[31] The ballroom, turned into a dining room with red-checked tablecloths, was a popular place from which to watch a melodrama on the stage.

Much publicity accompanied the opening of the Windsor safe,[32] which was embedded in the wall high above the lobby desk. To open it, one had to climb a ladder. (One wonders if in the long history of the Windsor Hotel any would-be robber ever assumed this conspicuous position.) In 1937, workmen chipped away layers of paint and then drilled the safe open, since the combination had been lost long since. What they pulled out of the vault was books. They were, alas, non-rare Victorian novels and not the old Windsor registers.

For a few months in 1946 Maxcy Tabor's daughter, Persis, conducted tours through the hotel. Also in 1946 the City Building

151

Inspector threatened to jail the leaser if she did not remove from the roof the corner tower and iron grill which were considered dangerous to public safety.[33]

About 1956 a Kansas City company acquired the Windsor with the idea of restoring it for the Colorado centennial celebration. But this project, like the efforts of the historically-minded women managers before it, fell through. In the spring of 1958, the seventy-eight year old Windsor Hotel closed its doors. Restore or raze? Its fate is still undecided. The diamond-dust mirrors in the entrance hall reflect nothing.

NOTES

[1] Letter from James Duff to J. W. Barclay, Dec. 22, 1878. Quoted by J. W. Buchanan in his *A Story of the Fabulous Windsor Hotel* (Denver, Hirschfeld Press, 1956. 2nd ed., pp. 5-6).

[2] A copy of the incorporation papers of the Denver Mansions Company is in the Colorado State Archives.

[3] Some of the Metropole rooms are now incorporated in the southern part of the Cosmopolitan Hotel. South of the Metropole stood the Broadway Theater.

[4] The 1890 edition of the fire insurance maps called Sanborn's *Atlas of Denver*, v. 2, specifies "cellar extending under alley" behind the Windsor Hotel. The 1929-30 edition says "open under alley." In 1957 the Public Relations officer of the Mountain States Telephone Company dug into old files and came up with a map "redrawn 11-29-35." On it is printed "Windsor Hotel Subway. Tunnel filled in and no ducts through . . . 138 feet long." This map was given to the Western History Department of the Denver Public Library. We have seen no maps of any other tunnels running from the Windsor.

[5] The Barclay Block was built by the Denver Mansions Company. It was named for J. W. Barclay, M. P., president of the company. Monograms on the outside walls of the Barclay Block display the company's initials, D. M. C.

[6] Pictures of the wrecked baths appear in the *Rocky Mountain News* for Jan. 20, 1949, p. 6A.

[7] It was not until August, 1949, that the Windsor Hotel was connected to the steam heating system of the Public Service Company of Colorado, according to Mr. Hancock of that company.

[8] One of the longest reports was on p. 8 of the *Rocky Mountain News*, June 23, 1880. See also the article by Caroline Bancroft called

"Debut of the Windsor" in the *1951 Brand Book* of the Denver Westerners, p. 291 ff.

[9]A report of an investigation of the Windsor Hotel dated Apr. 28, 1950, is in the City Assessor's office. The heights of the ceilings are quoted from this report. The number of rooms in the hotel varies in each newspaper account, one giving it as large as 300. The assessed valuation in 1950 was $26,810.

[10]The number of bath tubs reported in 1950 by the City Assessor's office was thirty-four in three-fixture bathrooms, and four public baths with tiled floors. The tubs are narrow and only about three feet long at the bottom, sloping up to about four-and-a-half feet at the rim. The tubs are on legs, of course.

The hotel advertised running water on all five floors at its opening. The Denver Water Board has a record that a four-inch pipe was put into the Windsor by the American Water Company in 1882. One of the legends of the Windsor Hotel is that bellhops carried water in buckets to Baby Doe's bathtub whenever she wanted to bathe, and afterwards emptied the buckets into the alley. Since the hotel was equipped with running water and sewers, this seemed a bit demanding of Baby Doe.

[11]*RMN*, Oct. 16, 1946. The City Inspector ordered this tank removed from the roof of the Windsor as being "too heavy for its underpinnings."

[12]*Denver Post*, November 8, 1939, p. 5, col. 1. The fire started in a pawnshop on the first floor.

[13]Report of the City Assessor, op. cit.

[14]*Denver Post*, May 27, 1939, p. 2, col. 6.

[15]*Denver Tribune*, Feb. 2, 1881.

[16]The scrapbooks of Mrs. John F. Spalding, wife of Bishop Spalding, are at St. Luke's Hospital. From them it appears that balls given by the Ladies' Relief Society at the Tabor Opera House and the Symes Building pre-dated the St. Luke's Charity Ball. The Charity Ball was held at the Windsor from 1882 to 1893. The next year it moved to the Broadway Theater which had ample room for sixteen sets. In 1895 and later it was at the Brown Palace Hotel. One year it was at the Kassler Building, once at Nathan Hall, and at El Jebel Temple.

[17]*Denver Post*, May 20, 1938, p. 23, col. 1.

[18]The full story of Lord Ogilvy has yet to be written. Mr. Birch, who shared an office with him at the *Denver Post*, said that "The Captain" started to write his memoirs but threw the unfinished manuscript away. One of the articles about Ogilvy is by E. L. Howe, called "Prince Hal Rides the Rockies." In *1952 Brand Book* of the Denver Westerners, pp. 241-278.

[19]Renard's obituary was in the *Denver Post,* Aug. 17, 1918, p. 4, col. 2. From the Windsor, Renard progressed to hotels in New York and Florida. He wore an Elk's insignia in which was imbedded a yellow diamond given him by the King of Hawaii. His son spent his childhood at the Windsor from 1890 to 1902. In an interview Nov. 8, 1956, the son declared that the tunnel from the Windsor to the Barclay Block was not intended for pedestrians.

[20]*Empire Magazine,* Feb. 12, 1956.

[21]E. S. Kassler remembered, Nov. 1, 1956, how he and Merritt Gano used to borrow the Kassler buggy and drive to Smith's Lake. Their proceeds from the frog legs was spent to buy bullets to hunt ducks.

[22]E. S. Kassler has a large photograph of the Rho Zeta Club.

[23]As a sample of the geniality of the Candlelight Club let us quote from Chairman Henry Rogers' opening remarks as reported in the *Minutes and Speeches of the Candlelight Club* at the Colorado State Historical Museum Library. Mr. Rogers referred to the poetic motto which the Club had borrowed from the Sunset Club in Chicago thus: "The Candlelight Club knows a good thing when it sees it (Applause) and therefore knowing it was a good thing, it seized it. (After a short pause, laughter.) That was a little late, gentlemen, but I thank you." By 1900 the attendance at the Candlelight Club was down to fifty.

[24]*Denver Times,* March 9, 1883, p. 4, col. 3.

[25]*Denver Times,* April 7, 1883.

[26]This quotation, and the prices of rooms, are from a full-page advertisement for the Windsor that appeared in a magazine published in Kansas City called *Kings and Queens of the Range,* April-May 1898, p. 139.

[27]Report of the City Assessor 1950. op. cit.

[28]Bennett and Myers were the new owners. If there had been a tunnel from the Union Depot to the Windsor, surely the advertisements would have played it up!

[29]*Denver Post,* May 23, 1922, p. 1, col. 4.

[30]Article by Eva Hodges in *Empire Magazine,* Dec. 15, 1946. Also *Denver Post,* July 30, 1933, p. 13, col. 3.

[31]Legends persist that U. S. presidents stayed at the Windsor, including Grant and Taft—the latter is said to have stuck in the narrow bath tub. Caroline Bancroft, after much research, refuted these legends. Her article was in the *Denver Post,* July 4, 1954, p. 3, col. 4.

[32]*RMN,* Oct. 12, 1937.

[33]*RMN,* Oct. 16, 1946.

SLICE VIII

The Baron of Montclair

A few blocks from the northwest corner of Lowry Air Force Base in Denver is a short street called Richthofen Parkway. From it angles even shorter Richthofen Place, on a corner of which stands a stone fountain carved with the name Richthofen. People who are curious about this name learn that the gray stone house at 12th and Pontiac was built by a Baron Walter von Richthofen, whose coat of arms is still embedded high on the square north tower. Further, they find that a real estate subdivision in southwest Denver is named Richthofen.[1]

Who was this Richthofen who left his name all over the map of Denver? He was Prussian, christened Walter at his birth in 1848 in Kreisenitz, Silesia, in eastern Germany. He grew up on the high plateaus of Silesia, a green country, but otherwise not unlike the plains east of Denver, Colorado, U. S. A. where Walter von Richthofen was to spend years of strenuous life. He was a typical Junker, a dashing fellow around whom legends were bound to gather. The facts seem to be that he did not attend the University of Heidelberg,[2] nor did he ever fight a duel,[3] but he saw action as an officer in the Franco-Prussian War of 1870. Exactly why or when he came to Colorado is uncertain. It is known that he tried his hand at cattle raising, even wrote a book about it. In the late 1870's, he put his tremendous energy to work in young Denver, promoting horse racing, railroads, the Denver Chamber of Commerce, real estate subdivisions, a beer garden, an art gallery, a spa, and a zoo.

In March of 1878, the Baron and Baroness von Richthofen met

On the opposite page is an airview of Richthofen Castle and the vacant lots of Montclair in the 1930's. In the photograph 12th Avenue runs from 6 to 8, and Pontiac Street from 7 to F. Some historic sites are:

A - 1, site of St. John's Episcopal School for Boys (Jarvis Hall) from 1888 until it burned on November 4, 1901.

B - 6, between the sidewalk and the wall, Gertrude Gibson Patterson murdered her husband in 1911, but was acquitted in a notorious trial.

D - 5, Richthofen Castle, called Louieburgh by the Baron, Castlewood by the Hendries.

F - 6½, where the moat, with water from Windsor Lake, left the castle grounds.

F½ - 6, bridge over the moat with capstones dated 1887-1888.

From F to H at the top of the picture is a block that was John Denison's legal fee from the Baron. Most of the block is still owned and occupied by Judge Denison's descendants.

L - 3, the Richthofen Fountain, built in 1900, stands at the point of this triangular lot. The ashes of the Baroness Louise were placed in the stonework in 1934.

To the right of 7, off the picture, stands the Baron's Molkerie, used since 1910 as the Montclair Civic Building.

157

BARON

WALTER VON RICHTHOFEN

1848-1898

He built a stark castle on
the plains east of Denver.
The picture below shows
it about 1889 with newly
planted trees. Note the
white marble fountain be-
tween the gate house and
the castle, the coat-of-arms
on the tower, and the sandstone head on the right
hand corner of the second
story front.

BARBAROSSA, FRITZ
REDBEARD
1123-1190

His portrait (right) is on Richthofen Castle and his beard
matched the Baron's. In 1910,
when the architect softened the
castle by the use of timbers and
peaked roofs (see picture below)
he was careful to place the head
of Barbarossa on the new wing,
so the German emperor could
continue to look northwest toward Longs Peak.

(Photos by Orin A. Sealy for the *Denver Post, from Mrs. Etienne Perenyi, Denver Public Library.*)

159

The Baron built the Sans Souci Concert Gardens on the Denver Circle Railroad at Virginia and Broadway in order to catch trade from visitors to the Mining Exposition of 1882. (*Denver Public Library*.)

The Baron built an Art Gallery at 8th and Monaco to house his collection of European paintings which downtown Denver did not appreciate. The building was used as a clubhouse after 1901, called the Montclair Casino. It burned in 1906. (Photo from the Casino's year book for 1902. *Denver Public Library*.)

The Baron built a Molkerie at 12th and Oneida where tubercular patients drank milk from imported kine stabled on the ground floor. Since 1910 this building has been the Montclair Civic Building. (*Denver Public Library*.)

with a carriage accident. The injuries were minor—the Baron broke two ribs and had to be taken to Wentworth House where Dr. Bancroft tended his injury—but the news item is of interest because it is the first mention of the Baroness in Denver. The Baron, the paper reported, "had lately returned to the city with his bride. A few days ago he purchased one of the cottages on Cheltenham Heights in North Denver."[4] The bride was Jane Oakley of London, a mousy little woman with a substantial dowry. In Denver she bore the Baron two daughters, Margaretha (Daisy) and Charlotte.

Though the Baron lived in North Denver, he invested in South Denver real estate. The proof of this is on the real-estate maps which show Richthofen Subdivision. Now South Denver was way out in the country. To provide transportation to prospective buyers the Baron helped to promote the Denver Circle Railroad, which eventually went both to Jewell Park (present Overland Park) and to University Park, but did not circle the city as its name indicated and its promoters hoped.

When a fine exposition building was erected in South Denver (on a lane still called Exposition Avenue), the Baron built a beer garden nearby, naming it Sans Souci. He thought the solid citizens of Denver with their families would quietly enjoy the garden. He forbade public dancing and served only imported beer and liquors. That the drinks came from overseas (and then overland) was somehow supposed to make the place refined. Strawberries and cream were served to the ladies. But bourgeois families failed to flock to Sans Souci to spend afternoons listening to the band and admiring the nasturtiums.[5]

Now the Baron was well acquainted in another stratum of Denver society. Disgusted with the lack of patronage for his respectable beer garden, he sent invitations for one special night to the gamblers, fancy ladies, and sporting men of town and threw his joint wide open. It was a crowded, lucrative, and long night, thoroughly enjoyed by a number of respectable men who would never after admit they had attended.[6]

Evidently the married Baron found it difficult to forsake the free life of a young bachelor which he had enjoyed earlier in the

West. In 1882 he took the Baroness and their two babies to visit his father at an estate called Carlowitz in Prussia and then to London to visit his wife's family. While there, he begged Jane to divorce him. He returned to Denver alone. Judge LeFevre arranged the divorce, making sure that the Baroness' dowry (dowries legally belonged to the husband) went with the Baroness to Germany where she reared her two girls.[7]

Even without the dowry, the Baron managed to amuse himself in the exciting Denver of the Silver Kings.[8] For one recreation, he belonged to the Corkscrew Club. Membership in this club was limited to well-born foreigners, many of whom were foot-loose in early Denver.[9]

In 1884, the Corkscrew Club arranged a race at Overland Park to be preceded by a parade in which the Baron, dressed in his hunting pink, was to ride. Cantering out to the Park on his spirited horse, he met a carriage in which sat a blond with peaches and cream complexion that could have come only from England. This Englishwoman was not at all mousy like the Baron's first wife. Seeing this vision, Baron Walter became lost. He, who had practically laid out the Denver Circle Railroad to serve Jewell Park, was forced to ask the lady to set him right on his direction. The lady courteously pointed out the way to the red-bearded gentleman with the military bearing, and drove on. That night, at the Club dinner that followed the race, the Baron managed a formal introduction to Mrs. Davies and started a tempestuous courtship.[10]

The lady told the Baron she might marry him if he would establish himself in a career. He was thirty-six and she considered he had been a playboy long enough.[11] Within a year the Baron could proudly bring her a copy of his book whose title page read: *Cattle Raising on the Plains of North America*, by Walter Baron von Richthofen. (New York, Appleton, 1885.)[12]

The Baron's South Denver project was not flourishing. He looked east for new worlds to promote. On the high plateau east of Denver, the Western Land and Colonization Company, headed by Matthias Cochrane, was starting a town named Montclair. The Baron became the animating spirit of this project. *Animating* is the exact word for the Baron. Under his direction, the company published a map of the streets even before they had been defined by a single plow track. The lots sold for $150 to $200, five per cent off for cash, eight per cent carrying charges. Clients were persuaded to buy whole blocks and surround them with box elder trees. John Denison, the young lawyer who cleared the title of the Joslin homestead for the Baron, accepted an entire block as payment. His house still stands at 10th and Olive.[13]

The first problem was how to get the customers to Montclair. It was a long way from Denver. From York to Geneva (Oneida) Street, the company widened the Kansas City Road (Colfax Avenue) and lined it with trees. They advertised in March, 1885, that every morning a carriage would transport prospective buyers from the heart of Denver to Montclair "if the weather turns fine." Business was so good that carriages were replaced by herdics which left the Opera House corner at nine-thirty a.m. and two p.m. each day. But herdics, horse-drawn taxicabs that opened in the rear, were not colorful enough for the Baron. He provided tallyhos to run between Denver and Montclair. The Baron often acted as outrider, his hounds leaping beside his capering horse and barking when the horn tallyhoed. The citizens of Denver dubbed this the Baron's Circus. It became even more like a circus when tents were pitched on the dry plateau to house excursionists brought from Nebraska by the railroad. They were fed by Denver caterers and entertained by a brass band.

In the late 1800's, consumptives were to Denver economy what tourists are today. The Baron knew how to entice health-seekers or "chasers" as early Montclair called them. At 12th and Geneva he built a wooden structure of two floors. On the first floor were stabled imported cows. Porches, their floors pierced with grills, surrounded the second floor. The theory was that tubercular patients would benefit by resting on cots on the porch while they ate whey and drank milk, at a penny a mug, and breathed the effluvia that arose through the grills from the imported kine.[14]

This building the Baron called the Molkerie (German for Milkhouse), a name still used by old timers though the building is now the Montclair Community House, a property of the City and County of Denver. Rumor says that the Baron could walk from the cellar of his home through a tunnel to the Molkerie.[15]

Between the time the Molkerie was the Baron's sanatorium and the time it became a civic center, it had a varied history. Around 1902 it housed the mentally incompetent, much to the perturbation of a Montclair resident who saw a woman in her night robe wandering the vacant lots in the cold of a winter night.[16]

Baron Walter's private plans were as grandiose as his business ones. For his home, to which he hoped to bring a new wife, he built a castle.[17] It was fashioned of sturdy gray stone quarried near Castle Rock, south of Denver. On the north tower was emblazoned the Richthofen coat of arms; on the west side was a rounded tower that looked like a donjon; and on the northwest corner was a large head sculptured in red sandstone to represent Barbarossa.[18]

The Baron brought water from Windsor Lake, east of Fairmount Cemetery. Locally known as an irrigation ditch, when it ran through the castle grounds it was called a moat. On the stone bridge that crossed this moat west of the castle, the Baron carved the dates 1887 and 1888, the years when the castle was rising on the plains.[19]

In three hectic years the Baron proved that he was a successful business man to the blond Mrs. Davies whom he had met going to the races in 1884. They were married on March 20, 1887, at the St. James Hotel, the bride gowned in electric-blue plush with hat to match.[20] After the honeymoon, the new Baroness refused to move into the castle until it was landscaped.

Landscaped it was! The Baron brought evergreens from Bear Creek Canyon and imported elms from the East. He fenced two whole blocks and put deer and antelope behind the fence. He even had a bear pit, with bears.[21] A newspaper reported that he let loose a shipment of wild canaries and other songbirds, which must have astonished the local meadowlarks. In November, 1888, the Baroness Louise von Richthofen consented to move from the Albany Hotel to Louieburgh, where she picked roses for their first dinner table. (It must have been a warm fall!)

They lived in the castle three years. One fears the Baroness

164

was lonely. Despite the elegance of her home, she was not accepted by the tight little social sets of either Denver or Montclair, though the neighborhood children were allowed to attend the Christmas parties, loaded with German traditions, that the Baroness gave for the son of one of their retainers.[22] Montclair children of those days watched the Baron stride across the prairie, fascinated by his whiskers and his coat tails blowing in the breeze.[23]

The Baron would try to cheer the Baroness by taking her to the city in a polished coach with footmen, the hounds scaring the prairie dogs among the sand lilies of a June evening. After dinner at Tortoni's (formerly Elitch's Palace) the couple would often attend the Tabor Grand Opera House where the Baron swept his opera cloak from his military shoulders.

Besides his interest in music and the theater, the Baron appreciated the graphic arts. On one of his trips to Europe he collected oil paintings which he exhibited in Denver at the Gettysburg Building near 17th and Champa. Though he charged a quarter for admission, his main object was to bring culture to primitive Denver. During the attempt, Denver discovered a nude or two among the pictures and raised a hullabaloo. So, about 1891, the discouraged Baron erected a gallery of his own on the northwest corner of 8th Avenue and Goodyear (Monaco) Street and carted his art collection to Montclair.[24]

It has been difficult to trace the subsequent history of the pictures, but the building was used at the turn of the century by some Montclair people as a genteel club where no liquor was served and no games permitted for wagers.[25] They enjoyed their Casino but it burned in 1906. Its ruins, including one high wall marked with smoke stains, stood untouched for years, a haunted landmark on the long trolley ride to Montclair and Fairmount Cemetery. In 1921, an attractive house rose on the old foundations. The ornate urns at the 8th Avenue entrance to the grounds may be relics of the Baron's art gallery.[26]

In the spring of 1891, after three years in the castle, the Richthofens left Denver for far places[27]—Southern California, Mexico, and Europe. After a hunt in Alaska, they settled down to an agreeable life in a house on Regent Street in London, their bills paid by the payments rolling in from Montclair real estate. The crash of 1893 stopped payments.

The Baron then turned his energies to a gold mine corporation in newly developed Cripple Creek. He sold stock in London. This company shortly proved to have more stock than ore.

In the middle 1890's the Baron was back in Denver with a grandiose and final scheme. Armed with Milwaukee money, he would turn Montclair into a spa, with hotel, games of chance, and baths. The water was to be piped twenty miles from a ninety-foot well that lies six miles southeast of Barr Lake.[28] For some time previously the Baron had been connected with a company that bottled and sold this water as "ginger champagne."[29] Full-page spreads, complete with architect's sketches, appeared in the Denver papers to advertise this Colorado Carlsbad of Montclair.[30]

Montclair citizens took one look at the Baron's plans and vetoed them. No drinking, no gambling, no watering place in Montclair.

The Baron then went beyond the town limits. South of 6th Avenue, his hotel was to stand on the highest ground. Later this rise was occupied by the main building of a sanatorium built by Senator Lawrence C. Phipps.[31] Today this building is the administration building of Lowry Air Force Base.

Things progressed nicely for the Baron and his Colorado Carlsbad until 1898, when the War with Spain rocked Denver. The Baron, who had started his manhood as a Prussian army officer, was military. He also was a flower-loving German. Combining these two characteristics, on a spring day of 1898 he stood erect on 17th Street in front of the Denver Club with a collection of flowers. He presented a bouquet to each soldier of the 7th U. S. Infantry from Fort Logan on parade before leaving for active service. To distribute 1,200 bouquets (red and white carnations with blue violets) must have been a chore to the Baron who was not feeling well.

Within a week he underwent an appendectomy and died from shock on May 8, 1898, at his rooms in the Hotel L'Impériale[32] (the present United Funds Buildings at 314-14th Street). The Baron would have been so proud had he lived to the First World

War when his nephew, Manfred von Richthofen, became the flying ace known as the Red Knight of Germany.[33]

Walter von Richthofen's funeral was held from the home of his friend Henry Bohm, at Colfax and High. The tramway company assembled trolley cars, perhaps including the funeral car draped with purple curtains, on Colfax Avenue to carry mourners beyond Montclair to Fairmount Cemetery. Later the Baroness took his body to Breslau where his daughters attended the military interment.

After this, the Baroness lived in Denver hotels for almost thirty years, the last years at the Cosmopolitan Hotel. In 1900 she donated $1000, and other Montclair residents added to this, to erect a fountain for beasts and bicyclists at Oneida and Richthofen Place.[34] The fountain still stands, though the watering trough is now used as a flower box. Mrs. Richthofen, as she called herself after World War I, loved to come from her hotel and sit beside the fountain. She died in November, 1934, and her ashes repose in a niche in the back of the fountain. She left an elaborate will and $500.[35]

But what happened to Richthofen Castle? From the time the Baron first advertised it for sale in January, 1891, it was sold and repossessed a number of times. Once it was a dancing club, frowned on by conservative Montclair. For eight years a Milwaukee man named von Mueller (Americanized soon to Miller) rented the place and there raised his dogs and children.[36]

Edwin Hendrie of the mining machinery firm of Hendrie & Bolthoff bought the place from the Baroness.[37] In 1910 he hired Maurice Biscoe, an architect, to enlarge it. Biscoe added plaster and timbering to the upper stories and a long music room with master bedroom above. He was careful to preserve and reset the head of Barbarossa in the northwest corner of the new wing, in full view of Longs Peak. In 1924 a southwest wing provided Mr. Hendrie's grandsons, the Grant boys, with independence in the form of an outside circular staircase to their living quarters.[38]

After W. W. Grant sold the castle in 1937, it went through various hands until 1946 when Mr. and Mrs. Etienne Perenyi bought the house and property. They have sold much of the land so that today the castle rises from a sea of low-roofed modern homes. The Perenyis, like the Baron, combine the West with middle Europe, for Mrs. Perenyi is a Coloradan and her husband is from Hungary. Surely Baron Walter von Richthofen would approve.

NOTES

[1]A mountain in the Never Summer Range, west of Rocky Mountain National Park, is named Mt. Richthofen. This seems to have been named, not for Denver's Baron Walter von Richthofen, but for a kinsman of his named Baron Ferdinand von Richthofen (1833-1905). He was a geologist and geographer, famed for his explorations in the mountains of China. From 1862 to 1868 he was in the United States and served on the California survey under Whitney. Clarence King of the 40th Parallel survey, having known Baron Ferdinand in California, probably named the Colorado mountain for him. A letter from this Baron to F. V. Hayden appeared in the *Rocky Mountain News* Feb. 3, 1878.

[2]On March 31, 1957, the Baron's daughter, Margaretha von Scheliha, nee Baroness von Richthofen, wrote to Agnes Wright Spring, Colorado Historian. Many of the details in this chapter are from that letter, such as the fact that the Baron did not study at Heidelberg.

[3]Edward Ring wrote in the *Rocky Mountain News,* Sept. 23, 1926, that the Baron was fond of telling how he almost fought a duel. An inebriated Russian challenged the young Baron who, being nervous, handed the Russian his mother's card instead of his own. The next day the Russian, believing he had challenged a woman, sent roses to the Baron's mother.

[4]*RMN,* March 26, 1878. The cottage was near Owen LeFevre's home on Federal Boulevard. The Richthofen girls and Frederica LeFevre (Mrs. Harry Bellamy) became life-long friends.

[5]*RMN,* June 30, 1882, "The Baron's Bower."

[6]*RMN,* July 17, 1921.

[7]Interview with Mrs. Harry Bellamy, 1957.

[8]"A gay dog if there ever was one" was W. W. Grant's comment on the Baron in *Such is Life.* (Denver, 1952, p. 212)

[9]Ring, Edward, "Clubs of the Past." In *Colorado Magazine,* v. 19, p. 140, July 1942. The 1885-87 *Denver Directories* show the Club Room at 1642½ Curtis Street, and the Baron's real estate office at 1642. Later the Corkscrew Club had rooms at 18th and Broadway.

[10]Article by Frances Wayne in the *Denver Post,* March 23, 1934, p. 7.

[11]Irwin Harrison wrote an article in the *Rocky Mountain News* July 24, 1927, after a personal interview with Louise von Richthofen.

[12]The timing of the book was unlucky. The winter of 1886-87 produced the storms that strewed the prairie with dead cattle. This disillusioned foreign investors in the beef bonanza. The Baron's book disappoints the modern reader because it is theoretical—full of tables on how many descendents one cow may be expected to have in ten years, etc. It specifically names few, if any, ranches or cattlemen and offers no personal data on the author. His farm may have been in Weld County. "A great portion of the stock of Baron von Richthofen's farm was disposed of at a private sale to E. L. Rolandett." (*RMN,* Aug. 14, 1879, p. 8, col. 1).

[13]Articles about the Baron's Montclair project appear in: *RMN,* March 20 and 22, 1885, and July 1, 1885; *Denver Tribune* and *Denver Republican,* May 30, 1885. Later articles include *Colorado Graphic,* v. 3, p. 3, Feb. 18, 1888; *Denver Republican,* May 1, 1890.

That many people bought blocks and built one large house thereon explains the look of Montclair today. Most blocks are full of low modern houses over which towers one old, large structure.

A map of Montclair was printed by the Denver Lithograph Company, (no date), for W. B. von Richthofen, 1116-17th Street. It shows a horsecar on Colfax. The street names of the Baron's subdivision were Goodyear (Monaco), West End (Magnolia), Belleville (Niagara), Newport (Newport), Geneva (Oneida), Saratoga (Olive), Manitou (Pontiac), East End (Poplar), Hyde Park (Quebec), and Dieppe (14th Avenue).

[14]Walters, T. E. *Talk before the Montclair Improvement Association,* 1924. Ms.

[15]W. W. Grant, son-in-law of E. B. Hendrie, who lived at the castle for years, said on March 30, 1956, that there was no tunnel. In the basement there was a trapdoor to a sewer, and in the dining room there was a sliding door to a walk-in safe.

[16]*RMN,* Feb. 2, 1902.

[17]Many people have written about the Richthofen Castle. Pictures augment the chapter in E. E. Kohl's *Denver's Historic Mansions.* (Denver, Sage Books, 1957)

[18]Barbarossa, "Fritz Red-Beard," the twelfth century emperor of the Holy Roman Empire, is to legend-loving Germans what King Arthur is to the English. What, if any, connection the Baron had with Barbarossa is not known, but those who knew the Baron said he also had a red and flowing beard. This presumably led Herndon Davis to state in the *Denver Post* Aug. 18, 1940, that the red sandstone head on the castle was a portrait of the Baron.

169

[19]The dated stones were preserved when the bridge was removed after the moat was filled up because of mosquitoes. The stones are now on the wall to the west of the front door of the castle.

[20]The bride's full name was Mrs. Louise Ferguson Woodall Davies.

[21]The bears were given to Elitch's Gardens, according to Helen Ingersoll in her ms. *I Remember,* 1947.

[22]Ingersoll, *op. cit.*

[23]Mrs. Hugh McLean (nee Rosamond Denison) has lived all her life in various houses on the block her father, John Denison, earned for his legal services. (He became the presiding judge of the Colorado Supreme Court.) Mrs. McLean provided me not only with reminiscences, like the Baron striding across the prairie, but with companionship in my journey to the Montclair of yesterday. Through her, the W. W. Grant family contributed information.

[24]*Denver Times,* Oct. 25, 1890; Harper, R. L. *Harper's Guide to Denver.* Denver, 1890, p. 66; Stone, W. G. M. *The Colorado Hand-book; Denver and its Outings.* Denver, Barkhausen & Lester, 1892, p. 68.

[25]*Denver Times,* Nov. 10, 1901; May 15, 1902. The Western History Department of the Denver Public Library has a copy of the Casino's yearbook, with rules.

[26]D. F. Burns, present owner of 815 Monaco Parkway, has the blueprints of his home. Made for Adamson in 1921, the plans show that the present house stands on the original foundations of the Art Gallery.

[27]The Baron offered his castle for sale in a three-column advertisement in the *Denver Times,* Jan. 24, 1891.

[28]*Colorado Geological Survey Report,* 1920, p. 203.

[29]Paul D. Harrison of Denver has investigated this water. He has been to the well and has picked up from the farmer's furrows two kinds of bottles used for the "ginger champagne" business. He said a Trinidad doctor organized the bottling company, the Baron joining later. The original plan was to have the spa near the well. The *Colorado Business Directory* of May 1893 lists, under Barr Lake, Colorado, Carlsbad Mineral Water Company, C. W. Thurlow.

Many people have written that the Baron planned to pipe the water for his spa from Idaho Springs. This tale probably originated with J. E. Smith in his "Personal Recollections of Early Denver." In *Colorado Magazine,* v. 20, p. 13, Jan. 1943.

[30]*Denver Republican,* Dec. 27, 1896; *RMN,* April 15, 1897 and Nov. 5, 1897, p. 10.

[31]The *Denver Republican* for April 26, 1903, outlines the plans for the Agnes Memorial Sanatorium to be erected by Lawrence C. Phipps in memory of his mother. The Sanatorium, under the direction of Dr.

George Walter Holden, was outstanding. The treatments its staff discovered for the cure of tuberculosis contributed to modern methods and lessened the importance of sanatoriums. The Agnes Memorial Sanatorium closed its doors in 1932. Its equipment was given to Sands Home and the Denver General Hospital. The buildings were acquired by the U. S. Army for Lowry Field in December, 1937.

[32]Obituary *Denver Times,* May 9, 1898; the funeral plans were in the *Denver Republican,* May 11, 1898.

[33]Three of the Baron's grandsons were killed in World War II and one of his granddaughters, her husband and their three children chose to kill themselves rather than be deported to Russia. (Letter from Margaretha von Scheliha, March 31, 1957, *op. cit.*)

[34]*Denver Times,* May 2, 1900. Harlan Thomas designed the fountain and Mayor Sylvester Williams of Montclair helped raise the money.

[35]Obituary *Denver Post,* April 7, 1934, p. 1. An article about the placing of her ashes in the fountain appeared in the *Denver Post,* Aug. 16, 1934, with pictures of Mayor Begole, Bishop Irving P. Johnson, and Mrs. Stephen Tyler Parsons, at whose home Mrs. Richthofen died.

[36]Obituary of John N. Miller, *Denver Republican,* June 20, 1902. Montclair children feared his Great Danes, according to Mrs. Hugh McLean and Miss Helen Ingersoll.

[37]The castle was sold to E. B. Hendrie, June 19, 1903, according to the *Denver Republican.* The price was not only $40,000 but included land near Hardin, east of Greeley. Baroness von Richthofen platted the town of Hardin, then sold it and built a buffet apartment house near 12th and Sherman, on land once owned by H. A. W. Tabor.

[38]The plans made by the architects, Biscoe and Hewitt, for the remodeling of the castle for E. B. Hendrie in 1910 are owned by Mrs. Etienne Perenyi. These show that the northwest wing was added in 1910. The Hendries called the house Castlewood. Architect J. J. B. Benedict made the plan for the addition of the southwest wing and outdoor stair in 1924.

Overland Park

Today Overland Park is an eighteen-hole golf course owned by the City and County of Denver. It is a spot of green in the industrial part of southern Denver. On yesterday's map it was so far beyond the city limits that one went *overland* to reach it.

It lies between present Santa Fe Drive and the South Platte River. The name of Santa Fe Drive[1] conjures up visions of the fur-traders in the Southwest, and the Platte brings to mind the gold-rush days of 1858. That year men from Lawrence, Kansas, built Montana City upstream from present Overland Park.[2] But the history of the site of Overland Park starts with something less glamorous than fur or gold. Potatoes!

On July 11, 1859 Rufus H. Clark[3] filed on a homestead of 160 acres on the South Platte River. Ten years before, he had shipped as mate on a sailing vessel in order to get to the California gold mines. He was not impressed, therefore, with the placer mining in Colorado of 1859. Someone probably showed him a large potato that had grown in the fresh soil and hot sun of the Platte Valley and that impressed him. He planted potatoes—great fields of potatoes—on his homestead that stretched east to present Pennsylvania Street. The first crop, dug in the fall of 1860, started him on his way to a fortune and crowned him the potato king of Colorado.

He was a character, this Potato Clark, a seafaring man "steeped in sin and prodigious profanity and the curse of drink."[4] But he got religion. Indeed it was he who in 1886 gave eighty acres and

$500 to the struggling Methodist college which has since become the University of Denver at University Park.[5]

Potato Clark was big and burly with an emphatic voice and a bushy beard. He had a kindly heart, even before his reformation. The day, for instance, that he heard about the Chicago fire of 1871, he loaded a wagon with potatoes and drove to Denver. At the Salomon Brothers' store he sacked the potatoes and auctioned them off, the profits to go to the victims of the fire. One sack sold for $270. When the spuds were gone he auctioned anything offered by other men—hats—cigars—boots. Late in the evening he collected a final seven dollars for the sign that advertised the auction. The proceeds he turned over to the mayor of little Denver who sent a check to Chicago for over $7,000.

A busy day like that was not unusual for Potato Clark. He drove himself and his employees. "One of the toughest fellows I ever met in spite of the fact that he 'Got religion' some time previous," was the comment made by one of his hired men in 1878.[6] Clark employed from seven to thirty men, depending on the needs of the season, and furnished them with whips to hurry the horses. One of his men wore out two teams in one day.

Potato Clark lived in a shack near the river. In 1878 his wife died tragically in a cloudburst. She was "hurrying in from the field when a storm overtook her. When they found her she was dead, with her long hair all entangled in a barb-wire fence."[7] His last wife (he was married four times) survived him and lived in the square brick house which he had built late in life at 1398 South Santa Fe Drive.[8]

The farm was beautifully located. To the west across the South Platte River rose Ruby Hill noted not only for its rubies (which were actually garnets and very small) but also for its wild flowers. Soaring above Ruby Hill was the distant Mount Evans. The farm itself, with the dark green of the potato plants relieved by an occasional cottonwood tree, looked like a park. When some Denver men decided to start a public park, they thought of that location and bought some of the land from Potato Clark in 1883. These men had built the Denver Circle Railroad, all six-and-a-half miles of it, two years before. As one can surmise from its name, the company planned to circle the city with the rails. One branch actually got to the University of Denver.[9]

The railroad company started the park in order to increase passenger use of the line. Potato Clark's old farm they christened Jewell Park, a contrast with the old name. It was named after ex-Governor Charles A. Jewell of Connecticut, a stockholder in the railroad and park, who died the spring the park was opened.[10]

The newspapers of that spring of 1883 reported the progress of the line as it built from Logan Street west along Jewell Avenue ending at the Platte, where there was a ferry. In May the race track, one mile, oval, was completed.[11] From 1883 to 1930 the dust on that track was whipped up by horses, sulkies, auto cars, motor cycles—everything but bicycles which seldom, if ever, were raced on this track because of the deep sand.

Also in May, 1883, a handsome depot and bandstand were completed. The company offered free use of the grounds for picnics, even provided seats in arbors and beneath the trees, free to all just so they did not hitch their horses to the shrubbery.[12] The aim was for beauty and respectability. Newspaper interviews usually ended "Again we warn disreputable characters from entering the park."

For picnickers, there was music. At the end of June the Jewell Park Orchestra gave a concert.[13] Three bands played for the Fourth of July celebration when a special train ran every half-hour from the Larimer Street depot. Fare was fifty cents round trip, twenty-five cents admission to the park.[14] Six large and numerous small balloons ascended skyward during the day; at night walks softly glowed with Chinese lanterns and, even though it rained just before dark, the fireworks were "the best ever seen."[15]

The next spring Jewell Park had 3,000 people at a May Day Fete which was not held until the end of May because of Colorado spring weather.[16] Always there were horse races, but a more unusual event was Professor van Tassell's balloon ascent. On August 7, 1886, he filled his bag with gas from the local gas company's main at Broadway and Deer Street (11th Avenue). More exciting than the ascent was the journey of the balloon from the gas main to the park. Into the body of an express wagon the basket of the balloon was placed and weighted with rocks. Drawn by slow horses, the whole thing was completely surrounded by small boys all the way to Jewell Park. The ascent was all right—no better than Ivy Baldwin was to do at Elitch's—but the crowd was disappointed because the Professor ascended alone. He announced that the pressure in the Denver main would not fill his balloon enough to support another passenger. This was a pity because a local reporter had publicly made his last will and testament in anticipation of the ascent to heaven.[17]

For this event South Broadway was crowded with carriages and wagons holding spectators who saw the show for nothing. Only 2,000 people paid admission. No wonder the Denver Circle Railroad and its subsidiary Jewell Park were glad to unload on buyers who came along in 1887. The Santa Fe Railroad bought the little circle route for its right-of-way into Denver. (Later the city refused to allow the Santa Fe to use the right-of-way.)

The promoters of the Denver Circle Railroad gladly sold Jewell Park to a group of Denver men looking for a site for a country club. The site was so far out in the country that they named it Overland Park. By 1889 Overland Park Club had built a clubhouse, later enlarging it.[18] Only members were allowed to live there but guests were welcome in the dining room. No tips, no dogs allowed, and no wagers except twenty-five cents per rubber point at whist, one cent per point at bridge whist, and ten cents per heart at hearts.[19]

Typical of the gala events at the clubhouse was the dinner dance held on Washington's birthday in 1899. The tables were patriotic with red, white, and blue hatchets. Despite the sub-zero weather, 150 couples came. Some used the Denver & Rio Grande railroad coaches to get there. Those who had made the long ride by horse-drawn carriages must have warmed themselves gratefully at the enormous fireplaces at either end of the large hall where four-foot logs were blazing.[20]

One of the active participants in all that went on at Overland Park was Henry Wolcott, a bachelor business man. He eventually bought up all the shares of the various organizations that owned the land. In 1915 his estate sold 164 acres of the land for $150,-

000.[21] This was a wise investment. However, among his contemporaries Henry Wolcott's claim to fame was not his business acumen. Nor was it that he largely financed the building of the Boston Building and the Equitable Building on 17th Street; nor that he was an officer in the Colorado Telephone Company and the Colorado Fuel and Iron Company; nor that he was a brother of Senator Ed Wolcott of Wolhurst; nor that he had financed Wolcott School for Girls where his sister educated the cream of Denver's belles[22]; but his fame rested on the fact that he introduced golf to Denver.

What year, month, day, and hour the first golf ball soared at Overland Park is not known, but in 1896 Henry Wolcott laid out a nine-hole course circling the Overland Park race track. He could water the turf from the Petersburg Ditch on the east and the Platte River on the west. The date was quite early in golfing history in the West.[23] Chicago had its first eighteen-hole golf course in 1893. Even when the sport was well established the West considered golf, like tennis, a sissy game. Nevertheless men of Overland Park immediately took up golf. And so did their ladies, much to the amusement of the press. For one ladies' tournament "society was out bright and early (for society) . . . beastly cold you know . . . to see the 16 contestants . . . jauntily clad in their jaunty caps and bright plaids."[24]

In December, 1901, some of the golfers incorporated the Denver Country Club. Any member of the Overland Park Club (there were about 100) automatically became a member of the Denver Country Club unless he refused in writing. This new club of 267 members rented the golf links at Overland Park from Henry Wolcott, and ran an omnibus (fare, five cents) from downtown Denver every afternoon except in bad weather, and a man was ready to care for members' horses any time after 12:30. There were also bicycle racks.[25]

At the end of 1902 the Denver Country Club did not renew their lease at Overland Park. Dissociating themselves from horse racing, they bought land on Cherry Creek in the deep country above present Downing Street bridge. The turf could be watered by the City Ditch. They hired Terry Boal, an architect

The clubhouse at Overland Park with the grandstand in the background and bicycle racks in the foreground. Overland Park, an eighteen-hole municipal golf course today, was Denver's first golf course. It was obviously appreciated by the ladies. (*Denver Public Library*.)

"THEY'RE OFF IN A BUNCH!" was the caption under the newspaper cartoon of society at the Overland races. "Six thousand pairs of eyes centered on the horses, 6,000 pairs of lungs heaved with excitement, 6,000 pairs of lips parted as the horses came under the wire, 12,000 hands applauded or handled field glass or toyed with programs. . . . The crowd arrived early, some over the D & R G, some by trolley, some in their carriages, on horseback, or on wheels. The stream of pleasure seekers stretched from the city to the park in one unbroken line." (*Denver Times*, June 16, 1901, p. 1.)

The photograph of a sulky at the City Park Driving Course is inserted for the benefit of those who have never seen a sulky race. (Photo by Joseph Collier. *Denver Public Library*.)

M. Paulhan, Famous French Aviator, Making His Flight [...] 50,000 People at Overland Park, Denver.

"M. Louis Paulhan gave Denver three marvelous exhibitions of flying with a heavier-than-air machine. The first day the enormous crowd seriously interfered. Later in the week he duplicated some of the stunts which won him the big purse at Los Angeles.... His record for actual height from sea level was made in Denver." (Photo and text from *Denver Municipal Facts*, v. 2, pp. 8–9, Feb. 1910.) The inset (both pictures from *Denver Public Library*.) shows M. Paulhan in his flying machine.

When America discovered the joys of the open road on wheels, Denver provided camping space for "motor gypsies" at various parks. Overland Park welcomed 11,087 cars in 1921. The picture shows how a veteran of World War I (see his campaign hat) set up a summer home. Evening lectures, and dancing to a Victrola, were provided at the clubhouse, as was a grocery store. (*Denver Public Library*.)

His wife could wash her white middy and skirt in the 1921 version of a self-service laundry, as shown in the picture below. (Photo from *Municipal Facts*, v. 4, p. 13, Aug. 1921. *Denver Public Library*.)

who was definitely country club caliber, to build them a clubhouse which was not completed until 1904.

The golf links and race track at Overland Park continued to be used after the departure of the Denver Country Club. For some time before this, Overland's clubhouse had stopped being fashionable for dinner dances. In fact the one-time elegant structure housed jockeys, and then it was a boarding house for workers employed at the Manchester Cotton Mills.[26] The building burned in January of 1903. Luckily no one was living there—it was being remodeled—no one, that is, except some tramp who was suspected of setting fire to the place in an effort to get warm.[27]

One may visualize the other buildings that once stood at Overland Park. First, probably Indian tepees stood among the cottonwood trees; then Potato Clark's shack; then the Jewell Park depots—the Denver Circle Railroad's at the south end of the park and later depots to the east; the bandstand and the rustic arbors lighted with Chinese lanterns. Though the race track was laid out in 1883 it was not until 1889 that the elegant clubhouse was built. Ten years later the association spent $6,000 improving the facilities at the park, but had to spend more after February, 1901, when the grandstand burned to the ground. The pyrotechnical effects during that fire were caused by the ancient lumber "which had dried in the sun 12 years."[28]

By summer of 1901, Merritt Gano, secretary of Overland Park, announced the completion of a new grandstand with twenty private boxes. The structure was extra safe because of thrust braces. The new betting shed, a building 80 by 120 feet, was not so strong as the grandstand. In July a freak wind, called anything from a tornado to a dust whirl, wound across the race track, which was fortunately empty though this was during a meet. The wind hit the betting stand, whirled its way between the judge's stand, the depot, and the grandstand, and ended in a miniature waterspout in the middle of the Platte River. In its wake were broken bones and bruised heads because the whirlwind had lifted the roof of the betting stand into the air and then dropped it down on the people within.[29]

Of the old buildings the stables lasted the longest. They stood south of the present, and recent, golf house until fire consumed them on November 22, 1934. They had been built and used for stables until the anti-racing law of 1908. Then they housed exhibits and concessions for fairs for a few years, but went back to stabling horses during World War I when the Colorado Cavalry tented at Overland Park.[30]

Now—Off to the Races! For of course the fundamental reason for Overland Park from its inception as Jewell Park in 1883 was the one-mile track. Horses ran on that track summer after summer. Sometimes the racing season lasted all summer, sometimes two weeks. When the sport was fashionable the audiences numbered six, seven, eight thousand. On racing day South Broadway was crowded with small traps weaving skillfully around the omnibuses and tallyhos. High-wheeled bicycles, later smaller wheeled, were sometimes barely visible through the dust.

Betting on the races had its ups and downs. Just as in the East, dishonest bookkeepers became so obnoxious that laws were passed to control betting, or abolish both it and racing. To follow the ups and downs of betting through Colorado history would be worse than riding a bicycle through the South Broadway dust. When betting was legal, official poolkeepers accepted wagers days before the races. There was a poolkeeper at the Windsor Hotel in 1892.[31] When betting was illegal but races were run, bookmakers went underground. When racing was stopped, great efforts were made to re-instate it. During one of the non-legal periods a man named Wahlgren was convinced that, through the influence of a local paper, betting would be voted back at the next election. He deposited $50,000 with Henry Wolcott on an option to buy Overland Park. The people voted against horse racing and the $50,000 was added to the Wolcott fortune.[32]

When the pari-mutuel system of betting was made legal in December, 1948, Colorado horse racing was put back on its four feet.[33] The timing was too late, however, to resuscitate Overland Park's race track. The present Centennial Track was built a little upstream from Overland, so near that the opening bugle call can again be heard at Overland Park.

What surprises the present generation of horse race enthusiasts is the kind of racing done at Overland Park. The horses were driven, not ridden. Harness races were the usual events. An entry in a harness race was a single horse hitched to a sulky in which sat the owner or driver. The sulky wheels were high in the 1880's, but after ball bearings were applied to bicycle axles in 1892, sulky wheels, using the same device, were reduced in size.[34]

The horses were bred to be pacers or trotters. Part of the joy of watching the race was to see the precise action of the horses' legs. The driver's skill with the ribbons prevented them from breaking their gait. This kind of horse, prosperous Denver men owned and drove around town hitched to shiny buggies, or, in pairs, to carriages.

For variety the high-stepping pacers or trotters at Overland Park were sometimes raced under saddle. Professional jockeys were hired but these races were not popular. To draw a crowd, the management introduced running horse races, under saddle, not in harness. Local entries included horses that had won in cowboy tournaments, but gradually well-bred running horses were imported from the East or bred locally to take their place beside the pacers and trotters. As late as 1914 a reporter wrote: "Any school boy knows all about harness races, trotters and pacers, but few have seen running horses."[35]

In an effort to popularize races under saddle, the manager tempted the sporting set of the town. He offered a choice of any horse in the Overland stables to "gentlemen jockeys." For a season or two the swagger set took up the fad. In one such race, riders included "society beaux" from the University Club, Denver Athletic Club, Denver Club, and the Army, two each.[36] To make the sport more sporting, hurdle and obstacle races were scheduled.[37]

We will leave horse racing at Overland Park now, with the understanding that every now and then horse races were held until the track was finally planted with grass for a golf course. The majority of the fickle public turned from horses to things mechanical. First there were bicycles. The wheel racks at the clubhouse stretched and stretched as more members wheeled out to the club over the pleasant path along Broadway and the City

Ditch. Bicycle races, however, were not held on the Overland track because of the sand.[38]

But motorcycle races at Overland Park? Yes![39] It even was the scene of a tragedy when the well-known racer L. A. Michaels was killed by his machine in 1909.

For Denver motorcyclists the big year was 1913. That summer downtown Denver streets were busy with parades. In July Buffalo Bill in a carriage, his white hair hanging about his shoulders, led the parade of his Wild West show. In August the Knights Templars rode down a much-decorated 16th Street on troops of all-black or all-white horses with hoofs burnished with silver and gold. On August 23, 1913, came a parade that may not have been as colorful but was certainly more audible—almost a thousand members of the Federation of American Motorcyclists.

Before this event, the first and only time the national motorcycle races have been held in Denver, the Colorado Motorcycle Club made extensive preparations. Committees were appointed for everything, including the greeting of guests who were expected to come by motorcycle. At Sedalia a local committee met forty members of the Kansas Short Grass Club whose wives were riding on tandem attachments or in sidecars. The daughter of the president, however, a seventeen-year-old miss, rode her own machine, one of about a dozen such daring females at the convention.

Contingents from farther east came tamely into the Union Depot by train. They had started on motorcycles but had found the muddy roads of the Midwest impassable. After driving on Colorado roads a few days, members declared "the roads hereabouts were designed by a clairvoyant Nature for the coming of the motorcycle."[40] Lookout Mountain's winding road was especially appreciated.

An argument as to whether the races were to be held at Overland or at the motordrome of the Tuileries (which had a permit for Sunday events) was settled only after the Federation officers arrived. The decision was Overland. This disappointed men like "Curley" Frederick since his machine was designed for board tracks. "Curley," still living in Denver, was one of the "greats" in national racing.[41]

184

For three days the "pop-pop speed kings" repaired to Overland's one-mile dirt track for professional and amateur races, the distance varying from one to ten miles. The professional ten-mile was won by Balke of Los Angeles, his time being eight minutes, forty-seven and two-fifths seconds. Two of the local stars were Red Armstrong and C. A. Odlorne.

The motorcyclists proved they were good sports on the last day of the meet when they canceled the final event in order to give time to stranded members of the Wild West Show. The impecunious actors had been begging Denver to let them give a benefit performance at the auditorium, a plea that was ignored by the city officials. At Overland the actors rode bucking horses, roped, shot, and generally put on a good entertainment. Then the cowgirls passed their Stetsons. When the money was counted there was enough to send at least some of the girls back home.[42]

The newspapers, reporting the motorcycle convention in detail, with pictures of beautiful girls and grimy racers, gave almost as much space to the election of officers and to the dance as they did to the races. The election was a contest between the East and the West. Hard words were "like tacks put under tyres," quipped a reporter. These arguments caused a rift in the local club after the convention was over.

At the dance, given at the Colorado Motorcyclists' clubhouse at 14th and Court Place, members did the tango and the fox-trot. The ladies were daringly garbed in slit-skirts![43]

Before leaving the subject of motorcycle races at Overland Park, we should look across the river to Ruby Hill. This hill, used as a testing ground for motorcycles, has made many a rider quickly slip from his cycle as it turned over backward on the steep paths.

As for auto racing at Overland Park and all the other race tracks of Denver, and on streets like South Logan or Federal Boulevard —why doesn't one of the old-time racers write its history? From the advent of the horseless carriage, Denver men vied with each other on the Overland Park track. Local mechanics built special engines, special chassis. Some of the early race cars were nothing but wagons equipped with two-cylinder engines. Professionals and amateurs raced at Overland as long as there was a track, and ate the dust and smelled the oil, and still love the taste and the smell which remind them of the early days when racing cars went thirty-five miles an hour![44]

On September 3, 1907, William Felker died instantly in a race at Overland Park. His death was especially mourned locally because he and his friend, Yount, had been the first men to drive a car—a Locomobile—to the top of Pikes Peak in August, 1901.[45]

Then came the time, more exciting than the breaking of the sound barrier, when Denver saw a car go a mile a minute. The date was 1904 and the driver was the "Dusty Daredevil." Before you belittle Barney Oldfield's feat of driving over sixty miles an hour consider that the dirt track of Overland Park was not banked.[46]

Every few summers thereafter Barney Oldfield stopped in Denver to race against time or other professionals. Once he announced he would race a Beachey airplane, but the plane, after doing a loop, did not act right and the race was called off.[47] Always with a cigar jammed between his teeth to act as a bumper, Barney Oldfield drove cars with wonderful names like the Green Dragon, the Winton Bullet, the Blitzen Benz, and the Golden Submarine. He became a legend to the horseless carriage age and in Denver, as all over America, backseat drivers called out, "Slow down, Paw! You think you're Barney Oldfield?"

When motor cars came in, they were watched by a little, courageous Denver man named Ivy Baldwin. As an aeronaut he had thrilled Denver for decades. His balloon ascents, usually from Elitch's Gardens on Saturday and Sunday, were more than ascents, since he performed trapeze acts in the air beneath the balloon. This of course was nothing out of the ordinary to a man who often walked a tightrope strung between cliffs above Eldorado Springs.[48]

Now Ivy was a good showman. He saw the attraction in motorcars, but was loyal to balloons. So, he anounced that he would combine the two—in this extraordinary balloon ascent "George Hering will be suspended from the gas bag in a Stanley steamer auto going at full speed." But trouble ensued. The first day this

186

was to take place, Baldwin's gas generator failed, the second day it filled the balloon until it burst.[49]

Even though the Stanley steamer did not take to the air, nor locomotives crash together as advertised, the fair and exposition of September, 1909, at Overland Park was a success.[50] The management broke even with 110,000 paid admissions for the week. The entertainment included the usual—Derby Day for horse lovers, auto races, prizes for the best jellies, pin cushions, and kims, also prizes for the best decorated auto car and electric car. The mineral exhibitors gave away samples of an ore containing pitchblende in which geologists predicted radium might be found. At night a spectacular was presented called "The Battle of the Clouds." It depicted a battle that was to take place half a century hence (1959, that is). A flying warship from Mars destroyed a City of Science on earth amidst cannonading from radium and chemical guns.

This flying warship, though prophetic, was make-believe; but on a snowy day of February, 1910, Denver saw a heavier-than-air contraption actually fly. A French aviator named Louis Paulham, accompanied by his bride and French mechanics, unloaded his Farman flying machine from a box car on the railroad tracks at Overland Park. The assembling and testing of the plane was watched all day by people shivering in the grandstand, or perched on the fence along the track, or roosted in cottonwood trees, and Ruby Hill was black with wet-footed free-loaders. The machine "was a rickety trap, strung together with piano wire. Paulham would pluck the wires as if he were tuning a harp. . . . The plane was magic. Boys who had scratched their initials on Barney Oldfield's Green Dragon and Blitzen Benz on the identical spot, made no effort to pluck the wires or touch the frail lacquered wings."

All day the people waited in the snow. "At sundown the little plane gave a couple of sputters, scooted up a runway, and disappeared toward Ruby Hill before anybody knew what had happened. A tremendous involuntary cheer gave way to frustrated mob silence. And as suddenly the plane reappeared and the show was over. . . . It was as if some troubled swamp bird had rustled into the air and fluttered back. . . . Denver had seen her first bird man."[51]

In November of the same year, 1910, three American barn-stormers unloaded their Wright biplanes at Overland Park. The first day of their three-day show, Arch Hoxsey ascended nearly 2,000 feet into the air and stayed up fully twenty minutes. The third day he flew to Lakeside and back. But the second day, November 18, 1910, was the day Denver long remembered when Ralph Johnstone plummeted to his death. He had flown off toward Fort Logan to gain an altitude of at least 1,000 feet. Then he made two turns in a spiral over the park, reducing his altitude to about 500 feet. The lower left wing of his plane collapsed. He struck the earth outside the fence east of the park on Delaware Street. The machine landed on him. Though he was killed instantly, the souvenir hunters were there almost as fast, collecting the blood-stained splinters of the wreck.[52]

The physical tragedies of Overland Park were matched by living tragedy when Buffalo Bill's Wild West Show was auctioned off in 1913, but since this is described in the next chapter we shall skip to the summer of 1917. From June to September Colorado's National Guard trained intensively at Overland Park, which was renamed Camp Baldwin for the duration of World War I.[53] Denver's pride was Battery B which later saw much action in France as part of the 148th Field Artillery. The First Colorado Cavalry Regiment later became part of the 40th Infantry Division, but when it trained, 1,183 men strong, that summer on the South Platte River its cavalry mounts were housed in the old stables of Overland Park.[54]

After the war the City and County of Denver bought Overland Park, acquiring the first acreage in 1919, and in 1921 buying land from the estate of Henry Wolcott.[55] In 1921 the park was turned into a motor camp for "gypsy motorists," as tourists were called.[56] This was the era when Americans first took to the road in hordes. Tourists motored West, bringing along their living equipment. They settled down for long stays at camps provided by the city at Rocky Mountain Park and City Park and the de luxe Overland Park.[57]

Here the Exposition Building was remodeled for their convenience, with a grocery store, a soda fountain, and a public laundry. A Victrola provided music for small dancing parties, but the main hall could handle 500 dancers. However, in 1923, Mayor Stapleton, urged on by the towns of Englewood and Littleton, banned public dancing. Part of the time the City of Denver hired a camp chaplain. Denver organizations gave concerts and lectures, like the illustrated lecture on wildflowers presented by the Colorado Mountain Club. Officials were happy when some of the motorists who had come to look decided to live in Denver. In 1925 the three Denver camps served 76,000 people.

During this time the last of the big auto races was held at Overland Park. Sponsored by the Press Club in July, 1925, it had publicity. It was a one-hundred-mile race—one hundred times around that mile track—with $10,000 in cash prize money. Eight of the greatest auto racers of the time drove in the race, one handling a Duesenberg with eight cylinders in a row.[58]

This was practically the farewell to the Overland Park race track. In 1930, when the City closed the auto camp, it closed the track. The track was plowed up for the turf of the nine-hole golf course, opened to the public in 1932. In 1957 the course was enlarged to eighteen holes. The present house on the links is of recent date, but cottonwood trees still watch the South Platte flow by, cottonwoods that look as their ancestors looked when Potato Clark planted his first field of potatoes one hundred years ago.

NOTES

Because the history of Overland Park is surprisingly complicated, the following outline may be helpful to the reader:

a. In 1859, homesteaded by Rufus H. (Potato) Clark. Even then it was between historic spots—upstream was Little Dry Creek and Montana City, downstream was Jim Beckworth's farm.

b. In 1883, the promoters of the Denver Circle Railroad bought it, laid out a race track, and changed its name to Jewell Park.

c. In 1887, Denver clubmen bought it and changed its name to Overland Park. Henry Wolcott eventually bought up all shares of the holding corporation. He rented the tracks, the links, and the clubhouse to organizations like the Overland Park Racing Association, Overland Park Club, Overland Park Riding and Driving Club, the

Denver Country Club (for two years, 1901-1902), the Corkscrew Club for its colorful corsos, and the Federation of American Motorcyclists.

d. In 1919, the City and County of Denver commenced to buy land for a park. It rented the race track, also made a camp for motorists.

e. In 1930, Denver opened a nine-hole golf course.

f. In 1957, the course was expanded to eighteen holes.

[1]The ancient road from Santa Fe came into Denver along Cherry Creek. In 1870 General Palmer laid tracks for his D & R G railroad far west of this in the foothills, crossing the divide at Palmer Lake. A wagon road paralleling the rails south of Denver was called Santa Fe Drive until 1904. Then Denver renamed the streets west of Broadway alphabetically, using Indian names: Acoma, Bannock, Cherokee, Delaware, Elati, Fox, Galapago, Huron, Inca, J—what to do for J? Jemez? Jicarilla? But they were Spanish J's, pronounced like H's. The officials chose to honor a Greek gold-rusher—Jason of the Golden Fleece. In 1912 western-minded residents of Jason Street petitioned City Council to restore to Santa Fe Drive that portion of their street south of West Colfax Avenue. About this time the street became the main automobile road to Colorado Springs. Overland Park was the motorists' camp and soon Santa Fe Drive was lined with auto courts. (Sopris, S. T. " 'Santa Fe Drive,' Denver." In *Colorado Magazine*, v. 5, p. 113, June 1928.)

[2]Montana City lasted about a year and then the lumber was re-used in the settlements at the mouth of Cherry Creek.

[3]Two articles on Rufus H. (Potato) Clark, (born 1822, died 1910) were most helpful; one in the *Denver Post* for Dec. 31, 1935; another in *Empire Magazine*, Jan. 2, 1947, by Mrs. J. J. Robbins.

[4]Smith, J. E., "Personal Recollections of Early Denver." In *Colorado Magazine*, v. 20, pp. 62-63, March 1943. Dr. D. F. Richards in August 1958 remembered a tale told about Potato Clark. After his drinking bouts in Denver, someone led him to the Petersburg Ditch. In this Clark walked until he hit a bridge and knew he was near home.

[5]Clark also financed a Methodist seminary on the West Coast of Africa.

[6]Harvey, James, "Cebert Alexander Trease, Engineer." In *Colorado Magazine*, v. 16, p. 223, Nov. 1939.

[7]*Loc. cit.*

[8]The Grant Watson Construction Company, finding Potato Clark's house unsuitable as an office building, pulled it down in 1957.

[9]Cafky, Morris, *Steam Tramways of Denver*. Denver, Rocky Mountain Railroad Club, June, 1950.

[10]*RMN*, April 5. 1883, p. 8, col. 3. Because of this man, Jewell Avenue in South Denver is still spelled with two l's.

[11]*RMN*, May 25, 1883.
[12]*Denver Republican*, May 26, 1883.
[13]*RMN*, June 28, 1883.
[14]*RMN*, July 4, 1883.
[15]*RMN*, July 5, 1883.
[16]*RMN*, May 30, 1884, p. 6, col. 2.
[17]*RMN*, Aug. 7 and 9, 1886.
[18]*Field and Farm*, Sept. 21, 1889.
[19]*Overland Park Club Handbook*, 1898.
[20]*RMN*, Feb. 23, 1899. This party was given by the Overland Riding and Driving Club.
[21]According to Henry Hanington, Henry Wolcott's business manager, in an interview in 1956, 164 acres of Overland Park were sold to the Colorado Agricultural Fair and Racing Association in November, 1915, for $150,000.
[22]Ferril, W. C. ed., *Sketches of Colorado*. Denver, Western Press Bureau Co., 1911, p. 158.
[23]*Denver Post*, June 5, 1934, p. 11B. The first golf course in Colorado was Lord Dunraven's in Estes Park in 1875.
[24]*Denver Times*, Sept. 26, 1900. The winner was Mrs. H. J. O'Bryan.
[25]*Denver Country Club Handbook*, 1901-02.
[26]Manchester was a short-lived hamlet near Overland Park. A paper mill started running there in July, 1891, the Midland Woolen Mills in 1893, and later a cotton mill, south of Overland, was equally unsuccessful. In 1903 the cotton mill took bankruptcy. At the auction of March 3, 1904, twenty carloads of cotton cloth were bought by a St. Louis firm. The newspaper reported that this marked the first time manufactured goods had been shipped from Denver to the Missouri River. Destitute families of unemployed workers were cared for by the city, some of them being housed at Overland Park.

During the reign of the Ku Klux Klan in the 1920's, the vacant cotton mills were infested with white-robed figures gathering for meetings. *RMN*, Feb. 2, 1936. As late as 1940 the "fiery cross" was again burned on Ruby Hill. During Warld War II, James D. Maitland purchased the old 500-foot building at West Evans and South Mariposa and started to manufacture three-inch armor-piercing shot. An explosion started a fire in the southern part of the building on December 19, 1942, causing a half-million dollar loss.
[27]*Denver Republican*, Jan. 10, 1903.
[28]*RMN*, Feb. 2, 1901.
[29]*RMN*, July 7, 1901.
[30]*RMN*, Nov. 23, 1934.
[31]*RMN*, May 28, 1892.

[32]Henry Hanington, interview, 1956.
[33]*RMN,* Dec. 22, 1948.
[34]*Encyclopedia Americana,* 1936 ed., v. 14, p. 408.
[35]*RMN,* May 28, 1914.
[36]*RMN,* June 6, 1889.
[37]*RMN,* June 22, 1900.
[38]Henry Hanington, interview, 1957.
[39]Information about motorcycle races at Overland Park came chiefly from two sources: The *Denver Republican* for July 22 through July 27, 1913; and interviews with M. L. ("Curley") Frederick in August, 1958. That he used board tracks is proved by the splinter cut out of his hand in 1958 which he had acquired from a bowl in 1921.
[40]*Denver Republican,* July 23, 1913.
[41]F. G. Menke's *The New Encyclopedia of Sports* (New York, Barnes, 1947, p. 723) lists "Curley" Frederick among the greats of motorcycle racers.
[42]*Denver Republican,* July 28, 1913.
[43]*Denver Republican,* July 27, 1913. Another article in the same paper attributes slit-skirts and "the undress craze in summer fashion" to women's suffrage militants.
[44]One of the early motor builders and racers of Denver was Arthur B. Heiser. Interview August, 1958.
[45]*Denver Republican,* Sept. 3, 1907.
[46]Barney Oldfield, 1878-1946, first clocked a mile a minute in Indianapolis on June 15, 1903, in a Ford 999. "He stopped off in Denver on the way out to the West Coast in 1904 and broke a number of records there," according to an article called "Wide Open all the Way" in *Saturday Evening Post,* Sept. 19, 1925. In an interview for the *RMN* on May 23, 1946, Barney said he was passing through Denver and a fellow named George Wahlgren, bicyclist, asked him to give a show.
[47]*Denver Post,* Oct. 9, 1914.
[48]Ivy Baldwin was one of Gene Fowler's boyhood heroes, as Fowler tells in *A Solo In Tom-Toms.* New York, Viking, 1946. See also an article on Baldwin by Forrest Crossen in the *Empire Magazine* for January 21, 1951.
[49]Gas was generated by burning iron filings and sulphuric acid. A man was stationed inside the balloon to douse sparks!
[50]*RMN,* Feb. 15, 1909. The papers before and after this date reported the Fair in full.
[51]Ferril, T. H., "When Icarus Came to Denver." In *Rocky Mountain Herald,* June 22, 1940. The author, now Denver's famous poet,

was one of the thousands of boys who wheeled to Overland Park in the mud to see the flight.

[52]Newspapers for Nov. 16-20, 1910.

[53]Major General Frank D. Baldwin, U. S. Army, retired, was the Adjutant General of Colorado in 1917.

[54]The authority on matters military in Colorado is J. H. Nankivell, *History of the Military Organizations of the State of Colorado 1860-1935.* Denver, Kistler, 1935.

[55]Information from the Parks Department of Denver, August, 1958.

[56]Real gypsies, also, used to camp at Overland Park. They hired out to dig dandelions from the lawns of Capitol Hill, Speer Boulevard, and the Country Club district.

[57]Information about these camps, of which the city was proud, may be found in Denver's *Municipal Facts* of the early 1920's.

[58]*The Road,* July, 1925.

Buffalo Bill in Denver

"Ladies and gentlemen! I give you the Wild West and Congress of Rough Riders of the World!"

Without benefit of microphone, Buffalo Bill's baritone voice rang across Arlington Heights at 10th Avenue and Grant Street, Denver, on September 6, 1898. Astride his spirited horse, he swept his Stetson from his shoulder-length hair as he proudly presented his company to Denver. At long last, Denver was to see the show that had taught a new game to children from California to Czechoslovakia, the entrancing game of cowboys and Indians.

The fifty-two cars that carried the show from Cheyenne to Denver employed three locomotives, one for each section. Almost 600 roustabouts and members of the cast were on the train, with Buffalo Bill at ease in his private car. The show unloaded at the Union Depot and was drayed to the vacant lots where the tent was erected.[1]

Water boys could lead the horses to drink from the small ditches running on both sides of Grant Street[2] or to the larger City Ditch that ran, instead of an alley, between Grant and Logan.

The parade—there was always a parade before the show—formed at nine o'clock on the 11th Avenue hill sloping toward Broadway. It marched north on Broadway to the Brown Palace Hotel, then down 17th Street in full view of Longs Peak at the end of the street. The parade turned on Larimer. Coming back, the bands found their second wind as they blasted up 16th Street. The homestretch was on Grant by the unfinished state capitol building, its dome then sheathed in copper. Surely every child in

194

Denver pressured his willing parents to take him to Buffalo Bill's parade. With a modicum of imagination, we today can see the Great Scout on 16th Street, riding his handsome horse—people said that he rode as though he couldn't help it—and shattering glass balls in the air with scatter shot from his rifle.

Performances were at two and eight o'clock, admission fifty cents, children half price, reserved seats one dollar. The tent covered only the audience; the arena was open to the sky. What was rain to cowboys and Indians? On those two September days of 1898 Denver must have produced a Colorado-blue sky for the matinee, bright stars for the evening show.

Let it be understood that Buffalo Bill's Wild West and Congress of Rough Riders of the World was not a circus. "No tinsel," stated the advertisements. In Kansas City, Colonel Cody said he would rather march his whole show off to jail than pay a circus tax. No, sir! His show was educational; it re-enacted history; it was the West.

The odd thing about these statements is that they were partially true. We can verify this by looking at the 1898 program for his Denver performance. After two pages of local advertisements twenty-four acts are listed. Some of them demonstrated the arts of the old West that were almost a thing of the past in 1898— target shooting not only by the Great Plainsman himself but also by Annie Oakley, known as Little Miss Sure Shot, and by Buffalo Bill's beloved foster son, Johnny Baker. Experts whirled lassos and cowboys fanned their bucking horses.[3] Not only American horsemen were featured, but also the audience saw horsemen of other countries. This was educational. A race was staged between an American cowboy, a Cossack from the Caucasus, a Mexican vaquero, a Peruvian gaucho, and a Red Indian, each mounted on a horse from his own country. The race was designed to prove who was the best of the world's riders, and one can guess the outcome.

The date—1898—meant patriotism was at wartime pitch. The show always featured military men on leave from various mounted organizations like the 6th U. S. Cavalry and the Royal Irish Lancers. This year it featured veterans of the Cuban battles on leave until their wounds healed.[4] Along with education the people were encouraged in patriotism.

And then there was history—Western history with cowboys and soldiers and Indians, real Indians (Sioux from the Pine Ridge Reservation)[5] who "whooped 'er up" in the scenes that re-enacted Custer's last rally on the Little Big Horn. The Indians also pursued a young boy who demonstrated the ride of the Pony Express. The most popular number was the Deadwood Mail Coach. As it lumbered across the tanbark, suddenly frenzied Indians attacked it. The driver whipped up his horses, the passengers screamed until help arrived in the person of Buffalo Bill and his intrepid hunters of the plains.

This Deadwood Coach act reveals that audience participation is no invention of the television age. Buffalo Bill always invited prominent people in each town to ride in the coach. In London in 1887, during a command performance for Queen Victoria, the capacious coach was packed with four kings and assorted princesses while the stalwart King of Greece galloped along as outrider. At some performances the passengers' screams were so realistic that the horses actually ran away. It would be interesting to know who rode in the coach in Denver in 1898.

The first evening performance was not a disappointment to the largest audience ever gathered in Denver up to that time. Twenty thousand came, according to the *Times*, 4,000 of whom were turned away. Major Burke, the show's publicity agent, was conservative for once in his statement that every one of the 14,000 seats was filled. Governor Adams and his lady had to duck under ropes to reach their reserved seats.

After two days on Arlington Heights, the Wild West rolled south to Colorado Springs, Pueblo, and Trinidad. The show returned to Denver many times after this glorious première. In 1902, when it was already starting to advertise its farewell appearance, Mrs. Crawford Hill gave a dinner "after which mobiles conveyed the party to the Wild West Show."[6] Each year thereafter the show diminished both in size and glamour until, in 1913, it expired in Overland Park.

Now, 1898 was not the first time Bill Cody had ever seen Den-

196

Copyrighted, 1895, by BEADLE AND ADAMS.   ENTERED AS SECOND CLASS MATTER AT THE NEW YORK, N. Y., POST OFFICE.   February 25, 1895.

No. 851.   Published Every Wednesday.   *Beadle & Adams, Publishers,*   Ten Cents a Copy.   **Vol. LXVI.**
98 WILLIAM STREET, NEW YORK. $5.00 a Year.

OR, THE

Great Scout's Big Three

A ROMANCE OF

THE PONY RIDERS of the OVERLAND.

BY COL. PRENTISS INGRAHAM,
AUTHOR OF "BUFFALO BILL" NOVELS, ETC.

CHAPTER I.
THE MYSTERIOUS WARNING.

"IF Buffalo Bill had not just made a double run because Jess Jordan was killed, he'd make the ride, boys."

"Well, plucky as I admit Buffalo Bill is—and none but a liar would say he wasn't—

BUFFALO BILL SEIZED THE LA ... AND WENT UP HAND OVER HAND.

This is the cover page of one of the many dime novels written by Colonel Prentiss Ingraham with Buffalo Bill as the hero. In real life, the Great Scout was better known for his feats on the plains than on cliffs! (*Denver Public Library*.)

This picture of Buffalo Bill on the chestnut "Duke" was taken about 1902, a few years before the middle-aged showman started to frequent Denver. "Duke" was a present from General Nelson Miles, the Indian fighter, who admired Colonel Cody. Note the saddle. The Great Showman never burdened his mounts with saddles heavy with silver. (*Denver Public Library.*)

2932 Lafayette St., Denver, Colorado. The facing on the lower walls was added in 1955, but the woodwork is the same as it was when Buffalo Bill died in the front room behind the upper porch at five minutes past noon on January 10, 1917. (Photo by Harry Smith, 1956. *Denver Public Library*.)

On June 3, 1917, five months after Buffalo Bill died, a white hearse carried his body to the top of Lookout Mountain, west of Golden. There he still lies buried despite protests from Wyoming and Nebraska, who consider him their property. Because they threatened body-snatching, the Denver Parks Department covered his coffin with tons of concrete reinforced with iron bars. (Photo by Ed Hickish. *State Historical Society of Colorado.*)

ver.[7] He himself said, and the *Dictionary of American Biography* accepts his statement, that he came to Denver, alone, in the 1859 gold rush, aged thirteen. Well—maybe so—but, as the *Dictionary* adds, "He dealt with facts in a large, free way."

William Frederick Cody was born in Iowa on February 26, 1846. He died seventy-one years later at 2932 Lafayette Street, Denver, if a legend as strong as Buffalo Bill can be said to die. Alive or dead, he was always the center of controversy.[8] For instance, did he or did he not ride for the Pony Express? Had he fearlessly killed many Indians or was the only Indian he ever killed too sick to care? All authorities agree that, as an army dispatch rider, he rode (walking when he lost his mount) 350 miles in less than 60 hours. As a scout he is said to have had the sharpest eyes and best sense of direction of any man on the plains. As a hunter some contend he was mighty; others assert he was merely a buffalo butcher hired by Goddard Brothers, meat contractors, to feed the construction gangs of the Kansas Pacific Railroad.

> Buffalo Bill! Buffalo Bill!
> Never missed and never will,
> Always aims and aims to kill
> And the Company pays his Buffalo bill.[9]

Denver men who remember Colonel Cody in his old age are divided in their opinion—was this man who walked the streets of Denver an interesting, dignified, elderly gentleman, or merely a flamboyant old fraud?

Everyone agrees on his good looks, especially as a young man when he was "discovered" at Fort McPherson, Nebraska, by the dime novelist Ned Buntline. Presently a serial started running in Street & Smith's magazine entitled *Buffalo Bill, King of the Border Men, the Wildest, Truest Story I Ever Told.*[10] It is said in Nebraska that no one waited more eagerly for the next installment of this tale than young Bill Cody.

Buntline, having discovered pay dirt, proceeded to work his mine. Then Prentiss Ingraham took over the rich vein and turned out Buffalo Bill novels by the dozens. The hero of the novels signed forty-seven of them himself, some of which he wrote.[11] Copies of these flimsy sheets must still be hidden in attics of old Denver homes where boys read and cherished them.

After he was discovered, Bill Cody went east to act in the melodramas Ned Buntline whipped up for him. In the late 1870's Colorado saw some of these hall-shows. At Central City a cultured critic was pained to note that the audience overflowed the opera house of that town to see "a third rate dramatic company . . . Buffalo Bill was remarkably fine but the support simply vile."[12]

The title of this melodrama was *May Cody, or Lost and Won*. The plot centered on a white maiden captured by Red Indians. "Thank Heaven!" cried the maiden, looking off stage, "Buffalo Bill has come! See the red devils quail before the terrible avenger!"[13]

On cue and a spirited horse, in rode the handsome hero, all six feet four inches of him clad in fringed white buckskin and red shirt. According to one authority, his eyes matched the color of his gold-brown hair (also his imperial and his moustache).[14] Sometimes on a summer evening of today, the ghost of Buffalo Bill rides his horse between the audience and the Metropolitan opera stars as they bring classical music back to Central City.

In 1884 Buffalo Bill was in "big time," with a supporting cast no longer vile, thanks to Major Burke, publicity agent, and Nate Salsbury, manager.[15] Buffalo Bill's Wild West and Congress of Rough Riders of the World toured America and then crossed the Atlantic for a four-year circuit. They made hundreds of one-night stands in Europe, staying longer in the cities.[16] Today, European visitors to the Denver Public Library, nostalgic for the days when Buffalo Bill introduced cowboys, Indians, and popcorn balls to the Continent, usually ask to see material about "Boofalo Beel."

As we have seen, in 1898 Cody got homesick and brought the show from its Old World triumphs to play in the small western towns of his youth. The Wild West continued to flourish until after the death of Nate Salsbury in 1904. Colonel Cody's only knowledge of money being limited to its expenditure, the show slipped down grade under his management. One winter, after an especially bad season when the horses all had epizootic, the Colonel borrowed $20,000 from H. H. Tammen and F. G. Bonfils, owners of the *Denver Post*. Tammen also owned the Sells-Floto Circus. For his beloved circus nothing was too good and he wanted Buffalo Bill. This is the way he got him:

On July 20, 1913, Buffalo Bill rode down 16th Street in Denver in his open buggy at the head of the parade of his show which was now combined with Pawnee Bill's outfit.[17] It wasn't much of a parade, nor was the performance much like the great show of 1898. When the show was ready to hit the road, the sheriff refused to let it leave town until it paid its bills, $86,000 worth of them. First there was the printing bill of $66,000 owing to the United States Printing and Lithography Company of Chicago; then a claim, filed by Attorney Bottom of Denver, for $20,000 from Tammen and Bonfils of the *Denver Post*.[18]

There was no money, not even to pay the company. About seventy-five people were still stranded in Denver after arrangements were made to send 114 Indians back to the Pine Ridge Reservation, where they arrived without their headdresses or beaded vests, having sold them for food. Some of the girls were sent home by means of the proceeds of the benefit the company gave at Overland Park during the motorcycle races. The man who owned the animals complained because the sheriff had seized them and placed them in the Sells-Floto quarters. Then the freaks complained because the animals were being fed and they were not. When the freaks were fortunate enough to get any food, they gave half to the fat girl since her chances of a job depended on her intake. With such publicity the papers were not exactly helpful to the stranded players.

In the middle of August the property of the show was moved to the barns at Overland Park and a notice of a Sheriff's Sale appeared in the papers.[19] The first two attempts to auction the property were snarled in legal red tape. It was not until the fifteenth of September that the sale was completed.[20]

Piece by piece, the show was auctioned off, animal by animal, until the 200 riding horses, the 143 draft horses, the yoke of sacred cattle, the 6 camels (they went to Missouri), the 45 railroad cars, the lumber, the 80 lengths of blue seats—everything was gone. Miller's 101 Ranch Show was the heaviest buyer. Tammen paid $915 for three spans of mules and spent a total of $2,800 at the auction, but what he was after, and got, did not appear on the bill of sale. Colonel William Cody—"Buffalo Bill in person"—was riding in the Sells-Floto Circus even before the completion of the auction.[21] For the seasons of 1914 and 1915 Buffalo Bill continued to ride in Tammen's circus, at $100 a day. There seems to be some doubt as to whether Tammen ever collected the $20,000 loan. Later, when the going was really hard for the Great Scout, it is said that Tammen provided him with pocket money.[22]

During his connection with the *Denver Post* owners, Colonel Cody often sat at the head of the steps leading to the editorial rooms of the paper at 1544 Champa Street, on Saturday mornings, to tell stories to spellbound boys and girls.[23] The story hour over, the children would follow their hero to the door of the Albany Hotel bar. His figure was still straight even in his late sixties, his clothes immaculate, his broad hat at the correct angle above his white hair (which was rumored to be a wig). Though not always sober, Colonel Cody was always the gentleman. His favorite swear words were "Dog-my-cats."

In 1915 Buffalo Bill toured the East in the 101 Ranch Show. He took his last public bow at Portsmouth, Virginia, on November 11, 1916. By this time Johnny Baker, his devoted protégé, had to lift the old man on his horse before the act and catch him as he dismounted, but in the arena Buffalo Bill overcame his arthritis and still rode as though he couldn't help it.

In January, 1917, the Colonel went to Glenwood Springs to take the hot baths. En route from there to his Wyoming ranch he became very ill. He stopped off in Denver and went to his sister, Mrs. Louis Decker, who put him to bed in the northwest room, second floor, of her home at 2932 Lafayette Street. His wife and daughter arrived one midnight and were motored to the house. Johnny Baker was sent for. Boy Scouts took turns waiting on the front porch in case of errands. The newsmen hung around the house, interviewing everyone who went in or out. They headlined the prognostications of the doctor who said on January 8th that Cody would not live through the night "because of the bio-dynamics resulting from the eclipse of the moon."[24] On January 9th he was still alive, asking for Johnny Baker. On January 10, 1917, at five minutes past noon, Buffalo Bill went to the happy hunting grounds.

Now the Speer administration was not one to ignore an opportunity. Publicity man Ed McMechen had an idea. W. T. R. Mills, Manager of Parks and Improvements, was delegated to meet with a committee of Elks, Masons, and friends of Colonel Cody, selected by the widow and Mrs. Decker.[25] The committee decided to hold a public funeral in Denver and later to bury the body on a foothill west of Denver, his tomb to be classified as an improvement for the Denver Mountain Parks. From Lookout Mountain, they said, his spirit could gaze toward his beloved plains of Nebraska, Wyoming, and Kansas. (General Carr of the U. S. Cavalry once said that Cody's eyesight was better than field glasses.)

Elaborate plans were made for the funeral, to which Mills especially invited the children of Denver.[26] On Sunday Buffalo Bill's body lay in a glass-covered casket on a purple couch at the foot of the stairs beneath the golden dome of the state capitol building from ten o'clock till noon and a little after, while Denver filed past. An estimated 18,000 people viewed the body. The doors closed on frustrated thousands standing in line in the bitter cold.[27]

That afternoon the funeral procession marched down 16th Street to California, then to the Elks Building on 14th Street. Procession is not the word—it was a parade. There were uniforms, military, Masonic, Elk, Knight Templar; Indians in war paint; people who had come by crowded trains from Kansas, Nebraska, and Wyoming; governors and ex-governors; and Johnny Baker, who had been unable to reach Denver in time to say good-bye to his lifetime hero. Bands played the Colonel's favorite song, "Tenting Tonight on the Old Camp Ground." The flag-draped[28] casket lay on a caisson and was followed by the traditional horse with an empty saddle. Those who knew the famous showman best half expected him to rise up and shoot glass balls as in the old parades on 16th Street.

From January to June, 1917, Colonel Cody's body waited in a crypt in Olinger's Mortuary in North Denver. On June 3rd, another parade of autos drove up the road that winds to the top of Lookout Mountain. Friends watched as the steel casket was lowered into the grave that had been blasted out of solid granite.[29]

But peace did not descend on Lookout Mountain. From Nebraska and Wyoming rolled mutterings against their hero's body being buried in Colorado, mutterings that caused the apprehensive Denver Parks Department to pour concrete over the casket, the concrete being reinforced with iron rails. This covering proved a nuisance when Mrs. Cody died, leaving a request that she be buried with her husband.[30] With great effort, the cement was broken and Louisa Cody's coffin placed on top of the Colonel's, an ironic situation considering the years Buffalo Bill had spent avoiding his wife.

The mutterings from Wyoming swelled to a roar in August, 1948, when the American Legion Post of Cody offered $10,000 to anyone who would bring Buffalo Bill back to Wyoming where, they said, he had wished to be buried.[31] Rallying to the defense, a Denver American Legion Post stood guard over the grave, night and day.[32] Under its tons of cement (some say seven tons, some say up to ten) the body remained unmolested and no blood was shed, but the mutterings still persist.

Colonel and Mrs. Cody lie under a simple bronze marker despite periodic agitations for a mausoleum.[33] Over the grave waves an American flag. Through the iron fence that surrounds the spot, tourists toss pennies or hairpins. The money goes toward buying new flags and maintaining the area.

Nearby is a museum, called by Buffalo Bill's Indian name, Pahaska, which means Long Hair.[34] This museum exhibits mementos connected with Buffalo Bill and sells curios. Admirers of the great showman visit his grave and Pahaska Tepee in such numbers as to prove the contention of Lee Casey, astute Denver columnist, that if Buffalo Bill "wasn't truly a great man, millions think he was and that amounts to the same thing."[35]

The Western History Department of the Denver Public Library owns the extensive Nate Salsbury Collection of Buffalo Billiana. It includes books, pamphlets, scrapbooks of press notices, programs, posters, photographs, original letters, dime novels, and an entrancing cardboard cut-out depicting some of the acts of the Wild West Show.

[1] Publicity was skilfully inserted in the Denver papers by Major Burke before and after the Wild West Show on September 6 and 7, 1898. One item obviously not furnished by Burke, the publicity agent, concerned a tragedy. One of the waiters of the show's kitchen shot one of the coffee makers. A twenty-five-dollar purse, collected from the help, was dedicated to the coffee maker if he recovered, to his funeral expenses if he died. *Denver Republican*, Sept. 7, 1898, p. 6.

[2] See Slice II, "The City Ditch." Water was still running in the gutters of Grant and Logan Street in 1898, according to J. C. Smiley in his *History of Denver*. Denver, Times-Sun, 1901, p. 375.

[3] Rome went wild when the American cowboys rode the Duke of Sermonita's horses which had been raised in the Pontine Marshes, according to the *Cincinnati Daily Gazette* for March 5, 1890.

[4] Colonel Cody offered himself and his outfit to the army in the Spanish-American War. Some of his horses were accepted and actually landed in Cuba. Teddy Roosevelt lifted the name Rough Riders from the Wild West Show.

[5] Always confronting the manager of the Wild West Show was the problem of homesick Indians. Toward the end of Buffalo Bill's career, Indians refused to hire out to him. Frink, Maurice, "Buffalo Bill's Last Raid on the Sioux." In *Empire Magazine*, Aug. 27, 1957.

[6] *RMN*, Aug. 8, 1902.

[7] One of the local legends that has no factual base, according to Caroline Bancroft, is that Buffalo Bill was in Denver at the ball given for Grand Duke Alexis of Russia in January, 1872. Had he been in town, Cody would not have danced with the belles because the hired help would not have been invited.

[8] Of the numerous books on Cody's life, one of the most careful studies is *The Making of Buffalo Bill; A Study in Heroics*, by R. J. Walsh in collaboration with M. S. Salsbury. Indianapolis, Bobbs-Merrill, 1928.

[9] *RMN*, Oct. 30, 1921.

[10] The serial began Dec. 23, 1869.

[11] Johannsen, Albert, *The House of Beadle and Adams and its Dime and Nickel Novels*. Norman, Univ. of Oklahoma, 1950, v. 2 p. 173.

[12] *Central City Register-Call*, July 31, 1879.

[13]This is paraphrased from an article in the *Denver Post,* Dec. 13, 1903, and has no documentary validity.

[14]Fellows, D. W. and Freeman, A. A., *This Way to the Big Show.* New York, Viking, 1936, p. 64.

[15]Salsbury, Nate, "The Origin of the Wild West Show." In *Colorado Magazine,* v. 32, pp. 204-14, July 1955.

[16]Itineraries of the show in Europe are among the items in the Nate Salsbury Collection.

[17]From July 20 through the end of the auction in September, 1913, the Denver newspapers carried articles about Buffalo Bill and his troubles. Anyone wanting a detailed account of the Denver parade should read an article in the *Denver Republican* for July 21, 1913. The reporter heard a woman describing the parade to some blind children.

[18]*Denver Republican,* July 24, 1913.

[19]*Denver Republican,* Aug. 20, 1913, p. 9.

[20]*Denver Republican,* Sept. 15, 1913.

[21]*Denver Post,* Sept. 3, 1913, p. 1, col. 6. In October Colonel Cody was happily escorting the Prince of Monaco on a hunt in Wyoming.

[22]Albert G. Birch of the *Denver Post.* Interview, 1956.

[23]Chauncey Thomas in *Outdoor Life,* May, 1917.

[24]*RMN,* Jan. 8, 1917 ff. The Cody deathbed story appeared in all local newspapers in detail and was headlined all over the world.

[25]In the *Rocky Mountain News* for Jan. 8, 1917, Buffalo Bill was said to have asked the Elks and Masons to select his final resting place. More about the selection of Lookout Mountain appeared on January 11. On that same day the *Denver Times* reported: "The decision to bury Colonel Cody on Lookout Mountain was made yesterday when Mayor Speer sent word to the family that the city desired to pay tribute to Buffalo Bill . . . by tendering a burial place that overlooks the great stretches of country which once were not dotted with peaceful homes . . . but were covered with cactus . . . etc." See also Lee Casey in *RMN,* Dec. 18, 1950.

[26]*RMN,* Jan. 13, 1917. After the services the floral tributes were broken up in order to give a flower to each school child in Denver.

[27]*RMN,* Jan. 15, 1917. The *News* gave committee names and lists of mourners. The *Denver Post* obituaries were eulogies by Courtney Ryley Cooper and Gene Fowler, who even contributed a verse.

[28]The flag was used because Cody had been an army scout during the Indian wars, and was an officer in the militia.

[29]*RMN,* June 4, 1917. The Masons of Golden held the services.

[30]*Municipal Facts,* Nov.-Dec. 1921, p. 14. Mrs. Cody's last letter asked for this.

[31]H. B. Sill and Victor Weybright state in their *Buffalo Bill and the*

Wild West (New York, Oxford, 1955, p. 254) that a will was found dated New York, 1907. In this Cody asked to be buried on Cedar Mountain above his Wyoming ranch with a native red sandstone statue of a buffalo above his grave. To date, no buffalo stands above his Colorado grave or on Cedar Mountain, but in Cody, Wyoming, there is a statue of Buffalo Bill on "Smoky" made in 1924 by C. V. Whitney.

[32]*RMN*, Aug. 1, 1948.

[33]The marker was erected October, 1918. Collections toward a large monument over the grave have been made. The children of the Maple Grove School in Arapahoe County sent forty buffalo nickels to the *Denver Post* for this purpose. *Denver Post*, Jan. 15, 1917. At the beginning of the first World War, Teddy Roosevelt requested that the project be put off. *Denver Post*, Dec. 4, 1917, p. 1. At present a trust fund for a monument is in the estate of Mrs. Johnny Baker. The city will make a decision about its expenditure when the estate is settled.

[34]Johnny Baker, Cody's foster son, asked the city if he could run a museum near the grave of Buffalo Bill on Lookout Mountain. In 1921 Pahaska Tepee was erected to be managed by Baker and later by his widow. The exhibits were willed to the city. The building was remodeled in 1957, the parking lots enlarged. It is now a concession, part of the income reverting to the city. (This information and part of that in the previous note came from the Denver Parks Department in August, 1958.)

[35]*RMN*, Apr. 2, 1946.

Elitch's Gardens

Just inside the gate of the Gardens the genial mayor of Denver, Wolfe Londoner, stood in the rain on a barrel which he resembled in shape, and waited for the signal to deliver the opening address. The gate opened, the crowds surged in, the signal was given, but few people heard the mayor's talk because Bandmaster Satriano thought the signal was his. The mayor's oratory was spoiled but not the day.[1] Soon the sun came out, creating diamonds on the apple blossoms, and the animals in the well-stocked zoo frisked after the rain. Everyone admired the flowers; the nautically inclined paddled canoes on the lake;[2] children rode the merry-go-round; and in the afternoon all gathered to see the free vaudeville show in the "Theatorium," a roundish structure with a roof but no sides. The newspapers commented on the fine view from this open theater, a view of "fair Berkeley and the distant Rockies on the horizon," at which the audience "said oh and ah just like they do at a display of fire works."[3]

Weatherwise, one of the traditions of Denver is cold rain on the day Elitch's Gardens opens. The tradition started that opening May Day of 1890, when John and Mary Elitch stood at the gate at what is now 36th[4] and Tennyson and searched the drenched plains to the southeast where Denver lay five miles distant. They feared that even their friends would not come to celebrate the opening of their amusement park which they had been preparing for two years. But the friends came—practically all Denver came. They were late because the mud slowed the horses and the bicycles. Even the steam train was late, the little locomotive with its open trailer for passengers.[5]

For almost seventy summers Elitch's Gardens has continued to provide amusement to the "respectable, orderly and moral people of Denver."[6] The effort to keep a public park orderly is demonstrated in the history of its dance floor. It was not opened to public dancing until 1920. Before that, clubs or classes used it.[7] This public dancing—to famous name bands like those of Glen Miller and Benny Goodman[8]—is closely supervised, and too much exuberance on the large floor of the Trocadero is controlled by a tap on the shoulder. A famous tap was on the shoulder of a young man who was dancing the newly invented "Turkey Trot" with his niece, a Denver girl named Mamie Doud. This was before she married Lt. Eisenhower.[9]

That Elitch's has always managed to be respectable and yet fun may be attributed to the original proprietor, Mary Elitch, who lived in the Gardens from 1890 to within a few years of her death in 1936. She had a warm personality, a large mouth which smiled readily; she loved children and animals; she had a keen sense of propriety and was stage-struck.

Mary Elitch had been strictly reared in California in a Lutheran household and educated in a Roman Catholic convent.[10] At church one day she met a young athlete, John Elitch, with Alabaman charm and black curly hair.[11] In 1872, without her father's consent, they were married in San Jose. On their honeymoon she saw her first play.

The very young couple settled in San Francisco, where John helped his father run a lunch counter in a theater building.[12] There John was spellbound by the show business. He soon invested in a vaudeville act and lost all his money.

About 1880 he came to Denver and ran a lunch counter at the Arcade Saloon until he heard of the boom town, Durango. Using his herculean strength, he crossed the snowy San Juan Mountains with a sheet-iron stove strapped to his back and arrived in Durango in time to elegantly feed the rich town promoters.[13] The money he made there he invested in a vaudeville act and lost it all.

Back in Denver, John and his father opened a restaurant on

211

Curtis Street.[14] In 1886 they moved to 1541 Arapahoe Street. This was quite an establishment. John decorated it with oil paintings by his wife, life-sized statues, and twining ivy. It was even equipped with electricity. They called it Elitch's Palace.[15]

The fifty-foot kitchen of the Arapahoe Street Palace enhanced John Elitch's reputation as a caterer. One of the clubs for which he cooked terrapin and other gourmet dishes honored his art by naming itself the Gout Club.[16] Among his patrons were all the athletes of Denver, who admired his muscles and his cooking.[17]

John wanted to invest the money he earned at the Palace in a vaudeville act, but Mary persuaded him to start an amusement park which would include his beloved vaudeville shows. After weeks of investigating sites in every direction from little Denver, they bought the Chilcott Farm beyond the town of Highlands (North Denver).

The Chilcott Farm appealed to the Elitches because Mrs. Chilcott, eight years before, with her own hands had planted rows of apple trees and bordered the sixteen acres of land with cottonwoods. To these the Elitches added a vegetable garden to furnish the Palace Restaurant with fresh produce. John planted hardwood trees and Mary started extensive flower gardens. The farm had good water rights, and in two years, by zealous irrigating, their house on the plains was surrounded by summer greenery.

They were so busy installing amusement features in their park, like a merry-go-round, that they sold Elitch's Palace Restaurant in 1888.[18] For the Gardens they collected a first-class zoo. John organized a vaudeville company with much pleasure. His interest in muscles led him to hire "Mons. Testo" who pitted his strength against that of two draft horses.[19] With gardens, animals, games, and vaudeville, their first summer, 1890, netted them $35,000.

With this money John, true to his pattern, took the vaudeville company on the road. This time the venture was succesful, but John became ill in California. Mary joined him there and was by his side when he died in March, 1891.[20]

Mary Elitch returned to Denver where she made the momentous decision to continue Elitch's by herself. To acquire money she sold subscription books, shares one dollar each, in the Elitch

Amusement Company. Her advertisement sprawled over eleven columns of the paper. It shows the feminine approach to business: "Both the rich and the poor, the fatherless, the widow and the orphan are advised and invited to invest their piles as well as their mites in this Company. WHY? Do you ask? BECAUSE . . ."[21]

Enough piles and mites poured into the company to enable Mrs. Elitch to keep the Gardens. Until the mortgage was foreclosed in 1916, she enjoyed her reputation as the only woman zoo keeper in the world and as a theatrical promoter of good judgment.

Her judgment was at fault in 1900 when she married Thomas D. Long, a man who had been her assistant for some time. They took a round-the-world wedding tour, collecting curios, but in a few years Mary was again managing the Gardens alone. Though she was never divorced, she was known thereafter as Mrs. Mary Elitch Long.

Let us return to 1891 when Widow Mary undertook to manage the Gardens. The first season or so she continued John's plan of showing vaudeville in the open-air theater. Presently she closed the sides of the building.[22] The walls blocked off the view as well as some of the noise from the amusement park. From vaudeville she turned to light opera with stock companies not only at Elitch's but also at Manhattan Beach, a rival amusement park on Sloan's Lake whose theater she managed for some years.

In 1897, she started a dramatic stock company[23]—no singing— which opened in a new play every Sunday night during the summer. This still happens. Today, Elitch's is the oldest continuously run summer stock theater in the United States. The outer lobby of the theater is lined with portraits of actors who have played there, such as Helen Mencken, Fredric March, Blanche Bates, two Denver boys named Harold Lloyd and Douglas Fairbanks, and, in 1951, a very pretty ingénue namd Grace Kelly.[24]

Mrs. Elitch hired competent directors. She helped them choose actors and plays in New York every spring, securing rights to both current and classical plays. Four of the original New York cast came to play in *Trilby* in 1899. That was the same year that *Cyrano de Bergerac* was produced at Elitch's with a hundred in the cast. Many Denver people acted as extras in this show.

Each summer, before or after the regular season, Mrs. Elitch provided an extra treat for theater-loving Denver. In 1905 the treat was Minnie Maddern Fiske and her troupe who played for a week. The next year Sarah Bernhardt came. For her the regular actors cheerfully played bit parts and ever after boasted that they had walked the boards with the immortal Sarah.[25]

So, in mid-continent Denver, summer theater became a tradition. One of the local rites of spring was—and is—the purchase of season tickets to Elitch's theater. In May, 1912, at least fifty-two women waited all night at the Tabor box office to get choice season tickets for Elitch's.[26]

The Gardens stage switched with ease from top professionals to the seniors of Miss Wolcott's School of Denver who presented a classical play, usually Shakespearian, every May. (The theater, unheated, was often cold that spring afternoon.) [27] The play was a climax to the annual field day when parents watched their daughters play games in white middy blouses, voluminous bloomers, and long black stockings. Miss Wolcott, head mistress, came to Elitch's in her electromobile.[28] Some girls came in a tallyho.

Music, also, both professional and amateur, was part of the Elitch tradition. The afternoon concerts in the lovely gardens gave them a Continental air. Friday afternoon was symphony concert time. Mothers bribed their children into music appreciation on Fridays by picnics before and merry-go-round rides after the concert. Serious music students formed the Symphony Club which, under Florence Taussig, studied on Tuesday the program scheduled for Friday.[29]

Music sweeter to the ear of the young shrilled from the steam calliope of the merry-go-round. (Its canvas sides were painted with European scenes.) The wooden animals have worn out and been replaced a number of times. The 1905 models cost $15,000 and whirled to music from "melodious pipes." The 1946 replacement cost three times that much because the management still insisted on hand-carved animals—but whirls to the music of records.[30]

214

Sadder to the older generation than the passing of the steam calliope is the lack of rings on the new merry-go-round. These rings were placed in a hollow tube which was fastened to a stationary part of the outer fence of the merry-go-round. A child could lean far out and grab a ring as he passed. The rings were usually iron but sometimes when the child looked in his hand he found a gold one. In that case, he had a free ride. The rings are no longer there. Too dangerous, say insurance men.

Mrs. Elitch did not consider ring-grabbing dangerous or she would not have allowed it. She was a careful baby sitter for hundreds of Denver children. Tuesday was children's day. All day long the electric trolley cars which replaced the steam trains jangled from the city. They were crowded with children climbing off or on at the Elitch gate. Non-sissies preferred to ride the open-air trailers whose seats ran lengthwise. There they could kick their short legs into space, not always missing the conductor who walked along the bottom step collecting fares.

All day on Tuesdays Mrs. Elitch played with the children, many of whom were not accompanied by grown people. She showed them the flowers, made the animals do tricks for them, taught them to dance, and even imported Ute Indians to instruct them in handicraft.[31]

She published a magazine for them, *The Child's Companion.* About 1906 this became part of her *Elitch's Weekly.*[32] Illustrated with photographs of the doings in the Gardens, the weekly combined publicity for Elitch's with pure reading matter for Denver homes. The tone may be deduced from a 1911 issue which, along with its usual caption, "no liquor served, no public dancing permitted," warned children that last year's Teddy Bear had grown up and should be addressed as Theodore Bruin.

Today Elitch's miniature train is pulled by gasoline engines disguised as Diesels.[33] The original steam train that tooted its way into the hearts of Denver young from 1895 to 1936 was smaller—twelve-inch gauge—and circled the theater. The original train was built by a man named Felker but later trains were built, owned, and operated by Frank Root.[34] One of the engines was 6' 7½" long and weighed 450 pounds. No wonder children thought Engineer Root loomed as big as a giant as he sat in the open cab with his hand on the throttle. The engine puffed coal smoke with authentic cinders to spot starched clothes. Frank Root had no children of his own. "My locomotives are my children," he used to say as he repainted his equipment in the winter, using his hand instead of a paint brush. After his death in 1936, the rolling stock and tracks were sold for $700 and shipped away from Denver. Who knows where?[35]

Another amusement beloved by Denver was the Old Mill. Out front was a large wheel that stirred the water in a ditch a foot or so deep, three or four feet wide. This canal ran a winding course through a tunnel-like structure. Shallow boats drifted through in complete darkness, scary to children, most opportune for lovers. Occasionally the boat drifted by a brightly lighted alcove in which was reproduced some fairyland scene. It would glow for a short time before the boat again entered the darkness. This Old Mill was in use before 1906, just how long before is uncertain, but its closing date is definite. On July 16, 1944, on Sunday afternoon, the Old Mill caught fire and six people died of monoxide poisoning. The Old Mill was not rebuilt.[36]

The roller coaster at Elitch's is a thrill. What may have been its ancestor was something which Mrs. Elitch found in Paris in 1905 and which she copied for her Gardens. Her description of the Parisian Helter-Skelter shows she was not above a little cheese cake:

"The first requisite to proper helter-skeltering is a pair of pretty, and well-shod ankles. You tuck your dress securely around you, seat yourself in the miniature toboggan, and take a firm hold and a deep breath and bang! you are off skimming through space at a perilous rate, banking around curves until you helter-skelter wildly in on the home stretch and land with a thud at the bottom of the slide."[37]

A less lady-like contraption was advertised in 1914 as "The Automatic Tango" which made you "dance the latest terpsichorean fads in spite of yourself," but usually the emphasis was on refinement. Even the "navel specticle of the Sinking of the Titanic" was advertised in June 1914 as "cheerful and heroic, not

216

Though many formal portraits of Mary Elitch are available, this picture seems to best illustrate the smile, the neatness of dress, and the interest in animal life of "the charming gentlewoman owner of Elitch's Gardens and Zoo." The ostrich was famous because once a day he ran a race with a cyclist. Hitched to a cart, the ostrich also pulled Mrs. Elitch around the Gardens. The bird died in agony in 1897 when a convention of bicycle salesmen fed him their celluloid identification buttons, complete with pins. (Photo from *Experiences of the Only Woman in the World Who Owns and Manages a Zoo,* by Mrs. John Elitch, Jr., n.d., p. 47, *Denver Public Library.*)

Elitch's Gardens has had a succession of gates. The first one was at Canby (West 36th Avenue) and Tennyson; the next on Prospect Avenue (West 38th) about where the present auto entrance stands. The next two, pictured here, were on the corner of West 38th and Tennyson. The rustic gate was replaced by the gate with the angels in 1909. This stood until 1958. Through these gates, and the modern one, have passed the happiest children in Denver. (Both photos by L. C. McClure. *Denver Public Library.*)

This early sketch of the theater at Elitch's shows why it was originaly called an open air theater. Mrs. Elitch soon enclosed the first floor against the chill of Denver summer evenings, then boxed in the second floor promenade. Nevertheless, the toot of the little train and the tunes of the merry-go-round still seep through the walls during dramatic moments on stage. The fence at the bottom of the picture enclosed the original bear pit. (The picture below is by L. C. McClure. Both pictures are from the *Denver Public Library*.)

This curtain may be the one that was raised on "Hélène," the first play, 1897, given by the first Elitch's stock company. The curtain is still in use and practically any old-timer in Denver can quote the verse lettered beneath the hedged-and-hollyhocked cottage:

> Ann Hathaway's cottage
> A mile away
> Shakespeare sought
> At close of day.

The original little train at Elitch's was little! Its track circled the theater. (Photo by Paul H. Berra. *Denver Public Library.*)

The merry-go-round was bought from the Philadelphia Tobaggan Company to be installed at Elitch's Gardens in 1905. It's handsome horses carried Denver children round and round and up and down to the loud music of a band organ. Replaced at Elitch's in 1928, this antique still operates at Burlington, a town in Kit Carson County on the eastern Colorado line. (Photo by *Gwen Goldsberry. Denver Public Library.*)

gruesome."[38] This unique interpretation of tragedy lasted until the first week in August when the building burned. No one in the Gardens was injured because the circular walls of the empty building fell inward.[39]

Mrs. Elitch, always eager for the latest in amusement, proudly presented the Edison Vitascope to a select group of friends on August 14, 1896. These were the first moving pictures shown in Denver.[40] The next day the public at both Elitch's and Manhattan Beach saw the Vitascope. Mrs. Elitch shipped movies hot from the battle fields of Cuba and the Philippines in 1898, showing them on something called the Waragraph, and at Elitch's, Denver saw its first movie of the Passion Play.

Though the drama evicted vaudeville from the theater, various acrobatic and animal acts performed outdoors, including midgets, dog shows, and the man who jumped a chasm in his automobile. Almost every Saturday and every Sunday of the summers from 1890 to 1907 Ivy Baldwin made a balloon ascent. Ivy Baldwin was a little, lithe man who varied his balloon routine by doing stunts on a trapeze as he went aloft. In 1902 he parachuted to earth for the first time.[41] One Fourth of July he slid down the rope of the captive balloon with his non-asbestos suit ablaze with fireworks and spent the next week recovering from his burns.[42]

In 1905 bears from the Elitch zoo made daily descents down a rope hitched to the balloon. This brings us to the Elitch's Gardens zoo. A good one it was! It included imported animals as well as local, such as the last buffalo calf captured in Kit Carson County, Colorado.[43] A rare albino buffalo named Kelly was allowed to roam the Gardens. The elephant was called Jess, the lion Rex. The lioness, named Gladys, was so tame that she rode on a float in the 1896 parade of the Mountain and Plain Festival. The float illustrated the proverb, "The lion and the lamb shall lie down together." Accounts do not specify whether the lamb was stuffed or alive at the beginning of the parade.

The first seals ever born in captivity (according to publicity) lived a year; after their death their heart-broken mother sank to the bottom of the pool and drowned (according to publicity).[44] There were monkeys, sometimes dressed in pink or blue pajamas.

221

There were mountain sheep, camels, kangaroos, and a white polar bear named Willie. Mrs. Elitch loved the animals, alive or dead. During their life she let them wander around her house;[45] and after their death, she had them stuffed or their hides tanned and installed in her home. After the polar bear died, she used his skin as a rug but always admonished her young visitors not to step on Willie.[46]

In an effort to maintain the highest standards for the gardens, the zoo, the amusements, the restaurant, and the theater, Mrs. Elitch became so financially involved that the Gardens were sold in 1916 to pay her debts. The high bidder was J. K. Mullen, Denver miller and philanthropist, who leased and then sold to J. M. Mulvihill. The new owner had come to Colorado for his health, which must have vastly improved or he could not have done the many things he did. He worked for the Gas and Electric Company while managing the Broadway theater in the winter and Elitch's theater in the summer. His grandsons, the Gurtler brothers, now own Elitch's Gardens.[47] They run it in the Elitch tradition by hiring a first-class stock company for the theater and keeping ahead of all the new-fangled contraptions for the amusement park. Hundreds of hanging baskets grace the extensive gardens—Mrs. Elitch loved hanging baskets. At the Trocadero, still one of the dance halls approved by Denver mothers, the Gurtlers offer free dance instruction, including baton whirling. There is no zoo.[48]

Mrs. Elitch was long a member of the Denver Woman's Press Club.[49] In 1916 when Elitch's fell under the sheriff's hammer, that organization, headed by Frances Wayne of the *Denver Post,* arranged a benefit for her. It was held in May at the City Auditorium and netted $5,250. More important than the money was the affection demonstrated by Denver toward Mrs. Elitch. Society filled every box; Wolcott School Girls sold $120 worth of flowers; Joe Newman, composer of popular songs, was there; Senor Rafael Cavallo led the orchestra; Father Bossetti produced a short opera; and a dancing class performed.[50]

To the end of her life Mrs. Elitch loved the theater. She talked entertainingly about the odd and the great she had known, from

Mr. and Mrs. Tom Thumb, who were her house guests in the 1890's, to Sarah Bernhardt, who had fearlessly stroked a lion.

Mr. Mulvihill, the owner, was happy to have Mrs. Elitch live in her house in the Gardens as long as she was able.[51] This house was packed with gifts from theatrical friends. These, and her mementos from her round-the-world wedding trip and from the zoo, were all itemized in her will. She left them to specified friends, most of them youngsters.

For decades Elitch's has been part of Denver's history. A distinctive amusement park, it has kept the spirit of the charming young couple who started it in 1890. Indeed, "not to see Elitch's is not to see Denver."[52]

NOTES

The statements that are not credited otherwise come chiefly from Caroline E. Dier's book, *The Lady of the Gardens* (Hollywood, Hollycrofters, 1932) which was based on personal interviews with Mrs. Elitch. Present day Elitch's is described by Alex Murphee in the *Saturday Evening Post* for March 12, 1956. Jack Gurtler, one of the present owners who are so ably keeping up with the times yet preserving the ancient flavor of the Gardens, has been most helpful in interviews.

[1]*Denver Post,* May 31, 1914. "Memoirs" by Mrs. Elitch.

[2]According to Mrs. Elitch in the above reference, the lake was on the southwest corner of the Gardens, a spot later occupied by the baseball field.

[3]*RMN,* May 21, 1890.

[4]*Denver Post,* May 31, 1914. Mrs. Elitch said the first entrance was on 36th Avenue.

[5]The Denver & Berkeley Park Rapid Transit Company had five steam locomotives and some open trailers. The track, laid in 1888, went from West 29th and Zuni to Berkeley Park. It ran up Tennyson from 35th to 41st Avenues. After Elitch's opened, the prospects for business were so good that the Denver Tramway bought the line late in 1890 for $100,000 and electrified it in the summer of 1891. Cafky, Morris, *Steam Tramways of Denver.* Denver, Rocky Mountain Railroad Club, June, 1950.

[6]Mr. Mulvihill is quoted in the *Denver Post* May 22, 1922, when the city tried to prohibit Sunday dancing at Elitch's. Mrs. Elitch in

her *Weekly,* during 1914, said the same thing in more words: "The ultra-best of clean-conscience entertainment specially providing for the safe and sane enjoyment of clean-living and high-thinking Denver."

[7]In 1914 the Thés Dansants were directed by Suzanne Perry.

[8]During the filming in December, 1953, of the movie called *The Glen Miller Story,* James Stewart and June Allison spent two days on location at Elitch's beneath artificial apple blossoms. Benny Goodman's first engagement at Elitch's was unsuccessful. His type of music was too new for Denver. He afterwards referred to his abbreviated stay as his "Denver Blues." Jack Gurtler, interview, 1956.

[9]Hatch, Alden, *Red Carpet for Mamie.* New York, Holt, 1954, p. 51.

[10]Her name was Lydia Houck, nicknamed "Lydsey." She changed to Mary Elizabeth when she became a Catholic.

[11]Two sources for the life of John Elitch are Frank Hall's *History of the State of Colorado* (Chicago, Blakely, 1895, v. 4, p. 436) ; and the obituaries in the Denver papers for March 11, 1891 which reflect genuine sorrow for the young man's death.

[12]Manning's Oyster Grotto. *RMN,* March 11, 1891, p. 1, col. 3.

[13]Camp, A. P., "Recollections." In D. A. R., *Pioneers of the San Juan,* v. 1. Camp recalls that Elitch first had a cafe on 2nd Avenue in Durango where he served everything from terrapin to champagne, meals costing sometimes fifty dollars. He later moved to a side street and ran a chophouse.

[14]The Denver *Directories* give: 1881—John Elitch works at Fisher & Slack Saloon, 399 Larimer (old style street numbering) ; 1883—John Elitch Jr. and Sr. Restaurant, 404 Curtis, residence 406; 1884—Elitch's Restaurant and Oyster House, 404 Curtis; 1887—Elitch's Palace Dining Rooms, 1541-47 Arapahoe (new style street numbering) ; 1889—John Elitch Jr., 1541 Arapahoe; John Elitch Sr., 1715 Champa; 1890—John Elitch Jr., proprietor Elitch's Gardens, Prospect Avenue (West 38th) and southwest corner of Canby, Highlands; John Elitch Sr., 810-15th Street, restaurant.

[15]*Denver Republican,* Aug. 7, 1886, p. 4.

[16]The Gout Club centered around Ward Hill Lamon who was finishing his biography of Abraham Lincoln at the St. James Hotel, 1528 Curtis Street. He and his cronies, Amos Steck and James B. Belford, the "Red-Headed Rooster of the Rockies," used to sit on the iron-railed balcony and eat meals prepared by John Elitch. *Rocky Mountain Herald,* Nov. 29, 1947.

[17]John Elitch helped organize the Denver Athletic Club, was its star performer and one-time president.

[18]Elitch sold the Palace to Rod Kavanagh and Henry and Numa Vidal who changed the name to Tortoni's. They made it *the* place to eat in Denver, "orderly, quiet and peaceful" and a bit elegant. Tortoni's obituaries in the *Denver Post,* for May 27, 1916, and July 18, 1916, say the bar could hold one hundred men knee to knee, and that it was "buried in the cemetery where Prohibition buries its dead."

[19]*Denver Republican,* July 6, 1890, p. 11. The acts on the opening day also included banjoists, knock-about comedians, a performer on the horizontal bars, and Bijou Mignon, child vocalist. Burt, W. P., *History of the Denver Theaters.* WPA Writers Program for Colorado, 1936-42 ms. The company's name was the Goodyear, Elitch and Shillings Minstrel Show. Hall, *op. cit.*

[20]*Denver Republican,* March 11, 1891, p. 1, col. 3. Obituary. John Elitch's body lies in Fairmount Cemetery, Denver. On his headstone is a bas-relief portrait of him, his curly hair enhancing his handsome face.

[21]*RMN,* May 3, 1891. Under "Because" are listed eleven reasons, one being that Elitch's was "the only Open Air Amusement resort in the city, as Denver has no park of its own where anybody but a donkey could enjoy himself."

[22]No record was found of the date the famous Elitch's curtain was hung in the theater. Age having weakened it, the management wonders how long it can be used. (See picture on p. 219.) At one time the wall panels on either side of the stage opening were painted with mountain scenery. The colors were subdued by stretching mosquito netting across the panels. Backstage was completely rebuilt in 1955.

[23]James O'Neill was the first leading man. His son was the playwright, Eugene O'Neill.

[24]From Denver in 1951 Grace Kelly went to Hollywood to star in *High Noon.* She is now the wife of Prince Rainier of Monaco. Does she ever remember the days when she washed her own laundry at 4020 Raleigh where her landlady remembers her as being quiet and ladylike?

[25]Bernhardt's Denver appearance was made possible because her San Francisco engagement was cancelled by the earthquake. At Elitch's she played *Camille* in the afternoon, *La Sorcerie* at night.

[26]*Denver Times,* May 20, 1912. Most of them were after their usual Wednesday matinee seats. Today daughters and granddaughters sit in the same seats on Wednesday afternoons that their mothers used to occupy. Friday night was society night, when the elite had dinners at Elitch's Restaurant before the play.

[27]*Denver Post,* May 11, 1922. The senior play that year was *The*

Merchant of Venice. In May 1955 and 1958 the Junior League of Denver presented their "Follies" in the Elitch's Theater.

[28]Elitch's, a pleasant drive from Denver, was a favorite with owners of the genteel electrics. The Colorado Electric Club (700 members) in 1912 used the old Katzenjammer Palace at Elitch's as their clubhouse. *Denver Times,* June articles, 1912.

[29]Williams, A. R., "Recollections of Music in Denver." In *Colorado Magazine,* v. 21, p. 146, July 1944.

[30]A steam calliope, silent, still sits at the center of the merry-go-round. The present managers obtained it from Barnum & Bailey's circus and would like to use it if they could find an old-timer who understands calliopes enough to mend it, reasonably. It might be interesting to note that the word merry-go-round, not carousel, was used in old Denver.

[31]Dave Day, editor of the *Solid Muldoon* of Ouray, later Durango, assured Mrs. Elitch that the Utes sent to Elitch's were the "flower of the tribe." Advertisement on Oct. 16, 1896, in Denver papers.

[32]The Colorado State Historical Society has broken files of *Elitch's Weekly,* v. 5, no. 1, June 13, 1911, through v. 8, no. 12, August 1914.

[33]The present engines and rolling stock were built to one-fifth scale by P. A. Sturdevant of Indiana. On the first run thirty passengers were spilled down a five-foot embankment on a curve near the main entrance to the Gardens, much to the astonishment of a man who was standing there admiring the flowers. *Denver Post,* May 23, 1940

[34]Arthur B. Heiser, interview, 1958, remembers Felker. A boy named Darrel Brumage worked for Root from 1926 to 1935. A letter from him on Nov. 17, 1956, reveals his affection for Mr. Root, who, he says, lived at 32nd and Clay Street where he ran his first locomotives on a small gauge in the yard. Later Root lived and worked on 38th and Tennyson, north of the Gardens. He built many locomotives. One went to a fair in Paris, one to Cleveland, Ohio. Two of the locomotives at Elitch's were steam, one was gasoline-powered disguised as a steam engine, to be used in emergencies.

[35]The court ordered the railroad tracks and equipment sold to Virgil C. Hardy for $700, according to the *Denver Post,* April 21, 1936, p. 26, col. 6. We have been unable to locate their present whereabouts. They are not at Saltair, Utah, nor in Phoenix, Arizona.

[36]*RMN,* July 17, 1944.

[37]*RMN,* May 8, 1905.

[38]*Elitch's Weekly,* June 9, 1914. The spelling is the original. Up to 1914 the spectacle at Elitch's was the *Battle of the Monitor and Merrimac,* but Mrs. Elitch deserted the Civil War when the Titanic sank.

[39]*RMN,* Aug. 11, 1914.

[40]Bloch, Don, "Flickerana in Denver." In *Westerners Brand Book*, Denver Posse, 1948, pp. 129-158. The first two reels shown in Denver were Ida Muller in a skirt dance and the kissing scene from *The Widow Jones*.

[41]*RMN*, July 27, 1902.

[42]For the occasion Baldwin had ordered an asbestos suit which failed to come on time, but he gave the performance as promised. No wonder the boys of Denver idolized a man like this. They used to chase his balloons from Denver to the foothills, hoping to help Ivy get the bags back to Elitch's. Baldwin made his 2,000th balloon ascent in August, 1901. In 1898 the U. S. Signal Corps utilized Sergeant Baldwin's service for the Spanish-American War. (See picture on p. 29.)

[43]Hoskin, H. G., "The Last Buffalo Hunt in Kit Carson County." In *Colorado Magazine*, v. 12, p. 185, Sept. 1935.

[44]Dier, *op. cit.*

[45]Mrs. Harry Bellamy (who sang with the Elitch Symphony Orchestra), interviewed 1957, remembered the pajamas on the baby monkeys. She also said that Mrs. Elitch let a half-grown bear wander around her house. One day the bear turned on the water in the kitchen sink. When Mrs. Elitch objected, he chased her around the kitchen table until she threw the sugar bowl on the floor.

[46]Betty Carlin, interview, Sept. 18, 1956. She was one of the neighborhood children who loved Mrs. Elitch during her last years when she lived with her sister, Mrs. Arnold. Betty inherited a red-headed doll valued by Mrs. Elitch because it was a gift from the actress Helen Mencken.

[47]The present Gardens include thirty-two acres, partially used to cope with the parking problem. The greenhouses, 160,000 square feet of glass, shelter flowers used in the Gardens and Colorado carnations for a large wholesale business. Jack Gurtler, interview, 1956.

[48]The bears were removed and their pit filled up after 1936 because of objections by the Humane Society. Jack Gurtler, interview, 1956.

[49]An oil portrait of Mrs. Elitch in a white dress hangs in the Denver Woman's Press Club house at 1325 Logan Street. (This house was built as a studio by George Elbert Burr, etcher.)

[50]*Denver Post*, May 9, 1916.

[51]Mr. Mulvihill installed the first gas furnace in North Denver in Mrs. Elitch's home. This house still stands though it is entirely surrounded by the walls of one of the amusement buildings. Jack Gurtler, interview, 1956.

[52]This is the well-known advertising slogan of Elitch's Gardens.

Eugene Field in Denver

For two years, from July, 1881, to July, 1883, Eugene Field was the managing editor of the *Denver Tribune*.[1] Having worked on the *St. Joseph Gazette*, the *St. Louis Journal,* and the *Kansas City Times,* he knew how to manage a newspaper, but his written contributions to the *Denver Tribune* were destined to be more important than his business ability.

Immediately upon his arrival in Denver he started to write verse for the *Tribune,* much of it on local subjects. After a while he had a column of his own called "The Old Gossip." From Denver he went to the *Chicago Daily News* where the children's verses he published in a column called "Sharps and Flats," later collected into books, made him famous. The poet laureate of childhood, he was called.

Perhaps his best known poem is "Little Boy Blue," beginning:

> The little toy dog is covered with dust
> But sturdy and staunch it stands. . . .

This was written after he left Denver. Few of the poems for children he wrote while in Denver were considered worthy to be included in his published books. Though not written here, one poem, however, has a definite Denver connection. This is "The Dutch Lullaby," better known by its first lines:

> Wynken, Blynken and Nod one night
> Sailed off in a wooden shoe. . . .

The local connection with this verse began two decades after Eugene Field's death. Mayor Speer of Denver was visiting Chi-

228

cago. In an art gallery he saw a statuette depicting the Field poem. Now Mayor Speer had three loves—children, sculpture, and Colorado. When he found that this statue of three children had been made by Mabel Landrum Torrey of Sterling, Colorado, he felt that he must have it. Just before his death the mayor commissioned Mrs. Torrey to make a life-sized copy in marble of the statuette, with the hope that some one in Denver would foot the $10,000 bill. Mr. and Mrs. Frank L. Woodward obliged[2] and the statue was placed in Washington Park in 1919.

Another connection between Field and Washington Park came years later. Some of Denver's bookish people were distressed to hear that the house in which the Field family had lived in Denver was to be pulled down. This was 307 West Colfax Avenue, across from the United States Mint. These people persuaded Mrs. J. J. ("The Unsinkable") Brown to finance the preservation of the house. She rented it with the expectation that Denver would furnish it as shrine to Eugene Field. Denver didn't. Finally Mrs. Brown bought the cottage and presented it to the City and County of Denver.

The gift baffled the city fathers until Librarian Malcolm G. Wyer suggested they move the structure intact to Washington Park and use it as the Eugene Field Branch of the Denver Public Library. Happily this was done in 1930.[3] The little cottage standing south of one of the largest cottonwood trees in the park is a busy library as well as a fitting memorial.

Everybody seemed happy about this solution to the problem of the Field house except the donor, Mrs. Brown. She stormed. A library! Why must Americans always, always be utilitarian? In Europe (where Mrs. Brown had lately acquired culture) homes of poets were revered. "Oh! Mais ça depasse tout! It is not a lapin agile I gave the city!" quoted the amused journalist who interviewed the irate lady.[4] This would have amused Eugene Field, too. He loved to poke fun at people who put on airs, such as Maggie Brown of Leadville talking French.[5]

Perhaps one reason Denver lacked enthusiasm for making a shrine out of the cottage on West Colfax was that Field had lived there such a few months, only when his family was in Denver with him. Part of 1881 and 1882 his wife "with velvet eyes" was here with Mary, aged six, Melvin, aged four, and the baby, Eugene Jr., who had been born in Kansas City earlier in 1881. Mrs. Field, with the children, went home to St. Louis toward the end of 1882 before the birth of another child.[6]

The few months in the cottage on West Colfax were probably happy ones. Julia Field "not only endured but seemed to enjoy the eccentricities of her husband."[7] Field was devoted to her, though he made gentle fun of her complaints about the money he spent on books and curios. Gene warned the lovely Julia that only those wives of bibliomaniacs who shared their husbands' enthusiasms would get to Heaven:

> But what of those who scold at us
> When we would read in bed?
> Or, wanting victuals, make a fuss
> If we buy books instead?[8]

Before and after his family was in Denver, Eugene Field lived in various rooming houses.[9] Because of his habit of playing the piano when he came home from work at four o'clock in the morning, he moved frequently.[10] Also, there was something about "taking a bath that seemed to stimulate his poetic activities."[11] He scribbled verses and cartoons all over the walls of bathrooms of his rooming houses. Now if these walls, or if the walls of his office at the *Tribune* at 1120 16th Street, which he papered with his own verse clipped from other newspapers,[12] could have been preserved, Denver would have a shrine to an eccentric genius, to supplement the Eugene Field Library Branch, the shrine to the poet laureate of childhood.

Gene was tall and gangly, with sunken eyes in a soulful face, the visage of a practical joker. It is easy to picture him at his desk in the second floor front room on 16th Street. With his legs stretched across the desk, he wrote on a lapboard. His handwriting was microscopic, too distinctive to be easily read. It had not always been small. His brother remarked that Gene wrote a fair-sized, legible hand which he refined when, at age thirty, he decided to become famous.[13]

230

At his *Tribune* desk Field worked prodigiously. He stopped at eleven o'clock sharp each evening to patronize "The Lunchman in the Alley" who sold "Apple-Pie and Cheese." Gene memorialized the lunch-cart interlude by writing verses with these titles. The poet liked food but all his life had dyspepsia. When one of his friends asked Dr. Lemen of Denver what ailed Field, the doctor replied "Cheese."[14]

After the coffee-break, Field turned out more copy, half of which, one of his staff said later, had to be censored.[15] Then Field went out-of-doors, sometimes for a short walk to a handy saloon,[16] or to the basement of Wolfe Londoner's grocery store where the Denver Press Club had its informal beginnings.[17] More often Gene went for a long walk. One of the young men on the *Tribune* loved to accompany Gene in the early morning hours to hear him talk of life and death as they strode across Prospect Hill (present Cheesman Park).[18]

Field returned to the *Tribune* to put the paper to bed, which was done only after Gene's vibrant bass voice had led the printers in the harmony of some current song like "My Old Kentucky Home."[19] When the presses rolled, Gene went to his rooming house, or home when his family was in Denver. Perhaps he stood on the steps of the white cottage to watch the dawn slide down the mountains propped up at the western end of Colfax Avenue.

He slept little. During the day he played with his friends or his children. Although all children unreservedly liked Field, Eugene said he liked children "insofar as he could make pets of them,"[20] a frank admission by a man whose fame rests on his love for the very young.

Gene invented games for children and played the same kind of games with grown-ups. For his little boy he perched a toy cat on a shelf, having first tied a silk thread to it. Every time the child took careful aim at the cat and pulled the trigger of his wooden gun, Gene pulled the toy off the shelf.[21] Field used this same technique when Mrs. Fiske, taking her curtain call at the Tabor Grand Opera House, stooped to pick up a bouquet of violets that Field had thrown on the stage.[22]

Gene's practical jokes were legion, thoroughly enjoyed by little, raw Denver. His most famous prank was perpetrated when Oscar Wilde was scheduled to deliver an address in Denver. Hearing that Wilde's train was late, Gene took the young editor-in-chief of the *Tribune,* O. H. Rothacker, "to the old Charpiot Hotel, registered him as 'O. Wilde, England,' got him a wig . . . overcoat with fluffy collar, and 'made up' Rothacker in imitation of the distinguished foreigner. Field then ordered an open carriage, guided Rothacker to it, and took a seat beside him. Together they drove all over town, Field being conspicuous by pointing with his cane to all the big buildings. They attracted general attention.

" 'There go Eugene Field and Oscar Wilde,' was whispered along Sixteenth Street, and some of Field's friends stopped the carriage and insisted on being introduced. Field did the honors in great form, and readily accepted the invitation of one of his friends to 'bring Mr. Wilde to dinner.' "[23]

A less subtle and therefore more typical Field joke occurred the day Eugene, dining in Colorado Springs, managed to insert in the turkey a giant firecracker, timed to explode as his hostess led him and other guests into the dining room. Another day a friend in desperate need of money showed Field some chemical bombs he had invented to smother fires. Helpfully, Gene arranged for an old shack to be burned that his friend might demonstrate his bombs. But the more bombs that were thrown on the fire, the hotter it got. Gene had substituted kerosene for the chemical in the bombs. Field thought this joke, that ruined his friend, a capital prank.[24]

These samples are enough to illustrate his sense of humor, but they fail to explain why so many people liked Field, even loved him. "He was adored in Denver, but it was love only that kept him from being lynched," wrote one of the women who had been a reporter on the *Tribune.*[25]

This vitriolic streak in Field was one reason he was hired by the *Denver Tribune.* That paper, like many journals of the period, was a weapon used by its owners to fight their opponents in political or business fields. In 1881 the current campaign of the *Tribune* was against the Denver and New Orleans Railroad, competitor of the Denver and Rio Grande, and against ex-Governor John Evans, the promoter of the New Orleans line.[26] John Evans was one of Denver's elder statesmen, a city-founder, an earnest Methodist. Field immediately seized upon Evans' religious beliefs to satirize "The Good Deacon John." He wrote in the *Tribune* that Evans had attended the theater, which no good Methodist would have done in those days. A day or so later Field gave scurrilous details. Evans threatened Field with jail. Field made fun of the threats. On September 29, 1881, Field used the technique of negative innuendo thus: "At the risk of 10 years more in the penitentiary, we will state that Deacon John was not at the show last night." With that, the Evans items dropped. We learned, though not from the *Tribune,* that Field actually was jailed.[27]

Being (temporarily) limited to the truth, Gene looked about for some other way to amuse himself and his readers. When he came to Denver the *Tribune* was running a Sunday column called "Our Little Ones." It was full of moral verse and insipid stories. Field, the future poet laureate of childhood, added verses to this column. They were sweet, "Mother rot," he sometimes called them.[28] He did not sign them.

Perhaps the column inspired Field in another, contrary, direction. From the middle of November there appeared sporadically in the *Tribune* a series of squibs in the form of the old-fashioned reading primer, the kind that started "A is for apple. Do you see the apple?" Field's first paragraph in this vein was called "The Lamp-Post:"

> See the Lamp-Post. By its Dim Rays you can Behold the Electric Light across the Street. There is a Man Leaning against the Lamp-Post. Perhaps the Lamp-Post would fall if it were not for the Man. At any rate, the Man would Fall if it were not For the Lamp-Post. What is the Matter with the Man? He appears Disquieted. He is trying to Work his Boots up through his Mouth. He will have an Headache to-morrow and Lay it to the Altitude.[29]

Gene fancied these items. He collected ninety-four of them into a pamphlet, entitled it the *Tribune Primer,* and had it printed and bound in flimsy pink paper.[30] The edition is thought to have been limited to fifty copies. The present whereabouts of fifteen of them is known, one of which sold for $600.[31]

Despite the title, the *Tribune Primer* was not for children. The type of humor in it appealed to part of the public in the 1880's. As soon as the pamphlet came to the attention of eastern publishers, it was reprinted. Publishers hired well-known illustrators to add their humor to the *Primer*. Some of the editions were pirated, some brought royalties to the author.[32]

In 1883, Eugene Field went off to Chicago with the well-wishes of Denver and Colorado. In his "Sharps and Flats" he immediately used his western experiences for copy. One of the Denver readers of his Chicago column was not pleased. He remarked that "Field's sense of humor seems to run through a deposit of bile when it deals with Colorado. Field says miners in Colorado are boorish Cornishmen, criminals from eastern states, or lung-spitting consumptives."[33]

Presently, and more pleasantly, Field was using his western experiences in verse.[34] In the style of Bret Harte crossed with James Whitcomb Riley, Field produced such verse as "Casey's Table D'Hote." He invented a character named Three-Fingered Hoover who was:

Good to the helpless and the weak, a brave an' manly heart
 A cyclone couldn't phase, but any child could rend apart;
So like the mountain pine, that dares the storm which sweeps
     along
 But rocks the winds uv summer-time, an' sings a soothin' song.

Three-Fingered Hoover had a number of adventures but no others so dramatic as the day he came down to Denver to see "Modjesky as Cameel" at the Tabor Grand Opera House. His tender heart being touched by the plight of the lady on the stage, he leaped over the footlights to rescue her.

Such stories in rhyme, along with poems about children (Gene's verse for the young had improved with practice) were published in 1889 in *A Little Book of Western Verse*. This set Field's feet on the path to fame.

But let us look at what Field wrote about Denver while he was

234

actually in the city. He immediately picked up the local topics of conversation like weather, water, and Tabor. In fact his work might be used as a resumé of what was happening in Denver in the early 1880's. For example, at the formal opening of the Tabor Grand Opera House when Emma Abbott sang the mad aria from Lucia, Field wrote:

> The Opera House—a union grand
> Of capital and labor—
> Long will the stately structure stand
> A monument to Tabor.
>
> And as to Emma, never will
> Our citizens cease lovin' her;
> While time lasts shall her name be linked
> With that of the Ex-Governor. . . .

One of Gene's best friends was Wolfe Londoner, on whom, therefore, he played endless jokes. When Londoner was running for mayor, Gene announced in his column that at ten o'clock that very morning any Negro who cared to call at Londoner's grocery store would be given a watermelon. Fortunately Londoner was able to buy a carload of melons. He afterwards credited the hoax as winning the election for him.[35] Field borrowed money from Londoner. When the ex-Mayor visited Chicago, Field announced in his column that Londoner was in the Windy City looking after a permanent investment.[36]

Then as now, the changeable Colorado climate was noticed. Gene squeezed the last drop of fun out of the local weather, both winter and summer. Concerning the vagaries of winter he wrote:

> This man with frozen hands and feet
> Is hurried off and put to bed;
> Another, prostrate by the heat,
> Wears cabbage leaves upon his head.
>
> Thus speeds the winter in our state
> A batch of contradictions rude;
> And we assign our varying fate
> To this peculiar altitude.

235

Summer, with its droughts and cloudbursts, also afforded him pleasure and copy. On June 3, 1882, he purported to have had a letter from Maxcy Tabor who was traveling in Italy. "He says there must have been a freshet shortly before he got there [Venice] for he found the streets flooded with water and the people paddling around in curiously shaped skiffs. He visited the Bridge of Sighs which he deemed inferior to the Larimer Street bridge over Cherry Creek in Denver."

The local dependence on irrigation ditches shows in Field's verse. Concerning a period of drought he wrote:

> And in this city, once our pride
> We see what ne'er before was seen
> Our trees no longer fresh and green;
> The grass is withered up and dead,
> And by the fire which burns o'erhead
> Each irrigating ditch is dried.

Field poked fun at Cherry Creek. He told about the man who "went bathing in Cherry Creek and would have been lost had he not with prodigious presence of mind waded ashore." Gene regretted after a flood had subsided that Cherry Creek was no longer navigable to sea-going vessels. For the Platte River, Field ran Marine Intelligence items in his column, noting sailing schedules and reporting one ship had foundered off the Boulder shoals. Once he wrote that the U. S. Navy had ordered three powerful modern warships to be constructed in the Denver shipyards. Field would have been amused to learn that, since the beginning of World War II, Denver has been fabricating ships for the Navy.

Tourists in resort towns, then as now, considered they were overcharged. Field wrote a verse about a rich man who had to give up his fortune to pay for one drink at a bar in Manitou:

> He signed a quitclaim to it all
> Then to the foothills he hied—
> "I will complete my dreadful fall
> By perishing," he cried.
> With that he made a fateful pitch
> Into an irrigation ditch.

Of course, Gene tried his hand at limericks, rhyming local names whose spelling amused him. With *Del Norte* he rhymed *forty* and *haughty; Sioux* rhymed with *dioux* and *hellabiloux.* One of the more successful of his printable limericks was:

A beautiful young man of Saguache
Once courted the charming Miss Sauche,
But when she was wed
To another, he said
"My life is a horrible bauche!"

Obviously, Field had a good time in Denver and nothing gave him greater pleasure than his final hoax. Needing money to move his family to Chicago, he went about raising funds in characteristic fashion.

First, he printed a letter in the *Tribune* which began: "Dear Mr. Field, Having heard of your early departure for Chicago, we, the undersigned, request an opportunity of hearing you on the lecture stand before you go. . . ."[37] The signatures, supplied by Gene, included names of fifty prominent Colorado men, especially those who had been targets for Field's poisoned buckshot.

In a few days he ran an advertisement for "An Evening with Eugene Field" at the New Academy of Music on 16th Street, tickets one dollar. The announced program was impressive. It included the "Zampa Overture" by the Koenigsberg Orchestra, solos by Belle Cole and Prof. Winter,[38] duets by Mr. and Mrs. D. J. Kelly, and a chorus of twenty-five voices.[39]

The evening was a success—Standing Room Only. The orchestra never played better, the soloists were in good voice, but the chorus of twenty-five voices was especially appreciated. For this Mr. Field came on the stage to anounce that he would substitute, the cast having been detained in Cheyenne. Thereupon he did a favorite parlor piece of the time called "Van Amburg's Show" which called for the imitation of the sounds of twenty-five animals. From then on, the evening was Field's. He "showed himself so versatile that the audience, when once he showed his pale, grave face, seemed loath to have him leave the footlights even for a moment. . . . He did everything. He imitated old men, old maids and small boys. He gave character sketches. . . . He played and sang the beautiful serenade 'She sleeps, my lady sleeps' and snored very naturally between verses. He imitated a tenor singer, a man sawing wood, and supplied a rooster in place of a mocking bird in one of the vocal and comic selections."[40]

There was one serious note in the evening. Eugene Stimson, former attorney general of the state, stood with his hands behind his back and gave a touching speech of farewell to Field. The sentiment was rather lost, however, when Field stepped behind him with head stooped, thrust his arms under General Stimson's armpits and made gestures.[41]

The next day a rival newspaper reported: "Last night the audience gave Mr. Field an ovation. He has a warm place in the hearts of Denver and he deserves it. His talk was what might be expected—bright, rollicking and ridiculously funny."[42]

Gene's own paper sent him off with a farewell written in mining terms, saying he had struck a genuine vein, light and individual, and that as he grew older he would strike less of drift and more of gold. "Beyond question he is the most brilliant journalist in the United States. . . . In the career that lies in his power he will have the hearty Godspeed of the plodders to whom he has endeared himself by his social graces."[43]

In the twelve years Gene had left to live, he made for himself a warm place in the hearts of Chicago readers and definitely fulfilled his own prediction that he would become nationally, indeed internationally, famous. But he probably never again had so good a time as he had in those two years in Denver when both he and the town were irresponsible.

NOTES

An extensive collection of Fieldiana was assembled by Willard K. Morse who managed the Tabor Grand Opera House and was the target for much of Field's sharpest humor. Mr. Morse collected words written about or by Field, including the mean remarks about himself. This collection was bought by the benefactor of the Denver Public Library, Frederick R. Ross, and is housed in the Special Collections Room.

The files of the *Denver Tribune* for 1881-1883 are in the library of the Colorado State Historical Society Museum.

[1]The *Denver Tribune,* 1867—1884, was "if not the most celebrated, surely the most picturesque paper" in Denver. (Stone, W. F., *History of Colorado.* Chicago, Clarke, 1981, Vol, p. 791). "Originally a religious paper," says D. C. McMurtrie in *Early Printing in Colorado* (Denver, Hirschfeld, 1935) the *Tribune* became "an organ of high literary merit and elevated moral tone." Field contributed to the former.

[2]*Denver Municipal Facts,* July, 1918. Mayor Mills closed the contract for this statue after Speer's death. Mabel Landrum was the gifted daughter of a judge in Sterling, Colorado, who went to the Chicago Art Institute. There she met and married Fred M. Torrey. They were part of the Midway Studios colony of Chicago until it was acquired by the University. About 1957 they moved to Des Moines where they teach and make statues. His specialty is portraying Abraham Lincoln, while she concentrates on small statues of small children. Her "Robin Song" has sold 10,000 copies. The "Wynken, Blynken and Nod" group in Denver's Washington Park is her largest work. A copy of it is in Wellsboro, Pennsylvania. Mrs. Torrey gave the original, small model to Mrs. Robert W. Speer. (Letter from Mrs. Torrey, Jan. 1959.)

[3]*RMN,* May 4, 1930, p. 4. Field had a connection with Washington Park long before the fountain or the library were placed there, in fact long before there was a Washington Park. In the dawn of a June day of 1882, Gene and two friends drove a carriage to Smith's Lake where they went swimming. Gene had cramps in the frigid water and almost drowned before his friends could pull him out. *Denver Republican,* June 19, 1882, p. 4.

[4]*RMN,* Sept. 3, 1930.

[5]Field had spent six months and an ample patrimony in southern Europe right after he came of age, and ever after had fun with the French language. One of his western characters he named Three-Fingered Hoover, probably because he wanted a rhyme for *chef-d'oeuvre,* pronounced *chef doover* in Colorado. In a verse called "Conversazzhyony" Gene tells how the boys in a mining camp refused to vote for Three-Fingered Hoover because he "spoke light uv wimmin folk" when he asked for:

> Oon peety morso, see vo play, de la cette Charlotte Rooz . . . .
> We never knew who Charlotte wuz, but Goslin's brother Dick
> Allowed she wuz the teacher from the camp on Roarin' Crick . . .

[6]The family Bible gives these dates. The fullest biography of Eugene Field was written by Slason Thompson of Chicago: *Eugene Field, a Study in Heredity and Contradictions.* New York, Scribner, 1901, 2v.

[7]Article on Field in the *Dictionary of American Biography*. New York, Scribner, 1928-36.

[8]From poem called "Dibdin's Ghost."

[9]At least four Denver addresses for Field are known. The Denver *Directory* for 1882 gives 307 West Colfax Avenue; for 1883 it gives the Clifford Block, which was at 1620 Lawrence Street. When the Leadville House, 1411 Blake Street, was razed after its immersion in Cherry Creek in the flood of 1913, the *Denver Republican* (July 24, 1913, p. 7) reported that Eugene Field had once lived there. The fourth location for Field in Denver was the Holzman house at 20th and Lawrence. J. Holzman said (*Denver Times*, Nov. 4, 1895, p. 6, col. 4) that Gene rented his house for six months before the Chicago move, and did not send for the books and curios he left therein for a year or more afterwards. This house was, according to the 1881 *Directory*, at 523 Lawrence Street. Translated into modern street numbering this is 2005 Lawrence Street, a site currently occupied by a Conoco filling station.

[10]Brown, J. G., "My Recollections of Eugene Field as Journalist in Denver, 1881-1883." In *Colorado Magazine*, v. 4, pp. 41-49, March, 1927.

[11]Vaile, H. T., "Early Years of the Telephone Company." In *Colorado Magazine*, v. 5, p. 127, August, 1928.

[12]*RMN*, Nov. 11, 1900.

[13]Field, R. M., "Eugene Field, a Memory." In *A Little Book of Western Verse*. New York, Scribner, 1896, p. xxx.

Gene loved to copy his poems in this acquired calligraphy, embellish them with colored crayons and give them to his friends. During World War I the original manuscript of "Little Boy Blue" was sold to one of the Chicago McCormicks at an auction for war relief for $2,400.

[14]Brown, J. G., *Address* before the staff of the Denver Public Library, 1928, ms. Mr. Brown, after retiring from active journalism, worked in the newspaper room of the Library.

[15]Jenny Hopkins Siebold in the *Rocky Mountain News*, July 27, 1918.

[16]"Field surrendered his ambition to become the champion winebibber of the century" when he went to Chicago. (Davis, C. C. *Olden Times in Colorado*. Los Angeles, Phillips, 1916.) One of the oft-told tales about Field was when the owner of Perrin's saloon, tired of Gene charging drinks, tore up his bill and announced that Gene would pay cash from then on. Gene immediately demanded a drink on the house, the custom when a patron settled an account.

[17]Smith, J. E., "Personal Recollections of Early Denver." In *Colorado Magazine*, v. 20, p. 70, March, 1943.

¹⁸*Denver Post*, Nov. 4, 1895. This young man, James McCarthy, later became known in Colorado under his nom-de-plume, Fitz-Mac.

¹⁹Brown, J. G., "My Recollections . . ." *op. cit.*

²⁰Field, Eugene, "An Auto-Analysis." In *The Complete Tribune Primer, containing 75 Original Drawings by F. Opper.* Boston, Mutual Book Co., 1901.

²¹Perhaps it was from this same shelf at 307 West Colfax Avenue that the old Dutch clock observed the fight between the gingham dog and the calico cat, later recorded by Field in a poem called "The Duel."

²²*RMN*, Feb. 2, 1947.

²³*Denver Times*, Nov. 4, 1895, p. 6, col. 3. Another version of this hoax tells that Field himself took the part of Wilde, with a sunflower in his lapel and a calla lily in his hand. A third teller of the tale says it was a publicity stunt engineered by Wilde's publicity agent. When Oscar Wilde actually got to town, perhaps he was in no mood to appreciate the Tabor Grand Opera House. When asked what he thought of Denver's pride, he shrugged.

²⁴The turkey and the bomb stories come from C. C. Davis, *op. cit.*

²⁵Siebold, *op. cit.*

²⁶Before Field arrived in Denver, Evans was suing the *Denver Tribune* for libel. *RMN*, July 20, 1881.

²⁷Rothacker and Field were indicted for libel. *RMN*, Sept. 23, 1881, p. 8, col. 1.

Further information comes from the photostat of a letter in the Morse Collection: "Dear Colonel Reed, The person who caused my arrest for libel was ex-Governor John Evans of Denver. My bondsmen were Gov. Routt, Gov. Tabor and Senator Hill, representing $20,000,-000. The alleged libel was in the printed statement that Evans attended the Abbott opera and loomed up in the front row of the parquette like a bald-headed rooster. Hastily yours, Eugene. Jany 18th, 1886."

²⁸Davis, *op. cit.*

²⁹If one looks hard for local significance in this paragraph, one finds two references. The newfangled electric lights were hung, three of them, from the roof of the Windsor Hotel in February, 1881. Though Field says you had to look at them with the aid of the gas lamp on the corner, the *Rocky Mountain News* for Feb. 18, 1881, said "They rivalled the stars and put the moon to shame." As for attributing hangovers to the altitude, it was (and is) a local cliché.

³⁰The title page reads: Eugene Field/ *Tribune Primer*/ Denver/ Tribune Publishing Co. (No date is given and it was not copyrighted.) At head of title: Tribune Series no. II. (The first of the series was O. H. Rothacker's *Ingersoll, His Arguments and Method.*)

[31]Wyer, M. G., *Address* at opening of the Special Collections Room of the Denver Public Library on March 8, 1956.

[32]The first eastern edition was *The Model Primer,* published by Fred Tredwell in Brooklyn in 1882 This was pirated, according to Field's *Auto-Analysis, op. cit.* The Morse Collection includes six of the original illustrations for this edition, as well as the originals for the edition published by Mutual and illustrated by F. Opper. He was the artist who not only illustrated the humor of Mark Twain, Bill Nye, and Mr. Dooley, but also drew the comic strip "Happy Hooligan."

[33]*Denver Republican,* Dec. 10, 1883.

[34]Fortunately, J. G. Brown collected the verses and humorous prose paragraphs from the *Denver Tribune,* so the reader need not tax his eyesight by reading the original newspaper column. Most of the quotations in this chapter are from Brown's two collections: *A Little Book of Tribune Verse,* Denver, Tandy, Wheeler & Co., 1901; and *Eugene Field in Denver, Gleanings from his Humorous Writings,* 1927 ms.

[35]*RMN,* Feb. 2, 1947.

[36]*RMN,* July 9, 1936. In Lee Taylor Casey's column.

[37]*Denver Tribune,* Aug. 1, 1883.

[38]Arthur H. Winter, a musician, was imported from England by Dean Hart for the choir of St. John's Church in the Wilderness. From 1882 to 1884 Winter's golden bass voice was heard at Denver churches, Elks socials, G.A.R. concerts and at benefits, such as Field's. Winter organized the local bicycle club and amateur theatricals. He belonged to the Colorado Press Association and the Art Club. He brought with him to Denver his wife, a wealthy Welsh widow whom he had married bigamously. This was one of many crimes on record in Winter's Scotland Yard dosier. The disillusioned Dean Hart, in his *Recollections and Reflections* (New York, Gibbs Bros. & Horan, 1917, p. 149) quotes an officer of the Yard as saying, "Winter was one of the most astute criminals who ever came under our observation." One wonders what Eugene Field thought of him. They were alike in their charm, acting ability, bass voice, and exhibitionism, but where Field played for fun, Winter played for keeps.

[39]*Denver Tribune,* Aug. 6, 1883.

[40]*RMN,* Aug. 7, 1883.

[41]Siebold, *op. cit.*

[42]*Denver Republican,* Aug. 7, 1883.

[43]*Denver Tribune,* July 30, 1883.

Some of his fellow-workers heartily disliked Field. He was an I-writer, as Lee Casey noted, and his assistants had to supply copy when Field did not turn up at the office. One hopes that the employees of the *Denver Tribune* knew one of Gene's verses about climbing Pikes

Peak on a burro. When the climber felt inclined to boast of his feat, the burro asked:

> What brought you up, good sir, this mountain high?
> Was it your legs or mine the journey made?
> There is no peak as high and steep as Fame's,
> And there be many on its very height
> Who stride in pride and vaunt their empty claims,
> While those who toiled with sturdy, honest might
> And placed them there, have unremembered names.

In August, 1884, the owners of the *Denver Republican* hushed competition from the *Denver Tribune* by merging the two papers. In this so-called merger all ninety employees of the *Tribune* were fired, including the brilliant young editor, Rothacker. (*RMN*, July 9, 1936.)

OUR LADY OF THE MINE

The Blue Horizon wuz a mine us fellers all thought well uv,
And there befell the episode I now perpose to tell uv;
'T wuz in the year uv sixty-nine,—somewhere along in summer,—
There hove in sight one afternoon a new and curious comer;
His name wuz Silas Pettibone,—a artist by perfession,—
With a kit of tools and a big mustache and a pipe in his possession.
He told us, by our leave, he'd kind uv like to make some sketches
Uv the snowy peaks, 'nd the foamin' crick, 'nd the distant mountain stretches;
"You're welkim, sir," sez we, although this scenery dodge seemed to us
A waste uv time where scenery wuz already sooper-*floo*-us.

All through the summer Pettibone kep' busy at his sketchin',—
At daybreak off for Eagle Pass, and home at nightfall, fetchin'
That everlastin' book uv his with spider-lines all through it;
Three-Fingered Hoover used to say there warn't no meanin' to it.
"Gol durn a man," sez he to him, "whose shif'less hand is sot at
A'-drawin' hill's that's full uv quartz that's pinin' to be got at!"
"Go on," sez Pettibone, "go on, if joshin' gratifies ye;
But one uv these fine times I'll show ye sumthin' will surprise ye!"
The which remark led us to think—although he didn't say it—
That Pettibone wuz owin' us a gredge 'nd meant to pay it.

One evenin' as we sat around the Restauraw de Casey,
A-singin' songs 'nd tellin' yarns the which was somewhat racy,
In come that feller Pettibone, 'nd sez, "With your permission,
I'd like to put a picture I have made on exhibition."
He sot the picture on the bar 'nd drew aside its curtain,
Sayin', "I reckon you'll allow as how *that's* art, f'r certain!"
And then we looked, with jaws agape, but nary word wuz spoken,
And f'r a likely spell the charm uv silence wuz unbroken—
Till presently, as in a dream, remarked Three-Fingered Hoover:
"Onless I am mistaken, this is Pettibone's shef doover!"

243

It wuz a face—a human face—a woman's, fair 'nd tender—
Set gracefully upon a neck white as a swan's, and slender;
The hair wuz kind uv sunny, 'nd the eyes wuz sort of dreamy,
The mouth wuz half a-smilin', 'nd the cheeks wuz soft 'nd creamy;
It seemed like she wuz lookin' off into the west out yonder,
And seemed like, while she looked, we saw her eyes grow softer, fonder,—
Like, lookin' off into the west, where mountain mists wuz fallin',
She saw the face she longed to see and heerd his voice a-callin';
"Hooray!" we cried,—"a woman in the camp uv Blue Horizon!
Step right up, Colonel Pettibone, 'nd nominate your pizen!"

A curious situation,—one deservin' uv your pity,—
No human, livin' female thing this side of Denver City!
But jest a lot uv husky men that lived on sand 'nd bitters,—
Do you wonder that that woman's face consoled the lonesome critters?
And not a one but what it served in some way to remind him
Of a mother or a sister or a sweetheart left behind him;
And some looked back on happier days, and saw the old-time faces
And heered the dear familiar sounds in old familiar places,—
A gracious touch of home. "Look here," sez Hoover, "ever'body
Quit thinkin' 'nd perceed at oncet to name his favorite toddy!"

It wasn't long afore the news had spread the country over,
And miners come a-flockin' in like honey-bees to clover;
It kind uv did 'em good, they said, to feast their hungry eyes on
That picture uv Our Lady in the camp uv Blue Horizon.
But one mean cuss from Nigger Crick passed criticisms on 'er,—
Leastwise we overheerd him call her Pettibone's madonner,
The which we did not take to be respectful to a lady,
So we hung him in a quiet spot that wuz cool 'nd dry 'nd shady;
Which same might not have been good law, but it *wuz* the right maneuver!
To give the critics due respect for Pettibone's shef doover.

Gone is the camp,—yes, years ago the Blue Horizon busted,
And every mother's son uv us got up one day 'nd dusted,
While Pettibone perceeded East with wealth in his possession,
And went to Yurrup, as I heerd, to study his perfession;
So, like as not, you'll find him now a-paintin' heads 'nd faces
At Venus, Billy Florence, and the like I-talyun places.
But no sech face he'll paint again as at old Blue Horizon,
For I'll allow to sweeter face no human soul set eyes on;
But when the critics talk so grand uv Paris 'nd the Loover,
I say, "Oh, but you orter seen the Pettibone shef doover!"

EUGENE FIELD

(From *A Little Book of Western Verse*. New York, Scribner, 1890. pp. 69-74.)

Eugene Field, age thirty, two years before he came to Denver. His pale, grave face belied his sense of humor. (Portrait from *McClure Magazine, Sept.* 1893, p. 315. *Denver Public Library*.)

When he worked, Gene always put his feet in carpet slippers, which where nailed to the wall, and he often drew pictures when he should have been writing. At the upper left hand corner of the sheet is an insect he has just drawn. Could it be the cockroach who came across the alley because the owners of the *Denver Republican* were so stingy with their paste? Perhaps the cockroach, and the mouse Gene is drawing, are the ancestors of Don Marquis' archy and Walt Disney's Mickey Mouse. (Cartoon by Selanders in Slason Thompson's *Eugene Field*, 1910. v. 1, p. 218. *Denver Public Library*.)

It was not Field's humor that made him beloved by a generation of readers but his poems about children. In them may be traced the influence of his wife, Julia, "the girl with velvet eyes." She must have graced the little cottage at 307 West Colfax Avenue, and she would have loved the statue of her Gene's "Dutch Lullaby" in Washington Park. One can see her looking at Wynken and Blynken in the wooden shoe and then walking around the other side to see Nod, who is a little boy fast asleep. (Portrait from Slason Thompson's *Eugene Field,* Scribner 1901. v. 1. p. 110. Portrait and picture below from *Denver Public Library.* Picture on opposite page from *State Historical Society of Colorado.*)

Field came to the *Denver Tribune* too late to work in the building shown above. H.C. Brown built it in 1868. The *Tribune* moved into it in 1872 and out in 1880. One of the few relics of the 1860's, it now stands vacant at 16th and Market, sagging under its ninety years. (Photo by Duhem Brothers about 1875. *Denver Public Library*.)

The *Tribune* moved to 1120 16th Street, between Arapahoe and Lawrence. Here Field worked in 1881-1883, in a building that antedates the one shown to the right of the alley in the picture below. This is 1120 16th Street but was built in 1892. However, Field doubtless walked down the alley, know as Newspaper Alley because the *Tribune* was at the right, the *Republican* at the left, and other newspapers were nearby. (Original water color by Herndon Davis, 1940. *Denver Public Library*.)

Index

249

253

257

258

259

260

DYNAMITED in 1950. The Grant Smelter stack towered 350 feet into the air when it was built in 1892. It stood west of the present Stock Show Stadium until it was condemned as dangerous. It was dynamited, and reluctantly crumbled on February 25, 1950, before the largest crowd of cameras ever assembled in Denver. (Photo by D. F. Wiederspan *Denver Public Library.*)

RAZED in 1933. The Arapahoe County Court House was built in 1883. Two things remind Denver of this building that used to occupy the block where the May-D & F store now stands: The name of the street—Court Place; and the statue of Justice from the top of the dome. Now painted aluminum, she leans against a prop on the roof of the Denver Post building. (*Denver Public Library*.)

BURNED. The Grand View Hotel stood above the city smoke at 17th and the Boulevard. In 1874 Denver excursionists could ride a horsecar to the hotel and there board a steamship waiting in the lake to take them, via a man-made canal, to Sloan's Lake. From 1881 St. Luke's Hospital used this building for ten years. It held 60 beds. (*Denver Public Library.*)

JUNKED December 1931. For twenty-five years the Welcome Arch greeted travelers at the Union Station. Strangers felt a western warmth as they passed under it to enter Denver's 17th Street. When the arch was built, the word WELCOME in electric lights shone from both sides, but in 1908 the word MIZPAH was put on the eastern side, as more appropriate to those departing Denver. The word is from Genesis 31:49. "Mizpah: The Lord watch between me and thee when we are absent one from another." (*State Historical Society of Colorado.*)